Ramadan Sermons

A compilation of speeches and lectures by

Dr. Sayed Ammar Nakshawani

SAYED AMMAR PRESS

Contents

About the author   5

Acknowledgments   6

Foreword   7

Introduction   9

1. Prophet Jesus and Heavenly Food   13
2. Enjoining the Good and Forbidding the Evil   21
3. The Philosophy of Du'a   29
4. The Philosophy of Jihad in Islam   37
5. Islamic Concept of Brotherhood   45
6. The Power of Salat al-Layl   53
7. Rizq or God's Sustenance in Islam   65
8. Lessons from the Biography of the Holy Prophet   73
9. The Disease of Backbiting   89
10. The Biography of Lady Khadijah   99
11. Charity: the Welfare of Humanity   109
12. Envy and Jealousy   117
13. The Prohibition of Pork   125
14. The Prohibition of Alcohol   133
15. Imam Hassan and the Treaty of Hudaybiya   141
16. The Rights of Neighbours in Islam   153
17. The Battle of Badr   163
18. The Case of the Pleading Woman   173

Ramadan Sermons

A compilation of speeches and lectures by

Dr. Sayed Ammar Nakshawani

SAYED AMMAR PRESS

Acknowledgments

As always, I wish to thank my hard-working editor, Kawther Rahmani, for her dedication and diligence under perpetually hectic deadlines. She heavily edited (and rewrote) this manuscript from audio transcriptions of my Ramadan lectures. My special thanks extend to Kawther Masood for her hard work transcribing the lectures at the beginning of the project and to Tehseen Merali of Sun Behind The Cloud Publications for her help in publishing the work. I would also like to thank Sayed Mourtada Mourtada, representative of Ayatollah Sayed Ali al-Seestani, for his endorsement of the work and helpful comments and to Kazim Sajan who helpfully translated his introduction. Your rewards are with the Almighty.

The project would not have been completed were it not for the generous donations of the Hamam and Dharamshi families, may Allah (SWT) reward you and bless your departed family members.

Lastly, I am grateful for the constant support of my family and Murtaza Kanani, Haider Ali Hashmi, Nisar Visram, Zahid Khimji, Zafar Azam and all at the Hyderi Islamic Centre and USA Foundation.

19. The Similarities between Prophet Jesus and Imam Ali	183
20. Imam Ali (AS) and his Concentration in Prayer	191
21. Examining the Final Will of Imam Ali (AS)	199
22. Imam Ali (AS), the Voice of Human Justice	207
23. Is Qur'an the Word of God?- Arabic Linguistics	217
24. Is Qur'an the Word of God? - Predictions & Prophecies	225
25. Is Qur'an the Word of God?- Scientific Principles I	235
26. Is Qur'an the Word of God?- Scientific Principles II	241
27. Is Qur'an the Word of God?- Historical Accuracy	249
28. Dhikr-the Importance of Remembering God	255
29. Examining Prophet Dawood's Judgement	265
30. The Islamic Philosophy and Definition of Eid	275

About the Author

Dr. Sayed Ammar Nakshawani is regarded as one of the most powerful speakers in the Muslim world. He was born in 1981 and graduated from the University College London, as well as the London School of Economics. He was then awarded with an MA in Islamic Studies from Shahid Beheshti University in Iran. Dr. Nakshawani completed his PhD thesis at the University of Exeter He has lectured at the university in Classical Islamic History and then pursued further studies at the Islamic Seminary in Damascus, Syria. Currently he is a visiting scholar at the Centre of Islamic Studies, University of Cambridge.

Foreword

Ramadan Sermons is a fascinating collection of speeches which Dr. 'Ammar Nakshawani delivered to a live audience during the blessed month of Ramadan. The thirty sermons, spread over the thirty nights of the holy month, deal with a wide variety of subjects. Common to them all is a framework of popular piety and traditional learning. The sermons also present an irenic tone of interfaith and intra-faith dialogue.

The order of the lectures remind the reader of the fasting (siyam) of Ramadan and joy of Eid al-Fitr, when Muslims bid the blessed month farewell and look forward to its return as the ninth month of the following year. Fasting is a humble act of worship in all the monotheistic religions. In Islam it is both a month-long social occasion with its own culture, and a personal relation between "the Lord of all beings" and His faithful servant. In a hadith qudsi (divine utterance) God says, "All the actions of the child of Adam belong to him-her except fasting. It belongs to me and I will reward her-him for it." In another hadith tradition we are told that "To the fasting person belong two joyous occasions: when he breaks his fast and when he meets his Lord."

The Sermons open with an interesting lecture on food. It reflects on the prayer of Jesus to God to send down from heaven a "table spread" (ma'idah) to him and his doubting followers. This significant event in the prophetic mission of Jesus is described in Surah 5 of the noble Qur'an, which is known as surat al-ma'idah, that is the surah of the "table spread." The Sermons close with a few profound philosophical reflections on both the concept of Eid, and the major festivals in Islam. These of course include the festival of breaking the fast (eid al-fitr) of Ramadan. They also include some more particularly Shi'i festivals, such as eid al-Ghadir (the event of Ghadir Khumm, where the Prophet Muhammad PBUH declared the Imam `Ali to be his successor).

It is obvious that the author of the Ramadan Sermons is of the followers (Shi'a) of ahl al-Bayt, that is the people of the House of the Prophet Muhammad , peace be upon them all. Thus while he privileges the heritage of ahl al-bayt, he consciously avoids polemics. He presents the school of ahl al-bayt as a source of guidance for all Muslims, and even for all of humankind.

Mahmoud Ayoub

**Professor of Islamic Studies and Christian-Muslim Relations ,
Hartford Seminary
Professor Emeritus, Temple University**

Introduction

بسم الله الرحمن الرحيم الحمد لله رب العالمين والصلاة والسلام على المبعوث رحمة للعالمين سيدنا ومبينا وحبيب قلوبنا وطبيب نفوسنا النبي الامين محمد بن عبد الله وعلى آله الطيبين الطاهرين

بالمعرفة والثقافة كما اعتنى بها او نظام سياسي او اجتماعي من الأنظمة الحديثة او القديمة لم يعتن دين من الأديان السماوية الدين الاسلامي ولا اكد على طلب العلم وحث عليه كما فعل ذلك القرآن الكريم والسنة النبوية الشريفة

ففي الانظمة القديمة كان طلب العلم محصورا بطبقة معينة من الناس كرجال الدين وكهنة المعابد او ابناء الملوك والطبقات الحاكمة. ولم يكن ذلك يعني الكثير لعامة الناس بل كانوا ينظرون اليه على انه ترف لا يحتاجون اليه. اما الانظمة الحديثة فإن وفرت ما امكنها من وسائله وأدواته. أقصى ما توصلت اليه هو انها جعلت التعليم في بعض مراحله إلزاميا واعتبرتها حقا لكل فرد طلب العلم فيها بقي اختياريا اما الذي يرجع الى القرآن الكريم والأحاديث النبوية الشريفة فانه يجدهما يحثان على طلب . لكن ولا يقف عند حد معين او سن خاص بل هو العلم الى الحد الذي يصير معه واجبا على كل مسلم ومسلمة وليس حقاً فقط فريضة على كل فرد من المهد الى اللحد. كما ان تزويد المجتمع بكل ما يحتاجه من وسائل العلم والمعرفة وملئ كل الجوانب العلمية التي يحتاجها الناس هو واجب كفائي على المجتمع بأكمله

وحين نستعرض سور القرآن الكريم وآياته نجد فيها الحث الكثير على التعلم والتأمل والتدبر والتبصر والتفكر وغيرها ... مما يشير بوضوح تام إلى ان المجتمع المسلم الذي يراد له ان يكون تحت ظل الحكومة الاسلامية ينبغي ان يكون مجتمعا واعيا مثقفا سابقا وقد اتبع الاسلام أساليب متعددة ومتنوعة في نشر الثقافة والمعرفة بين كل أبنائه لكل المجتمعات الاخرى في شتى ميادين الحياة

وكان للثورة الحسينية دور أساسي في هذا المجال فمنذ الايام الاولى لفاجعة كربلاء بدا المنبر الحسيني يلعب دورا اساسيا في توعية المجتمع المسلم تقام مجالس العزاء الحسينية على مدار السنة الامة واصبح منطلقا لنشر الوعي والثقافة بين كل افراد حيث وخصوصا خلال شهري محرم وصفر من كل عام وفي ليالي شهر رمضان المبارك اضافة الى سائر المناسبات الاخرى كالاعياد الدينية ووفيات المعصومين وولاداتهم وغيرها من المناسبات ويعتبر القاء الخطب والمحاضرات فيها جزءا لا يتجزا من تلك المناسبات وأمرا اساسيا لا ينفك عنها فكان ذلك سببا في زيادة ثقافة المجتمع وتوعيته وأصبح خطباء تلك المنابر يقومون بدور الموجه والمربي. والمعرفة والمعلم الذي يزود افراد المجتمع بما يحتاجون اليه من ألوان العلم

والكتاب الذي بين يديك هو نموذج من تلك النماذج الدالة على الحركة الفكرية الناشطة لدى اتباع اهل البيت عليهم السلام والتي لا تكاد تجد مثيلا لها عند اية أمة من الامم الاخرى والمؤلف هو واحد من قلة قليلة تقوم بمهمة التثقيف والتعليم بين اوساط المؤمنين الناطقين باللغة الإنجليزية وقد لقيت محاضراته آذانا صاغية وتلقاها مستمعوها بشوق وارتياح كبيرين . وهذا الكتاب هو نتاج سلسلة من المحاضرات الرمضانية التي ألقاها المؤلف وسعى فيها الى تعميق الفكر والثقافة لدى مستمعيه فتعرض فيها الى موضوعات مختلفة ولم يقتصر على جهة معينة ولا موضوع محدد بل تطرق الى مجموعة من المجالات المعرفية التي يحتاجها الفرد والمجتمع على حد سواء فتحدث في والمجتمع الاخلاق وهو العقائد والإيديولوجيا السلوك عن الحديث يغفل ولم والتاريخ والسيرة وتعرَّض يهدف من ذلك الى الوصول الى مجتمع يتربى على القيم والاخلاق متزودا بالوان من المعرفة تصل به الى ان يصير مجتمعا واعيا متعلما ومثقفا وإنني إذ أتمنى له النجاح وتحقيق ما يصبو اليه على اشد على كلتا يديه مثمنا لجهوده شاكرا له اهتمامه بخدمة الدين الحنيف مشجعا له على الاستمرار في مسيرته التي اختارها له الله سبحانه وتعالى داعيا له منحه المزيد من التوفيق والتسديد.

In the name of Allah, the Beneficent the Merciful. Praise be to Allah, Lord of the worlds. May peace and blessings be sent upon he who was sent as mercy to all people; our Master, our Prophet, the beloved of our hearts and the physician of our souls; the trustworthy Prophet, Muhammed Ibn Abdillah and upon his virtuous and purified progeny.

No divine religion, or political or social system, modern or ancient, has placed more emphasis on knowledge and education than the religion of Islam. Similarly, the pursuit of knowledge and its emphasis has not been found anywhere more than in the Holy Qur'an and the Prophetic traditions.

In ancient societies, the pursuit of knowledge was limited to specific social classes, such as men of religion and the priests of the temple, or the children of kings and the ruling classes. Knowledge did not mean much to the general public, as they viewed it as a luxury that they did not need. As for modern societies, the furthest that has been reached is to make education compulsory for certain stages and to consider it a right for every individual. Thus they have done their best to provide as many means and tools for education as possible. However, the pursuit of knowledge has remained only optional. On the other hand, if one was to return to the Holy Qur'an and the Prophetic traditions, one would find a strong persistence on the pursuit of knowledge to such an extent that it becomes obligatory on every Muslim, and not just a right. Islam states there is no specific level or particular age at which this pursuit becomes optional; rather it remains an obligation on every individual from cradle to grave. Similarly, it is the collective responsibility of society to provide the means needed for the pursuit of knowledge and wisdom, and to satisfy all aspects of knowledge needed by its people.

When one examines the chapters of the Quran and its verses, one finds a strong encouragement to learn, ponder and reflect; showing with great clarity that the Muslim Society that aspires to be governed by an Islamic system needs to be a vigilant aware society, ahead of all other societies in all fields of life. Indeed, Islam followed numerous methods in spreading its culture and knowledge amongst its followers.

The revolution of Imam Hussain played a fundamental role in this regard. Since the early days of the tragedy of Karbala, the pulpit of Imam Hussein played a crucial part in educating the nation, as it became a platform in raising awareness and spreading knowledge among all members of the Muslim community. Gatherings were held commemorating the death of Imam Hussein throughout the year, particularly during the months of Muharram and Safar. In addition, they were held during the nights of the month of Ramadhan as well as on other occasions such as religious celebrations, and on the birth and death anniversaries of the infallibles. Delivering sermons and lectures is an integral part of these gatherings and inextricably linked to them. This has been a cause for increasing the knowledge and awareness of society, as the preachers from those pulpits played the role of the teacher and guide, providing members of society with all that they need with regards to science and knowledge.

The book in your hands is one of the examples which indicate the intellectual movement active among followers of the Ahlul Bayt (peace be upon them); a movement unmatched any other nation. The author is one from a selected few who are carrying out the task of educating English speaking believers and raising their awareness. His lectures have been received by attentive ears with great eagerness and satisfaction. This book is a product of a series of lectures delivered by the author in the month of Ramadhan in which he has strived to deepen the knowledge and enlightenment of his listeners. Rather than focussing on one specific topic, he deals with different subjects aiming to delve into a variety of fields which are needed at both the individual and societal levels. Thus, he talks about beliefs and ideology in addition to touching on history and biographies, not forgetting to discuss ethics and law. In doing so, he aims to arrive at a society brought up on values and ethics, supported by a diverse fabric of knowledge. With this, it becomes a society that it conscious, educated and knowledgeable.

I wish him all the success in achieving what he aspires. I praise him for his efforts, thank him for the interest he has in serving the religion and hope that his continues the path that he has chosen. I pray that Allah SWT grants him more success and guidance.

Sayed Mourtada Mourtada

Representative of Ayatollah Sayed Ali al-Seestani

Lecture 1

Prophet Jesus and Heavenly Food

"Jesus, the son of Mary said, 'O Allah, our Lord, send down to us a table [spread with food] from the heaven so that it may be a day of Eid for the first of us and the last of us and a sign from You. Provide for us, as You are the best of providers'" (5:114).

The discussion concerning the heavenly food, or al-Ma'idah, which was sent down to Jesus, son of Mary, from his Lord Almighty on behalf of his disciples is one of the most important discussions of food in the Holy Qur'an. It thus requires an extensive analysis as it provides us with different angles when understanding the ways in which different religions treat the subject of food. Indeed, the subject is of importance because Allah (SWT) names the fifth chapter in the Qur'an al-Ma'idah after this incident, in addition to being named after one of the most important needs of a human being. When one assesses the variety of needs within a human being, there are some needs which are easily satisfied whereas there are others which are not easily satisfied. An example of one of the needs which is easily satisfied is our need for clothing. Thus, the clothes that you wear in the morning will satisfy your needs for the whole day. However, the need for food is arguably one of the greatest human needs; throughout the day a human may have three or four different meals and may even take snacks in between those meals. This highlights how important food is in our development, for "a healthy mind produces a healthy body and a healthy body produces a healthy mind." Indeed, Islamic law values the human need for food to such an extent that it considers that need to be among one of the conditions which precludes punishment in Islamic law. For instance, if someone is caught stealing, according to the School of the Ahlulbayt, one of the conditions that would curtail the cutting of the fingers is whether the person was in a state of famine. Thus, Islam does not hastily punish someone that steals; indeed, one of the nineteen conditions that averts punishment is if the person who committed the crime is in a country that is in a state of famine, i.e., if the person has no food, then this leads to physical unrest.

Every religion throughout history has a particular law, or particular customs, in relation to food. Chapter 5, verse 114, highlights the position of food in Christianity and the necessity to not only understand the need of food in Islam but in other religions as well. With regard to globalization and the world becoming smaller, the interaction of people from different religions (in terms of food) is more likely, thus it is vital that we understand each other's laws and customs in relation to food so that we can respect each other's identity.

For example, if you were invited to a meeting with a Jewish businessman, there would be no dairy products alongside meat, as this is seen as unhealthy in Judaism. If you had a neighbour who was Jewish, you would not take them bitter herbs as they symbolise the plight of the children of Israel when they were oppressed by the Egyptian pharaohs. Furthermore, when something is kosher, that means it is clean. In Judaism they have their own set of laws under the system of kashrut.

Moreover, in relation to Christianity, you would not give food to a Catholic an hour before communion because all Catholics fast one hour preceding communion. Furthermore, the Mormons do not consume any kind of food or drink which has alcohol or caffeine in it as they consider it to be unlawful. Another sect of Christianity, known as the Seventh-Day Adventists (SDA), do not even eat meat. Therefore, in Judaism and Christianity they have their own laws in regards to food.

Even when one socialises with a Hindu, one finds they have their own set of laws as to which foods are acceptable and which are not. For example, Hindus value food so much that they state that with every food that you eat there is karma, and this karma has energy which affects you. The famous Hindu philosophical saying states, "You are what you eat." Meat is thus not allowed in Hinduism as there is slaughter involved which thus produces bad karma, whereas dairy products are viewed highly because they enhance spirituality. Garlic and onions are seen as reducing spirituality. Likewise with Buddhism, their Buddha was once an animal. Therefore Buddhists will not eat animals. Many Buddhist monks engage in fasting in the afternoon. Therefore it is seen as offensive to offer food to a religious monk in the afternoon.

Thus it is important to equally understand both our traditions in food, as well as those of other religions, in order to demonstrate respect. Also, it is important to understand that if another religion does not adhere to their traditions, we should not compromise our conduct towards our faith. For example, if a Christian was seen drinking alcohol (when their sect prohibits it), this does not mean that one should compromise their values and do the same.

Chapter 5 (Surah al-Ma'idah), verse 114, is seen as one of the greatest verses (during Ramadan) because the verse itself discusses the "heavenly Food" which Allah sent to Jesus on behalf of his disciples. Our analysis of this chapter will involve the following topics:

1. What are the benefits of reciting Surah al-Ma'idah?
2. Why does God say "Jesus, son of Mary" in the verse? Why is there a mention of his mother whenever he is mentioned in the Qur'an?
3. Why does Prophet Jesus say, "It will be a day of Eid for us...for the first of us and the last of us?"
4. Why does Prophet Jesus also say that the food you will send will be "a sign for us?"

Prophet Muhammad (PBUH) has stated, "If a person recites Surah al-Ma'idah every Thursday, Allah (SWT) will protect him from wrongdoing and will save him from associating partners with God. If a person recites this chapter, Allah (SWT) will give him ten good deeds, cancel out ten evil deeds and will raise the person ten stations higher than what he deserves."

The verse states, "Jesus, son of Mary, said, 'O Allah, our Lord, send down to us a table [spread with food] from the heaven so that it may be a day of Eid for the first of us and the last of us and a sign from You. Provide for us, as You are the best of providers.'" The verse starts off with "Jesus, son of Mary, said" and not "Jesus said" as firstly Allah (SWT) wanted to address the accusations that Mary performed an illicit act. At the birth of Jesus many people from the children of Israel believed that Mary performed an adulterous act. Another accusation that emerged from the Christians was that when Jesus was born he didn't have a father, therefore God was his father. Allah (SWT) thus began the verse with "Jesus, son of Mary" to highlight that He has power above all powers, that Allah can create a baby without a father. The Qur'an shows that before Jesus there were five creations who were born without a womb: Adam, Eve, the camel in the story of Prophet Salih, the sheep in the story of Prophet Isma'il, the snake in the story of Prophet Moses, and the birds were created from clay by Jesus later in his life. Therefore, when the verse began with "Jesus, son of Mary" Allah (SWT) wanted to say that I have already shown you five creations apart from Jesus who have been born without a father, so likewise Jesus was born fatherless.

Secondly, Allah (SWT) says, "Jesus, son of Mary" because Allah wants to tell us that if a Prophet of God can be born without a father from a virgin mother then never despair of His Mercy in your own lives. The human being always views Allah according to the same law of cause and effect as we put ourselves, i.e., when we make du'a whilst not wholeheartedly believing Allah can change things. "Jesus, son of Mary" is mentioned so that God reminds us that this was a miracle that broke the law of cause and effect so do not doubt if God can break human cause and effect.

The third reason why Allah starts the verse with "Jesus, son of Mary" is because there are some mothers who are even greater than their husbands, whereby Allah (SWT) always mentions their sons alongside them. Where Jesus is mentioned in the Qur'an, Mary is mentioned too, illustrating that Jesus would have never come about had it not been for one of the four women of Paradise. It is a response to those who believe that Islam oppresses women; Mary is constantly mentioned thereby refuting this notion. In history there are four women who Allah (SWT) has said are the women of paradise: Mary, Asiyyah, Khadijah and Fatima al-Zahra (AS). In the time of Prophet Muhammad (PBUH), there lived a man named Abu Talha al-Ansari who was one of the greatest companions of The Prophet (PBUH) and was of the "Ansar" of the people of "Medina" (i.e., not of the "Muhajiroon" from Mecca). Whenever The Prophet (PBUH) would lead prayer, Abu Talha would always be amongst the first to pray behind him, yet once he faced a severe test when his son became ill. He became preoccupied with his son instead of attending to *jama'ah*, and so his wife noticed this and reminded Abu Talha to go and receive blessings from the

Prophet by praying behind him. It so happened that same afternoon when he left to *jama'ah* that his son passed away. As soon as Abu Talha's wife witnessed this, she changed into her best clothes and she had told Abu Talha when he arrived that their son was resting. Abu Talha looked at her and noticed something different. He asked her if there was anything he had not given her. Abu Talha's wife told him that there was one thing he had missing which was that when someone gives him a trust he finds it hard to return it to them. She then explained how Allah (SWT) gave them their child and this afternoon he wanted it back. He replied in astonishment praising her patience. She was one of the many women in history who must be praised in Islam.

Prophet Jesus had a set of twelve disciples, Prophet Moses also had twelve disciples and our Prophet Muhammad likewise had twelve disciples. Prophet Jesus' disciples occupied a very high position, which was, that amongst their features, God could communicate to them through inspiration. There are certain of the creation of Allah (SWT) that God does not use an angel to communicate with, but instead does so through inspiration or "ilham" with a thought or piece of knowledge. In the Qur'an Allah says, "I revealed to the disciples of Jesus," which means this feature was amongst them. These disciples were the messengers between the people and Prophet Jesus; it is narrated that whenever Jesus would leave his house five thousand people would follow him. These five thousand were different in their composition; some were disciples, others were the lepers and the blind, a third group were his general followers and a fourth group of them were those who would mock him. Those who used to mock him came to the disciples of Jesus and challenged that if he truly was the Messiah, let God send down food from heaven to him. The disciples said to Prophet Jesus, "O Prophet of God, can your Lord send us down food from heaven?" Prophet Jesus replied, "Fear Allah, what you have just asked is not something of the pious." The disciples then said, "We do not doubt. We want our hearts to gain more yaqeen/certainty." This is because some yaqeen/certainty requires physical observation to have faith. Prophet Jesus then agreed to this and prayed to God for the Ma'idah/table spread from heaven. *"O Allah, our Lord, send down to us a table [spread with food] from the heaven so that it may be a day of Eid for the first of us and the last of us."*

Allah (SWT) answered his call and sent the heavenly food down on a Sunday. This is why Christians today take Sunday as their holy day. It also must be noted that if Prophet Jesus said a day that food was sent down would be celebrated as Eid, then how can the day that Prophet Muhammad was born in be a bid'ah and not Eid? The Eid of Jesus satisfied the stomach, however Eids such as Mubahila, Mawlid Nabawi or Ghadeer satisfies the mind of the human being.

Prophet Jesus also said that this Eid will be for the first of them and the last. This statement has highlighted that it is not bid'ah to remember an Eid every year. For instance, the birth of the Prophet should be an Eid every year. This word "Eid" was evidently used before Prophet Muhammad (PBUH). A further question arises as to why Allah gave it the name "Eid?"

There are four opinions as to why it is called the day of Eid. The first opinion is because the word Eid comes from the word "ya'ood" or "something returning," i.e., this day returns to us every year. The second opinion in the School of Ahlulbayt is that it is called Eid because Allah (SWT) returns His Mercy to human beings. There are certain days in the year where Allah sends His Mercy more than others, e.g., Laylat al-Qadr, a day where Allah sends down all His Mercy and removes all sins. Another such day is the hour on Friday where Allah sends His Mercy, or the Day of Ashura where Allah cures the people of their sins. The third opinion regarding the word "Eid" is because mankind returns mercy to each other, i.e., in Eid you tend to see everyone in the community. Our fourth Imam, on the night of Eid, would gather all the servants in his house and would ask them questions like, "Have I ever wronged you?" and "Have I ever been unmerciful towards you?" They would say, "No, Zaynul Abideen." The Imam would then reply, "Then I ask you to pray for me on the day of Eid, that in the same way I have not wronged you, then do not let me wrong Allah (SWT), and in the same way that I have been merciful to you, let Allah be merciful to me on the Day of Judgment."

The fourth opinion concerning the name "Eid" says that, because there was a horse in Arabia called "al-Khayl al-Eidiya," or "the Horse of Principle," as in generosity or honour, the Arabs decided to name their festivals "Eid" after this horse, just as the day of Eid is the day of principles, generosity and honour. Verse 5:114 then goes on to say, "*...and a sign from You.*" Prophet Jesus thus describes food as a sign from Allah (SWT). This is because when we look around the world we notice those who are in poverty and in need of food whilst there are those who partake in luxury meals. Food, according to Prophet Jesus, tried to highlight to the Christians of the time, and to the Muslims also (until the Day of Judgment), that any food given to you, whether it is from heaven or from earth, is a sign from Allah. Equally every sign of Allah needs to be protected. But how does one protect food?

The first point about protecting food is that if Allah says that food is a sign from God, then earn your food in a lawful manner and not through prohibited manner. One of the signs of our Holy Prophet Muhammad (PBUH) was that the Jews had known that the Final Messiah would never eat food which is unlawful or dubious (i.e., if one is unsure if it is halal). When the Jews had seen a seven-year-old boy walking in Arabia, having known the Prophet would come from Arabia whilst displaying the signs of Prophethood, they wanted to test what had been written in their scriptures. They tried to make two scenarios, one offering unlawful food and the other which had dubious food, i.e., it wasn't halal and wasn't haram either. The Jews had offered the Prophet stolen fowl for the first scenario and the Prophet would not allow the food to come near his mouth. For the second scenario, they took some fowl from their neighbour but they had the intention of paying him when he had returned. Whenever they tried to force this food towards the Prophet, the food would not come near his mouth. Those around the Prophet from then on knew that he was the Messiah, as unlawful and dubious food did not enter his mouth.

Al-Mansoor al-Dawaneeqi, one of the Bani Abbas caliphs who poisoned Imam al-Sadiq (AS), was known to be stingy, or "dawaneeqi." While he was caliph, Imam al-Baqir (AS) was in prison. Whenever they would bring food to the Imam, he would not eat it as it was from unlawful money and the family of the Prophet knew that food is a sign from Allah. One of the Shi'a ladies gave some food to the jail warden to give to the Imam. The Imam explained that he couldn't eat it because, although it had been lawfully made, it reached him unlawfully. Moreover, Harun al-Rashid would invite guests to his palace to eat his unlawful food and would then give the leftovers to Bahlool. However, Bahlool asked that the food be given to some dogs in front of them instead. The guards were angered saying "How dare you give the Caliph's food to the dogs. Bahlool said to them "Don't say that too loudly, because then even the dogs will not eat the food!"

Knowing that the food from God is a sign is also acknowledging the poor. Imam Ali (AS), whenever he knew there were those who didn't have food, he wouldn't eat until they were given food. This is why verse 5:114 was once used by Imam Ali and Lady Fatima al-Zahra (AS) when they did not have any food at all. One day, Amir al-Mu'mineen was leaving his house. He saw Fatima al-Zahra. Her face was pale, and he had asked what was the matter. Fatima replied, "There has been three days where me and my children have not eaten anything. I did not tell you as my father The Prophet (PBUH) had told me to not trouble you."

Imam replied that she should not worry as he will get a loan for them. When he had left the house he bumped into his companion Miqdad. Miqdad then told Imam how one of his children fell unconscious that day as they had nothing to eat and how he was shy to even look at Imam. Imam had just borrowed one dinar that he straightaway gave to Miqdad. When Imam had gone to pray, the Prophet told him he would be visiting them. Fatima al-Zahra knew that there was no food at home and she knew that food was a sign from Allah, whether it was from heaven or earth. She went into the kitchen and recited verse 5:114. "When Jesus, son of Mary, wanted food you gave him, Ya Allah," she said.

The hadith narrates that Angel Gabriel came down to her and said to her, "O Fatima, your Lord has answered your du'a. You wanted food from paradise, then open my wings." As soon as he opened his wings, the hadith says, there was food which had the scent of musk and amber. Therefore, this verse was used also by the Family of the Prophet to tell us that if there is no food on earth then ask for food from heaven, and Allah will open his doors.

Lecture 2

Enjoining the Good and Forbidding the Evil

Amr bil maa'ruf wa nahi an al-munkar, or "enjoining the good and forbidding the evil," is one of the most important acts in the religion of Islam. This act is both individual and collective, and is an act which is important in the social spectrum of the religion of Islam. It is an act at the very root of Islam as it is one of the Furoo' al-Deen or, the "roots of the religion." Therefore it is an obligatory act, just like the other roots of religion, such as prayer, sawm, hajj, zakat and khums. Any great community is one which constantly enjoins the good and forbids the evil. Throughout history, many of the successful communities were ones that built enjoining good and forbidding evil as a legacy. Weaker communities, however, were those who neglected this. Hence, in Islamic thought, enjoining the good and forbidding the evil is vital for every successful community.

The neglect of "amr bil maa'ruf wa nahi an al-munkar" is normally because of two reasons. The first reason is because of fear of the governor or caliph of the time. The greatest leaders in history were those who let their people speak out against their policies. When Umar ibn Abdel Aziz became caliph of Bani Umayyah, he said upon becoming caliph, "Many people choose a leader to rule over them, whereas I ask you to rule over me. Anytime you see me doing good, enjoin it and if you see me doing bad speak out against it." The second reason why people do not enjoin good and forbid evil is psychological. People say, as long as I am good why should I care about others? The Qur'an stresses that the best of communities is one in which no one remains silent. They speak out against wrongdoing. Surah 3, verse 104, says, "And let there be [arising] from you a nation inviting to [all that is] good, enjoining what is right and forbidding what is wrong, and those will be the successful."

Likewise, when the Islamic state was built in Medina by the Prophet, who stayed there for ten years, the aim of the state was not to be economically or military powerful, rather the aim was to enjoin the good and forbid the evil. Hence, we find in Surah 22, verse 41, that Allah (SWT) tells us what the aim of the Islamic state is: "(They are) those who, if We establish them in the land, establish regular prayer and give regular charity, enjoin the right and forbid wrong. With Allah rests the end (and decision) of (all) affairs." Thus, the aim of the Islamic state is to build the worship aspect of a community, as well as the social aspect – and this involves "enjoining the good and forbidding the evil." Likewise we find in the Qur'an that when Luqman spoke to his son, one of the first pieces of advice was to "establish your prayers and carry out the enjoining of good and forbidding of evil." The Qur'an here shows us that it is one of the roots of the religion that must be established at even a young age because this then builds a child who has a social vision of the world around them. Many times the child is taught dogmatic principles, merely following things without thinking, whereas a vision of enjoining the good and forbidding the evil will allow them to build society from a young age.

Scholars discuss enjoining the good and forbidding the evil in the areas of fiqh and aqa'id as well as in the area of kalam. In fiqh, we find that, in the front pages of the scholar's risaala, the discussion of enjoining good and forbidding evil already starts here because it is a social responsibility binding on anyone that passes buloogh. Buloogh is when a person has reached the age to carry out the roots of the religion and now they have a responsibility to enjoin good and forbid evil. The aim is that when you learn the laws of this religion, you should apply them and spread them. And when you see people not acting upon them, then speak out. Also, the scholars of aqa'id discuss enjoining good and forbidding evil under Usool al-Deen, part of Qiyamat, or the Day of Judgement (Usool al-Deen includes tawheed, adala, nubuwa and qiyamat). Enjoining good and forbidding evil is the best action to remind someone of death and the Day of Judgement.

Thirdly, there is a beautiful discussion on enjoining good and forbidding evil where there is a difference of opinion between Ayatullah Burujurdi and Allama al-Hilli. The discussion is deeply rooted in philosophy and forms the basis of this lecture. The question posed is the following – Is "enjoining good and forbidding evil" something natural or something which is learnt through religion? Would those from other religions have this trait already or would you have to be Muslim to carry it out? Burujurdi believed that enjoining good and forbidding evil is something naturally instilled within us, irrespective of whether someone is Muslim or not. He gave an example in Persian poetry about a blind man walking towards a well and two other people watching. One is a Muslim man and the other one is an observer watching if this Muslim will go help the blind man. Burujurdi believed that the observer does not have to be religious to go and tell the Muslim he was wrong if he did not help the blind man. Allama al-Hilli had differed with this opinion; he said enjoining good and forbidding evil is learnt through religion and is not natural. This lecture will analyse how al-Hilli proved this.

The Holy Prophet (PBUH) instructs us of the punishment that comes to those who do not perform the enjoining of good and forbidding of evil. One day the Holy Prophet was asked, "Who is the weakest person?" The Prophet answered, "The weakest person is the one who sees evil and does not speak out against it." To us, the weak are physically or emotionally unable to cope with matters, but the Prophet here states that the person who is weak is one who does not speak out against evil. In another hadith, our Holy Prophet says, "Beware that if you do not speak out against tyranny and oppression then one day the bad amongst you will rule and when you supplicate to Allah, your supplication will not be accepted." In a third hadith the Prophet has been narrated to have said, "Waylun (or Woe) to those people who do not enjoin good and forbid evil." Waylun is the deepest pits of Hellfire, thus if you do not carry the enjoining of good and forbidding evil then you will be in the deepest pits of Hell.

Now the question arises as to how should someone perform the enjoining of good and forbidding of evil. Also, what are the three conditions of enjoining good and forbidding evil? And what are the three levels of enjoining good and forbidding evil? How did Imam Hussein (AS) act out the enjoining of good and forbidding of evil on the tenth of Muharram? Firstly, the Qur'an instructs us to carry out the enjoining of good and forbidding evil in two ways. The first direction is that we must "invite the people to Allah with hikmah (wisdom) and good preaching." Plato used to also say, "A wise man has something to say, whereas a fool has to say something."

Many times when we try and bring people towards Allah (SWT), but we mess up the whole intention by performing it in an incorrect manner and without wisdom. Some may shout, act arrogantly or even be intimidating. Montesquieu used to say, "A good leader doesn't stand above his men but alongside them." This means that in the same way the Ahlulbayt have taught us, if we want to help a person by enjoining good and forbidding evil, then we should make them feel as if they are in the same struggle as you. For example, if your sister does not wear hijab, you can say how it is difficult in this day and age for both of you, but we can struggle to reach religiosity together. All they have to do is go that one step closer to Allah (SWT) by wearing the hijab. Rather than being arrogant one can talk to someone in a nice way with wisdom. Likewise for example there are lecturers who talk down to their crowd, but there are those that show the struggle is equally difficult for themselves as well as for others, yet if they can be religious, then so can everyone else.

The second way to perform "amr bil maa'ruf wa nahi an al-munkar," or enjoining the good and forbidding the evil, is to stroke then strike and not to strike and then stroke. If you immediately let someone know of their negative points, then the person will not listen to the rest of what you have to say. The Qur'an came and told the Prophet Muhammad (PBUH), "O Prophet of God, if you were hard-hearted (or severe) then everyone would have fled from you."

This means that The Prophet (PBUH) was able to bring everyone to the religion of Islam through his warmth and good preaching when enjoining good and forbidding evil rather than negativity. If you are trying to enjoin good and forbid evil, you should firstly think of all the good things they do or have, e.g., charity work, akhlaaq, etc. After this, you can then mention the one area which they seem to be struggling in. The fourth Imam was walking one day and Hassan al-Muthanna saw him and said, "You are a person who is not acting as he should be. You have neglected the message of your grandfather and you are a person who people should oppose."

The Imam looked at his companions, who thought the Imam would reply to al-Muthanna, but the Imam simply walked away. The next day the

Imam asked them to come with him to meet al-Muthanna, saying look at how I will act with him and take away some wisdom. Imam said, "O Hassan! I did not expect such an action coming out form you. If I am truly like what you have said, then ask Allah to forgive me. But if I am not as you have said, then I ask Allah to forgive you." In this way the Imam showed al-Muthanna that they are living in the same world, both struggling with the same aim. Then he said he "wouldn't expect this from him" as if to say he is better than this and for them to be forgiven as to whoever is wrong. This is what Islam, as well as enjoining good and forbidding evil, is all about.

Furthermore, The Prophet (PBUH) explains that there are three conditions of "enjoining good and forbidding evil." The first condition is to ensure that you have knowledge of what you are talking about. If you go to enjoin good and forbid evil about a certain aspect then someone can easily turn the tables on you and ask you why you haven't researched the topic fully, or they can even ask you a question which you do not have the answer to. The second caliph in Islam demonstrated this example one day when he was walking the streets trying to spot anyone doing anything unlawful in order to stop them. He came across a house where a man and woman were merrymaking and laughing. The caliph jumped over the wall of the house and found them sitting near a jar of wine, which they had been drinking from. The caliph asked,"How can you drink whilst I am caliph?" The seated man replied, "I may have committed one sin, but you have committed three. The first sin you have done is in Surah 49, verse 12, of the Qur'an which says, 'O ye who believe! Avoid suspicion as much (as possible), for suspicion in some cases is a sin. And spy not on each other behind their backs.' You spied behind my back without me knowing and the second sin is mentioned in Surah 2, verse 189, 'And it is not righteousness to enter houses from the back, but righteousness is [in] one who fears Allah. And enter houses from their doors. And fear Allah that you may succeed.' You must enter from the door but you entered by jumping over the building, and the third sin you have performed is in Surah 24, verse 61, 'But if ye enter houses, salute each other – a greeting of blessing and purity as from Allah.' When you entered you didn't even say Assalamu Alaykum. You tried to enjoin the good and forbid the evil against me, but you have done three wrong acts." The second caliph was embarrassed and made him promise that he would stop drinking alcohol and left. The idea here is that when we want to do "amr bil maa'ruf wa nahi an al-munkar" we must do it on ourselves first, and make sure we have enough knowledge to do it.

The second condition the Prophet gave was that you ensure that your actions do not contradict your words. For example, you cannot be a hypocrite when one day you tell someone to pray on time but the next day you pray three hours late. Amir al-Mu'mineen never contradicted himself with what he preached and what he practiced. On one day he would tell everyone to speak out against the oppressors and the next day he would oppose the oppressor and support the oppressed. It was narrated that one day he was walking the streets of Kufa, and would walk in the markets and ensure everything was fine. He happened to see a slave girl crying, he asked her why she was crying and she answered, "My master had asked me to get some dates, but when I gave it to my master he didn't like the look of these dates and asked that I return it to them and get my money back. But when I came here he will not return my money."

Imam asked her to take him to the man selling the dates. The people in the market didn't recognise him as they didn't think their caliph would be amongst them. Imam told the man about how this slave girl brought the dates from him, her master doesn't want them and all it costs is a dirham, give this to her and let her return. However, the man still refused to do so and the man pushed Imam Ali (AS). The companions of Imam let the man know who he had pushed. Ali ibn Abu Talib told the man he was trying to stop oppression and your role is to help this slave girl. The man apologised and returned the dirham. Here the second condition of enjoining good and forbidding evil is to practice what you preach. The Imam is infallible, so his actions are not different from the words which he states.

The third condition of enjoining good and forbidding evil is to not speak to someone who will not change as you are wasting your time with them. There are certain people who deserve the energy but then there are others who are arrogant from the beginning. The Qur'an says, "There are those who impress you when they speak but when you tell them to fear Allah, they take pride in going against Allah (SWT)." This verse was revealed about Akhnas ibn Sharee' who was one of the richest men in Arabia. Even when The Prophet (PBUH) was going towards Ta'if, he asked Akhnas to help him and stay in his residence. However Akhnas refused the entry of the Prophet (PBUH). Akhnas was the same man who killed the Prophet's cousin Abdullah in the battle of Uhud, yet the Prophet persisted in trying to bring him towards Islam. On the day Akhnas read his shahadat to become a Muslim, he saw a pasture with animals grazing; he thought to himself, how could someone else have the blessings he had, so he burnt the whole field with fire. The Prophet (PBUH) worked hard to bring him to Islam, but Allah (SWT) in this verse was trying to tell the Prophet to not waste time on those who were arrogant from the start.

In hadith the Holy Prophet gives us three levels to go through to enjoin good and forbid evil. The first way is for your heart to enjoin good and forbid evil. This is the lowest form, and is the very least that we can do. For example, when you hear the plight of Muslims around the world, you cannot help physically so at least you can allow your heart to burn for them. The hadith of the Holy Prophet states, "The one who wakes up in the morning and does not care about the affairs of the Muslims is not a Muslim." The second level to enjoining good and forbidding evil is to use your tongue, because Allah (SWT) gave you that tongue as a blessing to speak out against injustice. Martin Luther King used to say, "At the end we will not remember the words of our enemies but the silence of our friends."

When the seventh Imam died, like every Imam, he had a representative who looked after the khums of the believers. The seventh Imam had two representatives who were meant to give him the khums. One of them, Ziyad al-Qandi, had 70,000 gold coins, and another, Ali ibn Hamza, had 30,000 gold coins. When the Imam died, greed overtook them. Ziyad told Ali that the Imam after them is Ali ibn Musa al-Ridha and that the best option for them is to make a false accusation that Musa ibn Ja'far did not die and had gone into ghaybah. The two of them formed a sect called al-Waqifiyah, which can be translated as "those who have stopped" at Musa al-Kadhim. There was another companion of Imam al-Kadhim named Younis ibn Abdelrahman who was known for his "enjoining good and forbidding evil." Younis spoke out and said that Imam al-Kadhim had died in Baghdad and the Imam after him was Ali ibn Musa al-Ridha (AS). Ziyad and Ali ibn Hamza came to Younis and asked him why he was doing this as this could stop them from being so rich and they offered him 10,000 gold coins so that he would stop telling the truth. Younis refused the money and told them, "You will never stop Imam al-Ridha's mission. I do not care if you become my enemies because Imam al-Sadiq has said, 'If the elders and the leaders of a community do not speak out when they see evil, then know that the light of the guidance of Allah

(SWT) will leave that community.'" Ibn al-Sikeet lost his tongue defending the Holy Prophet and his Holy Progeny. Mutawakkil asked him, "Who do you love more, Hassan and Hussein, or my children?" Ibn al-Sikeet could have easily worried about his bank balance which was in the hands of Mutawakkil but he feared the bank balance of deeds held by Allah on the Day of Judgement, so he said, "I have more respect for Qanbar the slave of Ali than I have for your own children." This caused his death and the cutting of his tongue because he stood up against the unjust caliph to enjoin good and forbid evil.

The third level of enjoining good and forbidding evil is, that if you have used your heart and tongue, then if it means you have to use your sword to defend the religion, then so be it. This level can be seen in Ashura with the following statement of Imam Hussein (AS): "I have not left Medina and Mecca for fame or for glory or for wealth or for kingdom. I have left so I can follow the Message of my grandfather The Prophet (PBUH). I want to enjoin the good and forbid the evil. I want to follow the path of my father Ali and my grandfather Muhammad." This is why in Imam Hussein's ziyarat we admit that his martyrdom was nothing other than enjoining the good and forbidding the evil. This was the sole aim of the poet when he said, "If the religion of Muhammad (PBUH) will not stand except with my death, then oh swords come and take me."

In conclusion, Hilli believed that enjoining good and forbidding evil was learnt through religion. Hilli said that only through religion do you know that enjoining good and forbidding evil has three conditions and only via religion do you know there are three levels. Hilli also said that the true enjoining of the good and forbidding of the evil was conducted by Imam Hussein (AS) when he first showed that his heart was uneasy with the evil that was happening at the time, then he spoke out until the sword took him and he was victorious over evil.

Lecture 3

The Philosophy of Du'a

Supplication, or du'a, is regarded as one of the most important forms of worship in the religion of Islam, and indeed, it is one of the most beneficial. Supplication doesn't just exist in Islam, but it can also be seen in the life of virtually every human being. Thus the act of supplication is carried out in order to maintain a relationship with the Almighty Allah (SWT). The human being supplicates for many different reasons, such as an increase in wealth or an increase in health. The Roman Catholics view supplication as being one of the important aspects of their religion, and supplication in Catholicism is honoured in the Noveni, which translates in Latin as the number nine. Catholics come in to church on the nine days preceding Christmas Day (from the 16th to 25th of December) and supplicate everyday as they believe that when the whole Catholic community supplicates, then God will accept their combined supplication. Further than this, in the chapter of James in the Bible, Chapter 5, verse 13, there is a set of supplications which was left behind by the children of Israel.

There is a also chapter in the Bible called the Psalms, or Zaboor. Prophet Dawood is a prophet for the children of Israel as well as a Prophet in Islam. The Psalms are a collection of prayers which are read by the Christians. In the School of Ahlulbayt, we have the collection of "Saheefa al-Sajjadiya," which comes from the fourth Imam. It is the Zaboor of the Holy Progeny, and within it is equivalent of the du'as of Prophet Dawood. The words of Zain al-Abideen (AS) are put [by God] as equivalent to the

King of the Children of Israel. In the Munajat of Imam Ali (AS), he says, *"My Master, O my Master, You are the Guide and I am the astray. Who is there to help the astray one other than the Guide?"*

Every du'a has a specific time, place, etiquette, and value to its words. There is a beautiful conception of du'a in Buddhism. They believe that when one recites du'a they must do so with the etiquette that requires you to recite through contemplation. Thus in contemplating over the words there is more chance that they are attracted towards the supplication. The du'a following the Asr prayer states, *"Ya Allah, I seek refuge from you from a du'a which is not being heard."*

Some du'as are recited without paying attention to the words, but the essence of du'a is to allow us to contemplate, and if our Imams speak like this, then what are we meant to say to our Lord? Imam Ali (AS) teaches us to remember two points when it comes to supplication. In Du'a Kumayl he states, *"My Lord, I have faced you and you alone."* In other words, the recognition here is that this du'a is purely to Allah, and you are not getting distracted with your environment, but rather are submerged in the supplication. And then the Imam says, *"My hands are extended to you."* Our whole arms should extend to Allah to carry out the specific etiquette. The Imam has a third etiquette with du'a. He says, *"All that I have with these hands which I raise as a weapon are my tears."* One has to ask for their prayers to be answered with full emotion.

Du'a Mashlool came about when Imam Hussein (AS) was walking with the Commander of the Faithful as they were performing the tawaf of the Ka'aba pilgrimage. They heard the crying of a young man. Imam Ali (AS) asked Imam Hussein if he had heard this cry and asked him to find him. Imam had found him between rukun and maqam, and brought him to his father. He asked him why he was crying so loudly. The man replied, "I am crying because of my disobedience and sin as I have been unjust to my father. My father was a good man but whenever he would repeatedly tell me to be religious I wouldn't listen. One day I tried to take some money from the house, but my father spotted me. When he spotted me, he came towards me and pulled me down so as not to take the money. As he was doing this, I pulled him too and threw him. This caused him extreme pain, and when he couldn't get up, he told me he would curse me in front of Allah (SWT). Later I saw him holding the Ka'aba and complaining to Allah about me, asking for my punishment. As soon as he did this, I became paralysed on one side of my body. I begged my father for forgiveness, and I would cry. Three years later my father agreed to ask Allah to forgive me near the Ka'aba. On the way to our pilgrimage, however, a bird had come and hurt my father's camel whereby the camel fell, so my father fell too and died. Therefore I have come to ask Allah for my body to return the way it used to be."

Imam Ali responded to this man asking him to recite this du'a (Du'a Mashlool) – but when you recite it, do so with tears on the eve of the tenth of Thul Hijjah, i.e., the eve of Eid al-Fitr. The young man then narrates to have recited this du'a like he had never done so before. The tears were overflowing. "And on the first day of reciting it, I was going to go on to the second day when I heard a voice in my ear telling me that my du'a had been received." In his dream he even saw the Messenger of Allah touching the part of the body that was paralysed. From that day onwards he was able to walk again.

This highlights to us the importance of du'a. Amongst the etiquette of du'a is turning your face towards Allah mentally, with the hands being raised and letting the tears flow. When you examine history, Qur'an, and hadith, you find that du'a comes to us in many different ways. For example, in history, you find that the Arabs used to also indulge in du'a in the days of "Jahiliya," or Ignorance. However, they placed no concern as to the etiquette of du'a, and so their prayers were rejected. In Surah 43, verse 36, Allah describes the Arabs' du'a. "Those who you supplicate towards, those besides Allah, will never be able to help you."

So then we must ask, why did the Arabs, or people in general, worship idols? The human being has two pressures coming towards him, the pressure of the soul and the pressure of our senses. Every soul looks for an ideology; even the atheist has this pressure. The pressure of the senses is when your hands want to touch something and your eyes want to see something. Similarly, the Arabs wanted to see something physically in order to worship it. In Islam we believe that part of the worshipping of God is not just believing what is seen but believing in what is unseen as well. When the Arab would ask the idol if they would accept their du'as, they would get a bowl and put three pieces of paper in it, with the words "act" or "do not act," and the last one would be blank. Then they would go ahead and pick the first paper that their hands touched and follow it. This is why, when Abu Dharr al-Ghafari saw his tribe worshipping like this, he was sure that this was not the right way. His tribe then saw him converting to Islam early on, as he was the fourth person to convert to the religion. When they asked him why, Abu Dharr replied, "As a result of the fox that urinates." He had seen the idol standing there alone and this fox stopped past it and it decided to urinate on the top of what they had worshipped. If that which they worshipped cannot protect itself from the urine of the fox, then how would it protect Abu Dharr in the darkness of the night? Thus the Arabs did not have their du'as accepted as they had put partners with Allah.

In Surah 25, verse 77, there is one line which shakes the soul of the human being when it comes to du'a. Allah (SWT) says, "I would not care for any of you if it wasn't for your du'a." This is reflected in a Hadith Qudsi which states, "My servants, I did not create you for my needs. I created you so I could bless you with your needs."

Likewise, when one reads du'a, Allah isn't receiving anything which He does not have, instead it is us who are benefiting. Imam Hassan (AS) was once asked a question in which he answered only in a way that Imam Hassan would answer. He was asked, "What's the distance between the heavens and the earth?" To which the Imam responded with, "The distance between the heavens and the earth is the cry of an oppressed person in du'a." The Imam here didn't mean the heavens to be the planets, he meant the Lord of the heavens and the humans themselves. Prophet Muhammad (PBUH) even says, "A du'a is the key to Paradise." Moreover, in Surah 42, verse 60, Allah says, "Ask me, I will answer you."

What more of a promise do you need?

Again in the Qur'an, a beautiful verse in Chapter 7, verse 55, says, "Read du'a openly and privately." That is why there is a difference between du'a and munajat, the former is recited openly and the latter secretively, as munajat means "whispered prayers." Our Holy Prophet was once asked to define du'a and he replied, "Du'a is the weapon of the believer. The light which keeps the heaven and earth alight is du'a." There is no use to a weapon if it is left untouched. One of the names the Commander of the Faithful used to go by is "Da'aa." Wherever he used to go, he would supplicate.

A hadith regarding du'a says, "Those who leave du'a, they have committed a great sin." Some of those who have asked for something and it wasn't answered stop supplicating as they stop believing. In the Qur'an every Prophet of God has his own personal du'a related to his personal situation. This can then be used in our own lives. For example, for those who cannot have children, the du'a by Prophet Zakariya can be recited. Prophet Zakariya had reached old age and still didn't have any children so he asked Allah for a son in Surah Maryam. Similarly, Prophet Ibrahim prayed for an obedient son in Surah 37, verse 98, "Ya Allah, give me a righteous son." There is also a du'a of Adam and Eve for those repenting, in Chapter 7, verse 23, which says, "O Allah, we have oppressed ourselves. Therefore, if you don't forgive us, we will become of those who are lost."

The best verse in the Qur'an when it comes to du'a is, "When my servant asks you about me, tell him I am near. I answer the supplication of the supplicant when he supplicates towards me." This verse was revealed one day when a man had come to the Prophet (PBUH) and asked him if God was near to us or far away. As soon as the man had asked this, this verse came down. The beauty of this verse can be seen in the Arabic, because when Allah speaks about His human beings He does not speak as if humans are sinners, rather he speaks about them as if they belong to him as an "abd," or servant. Instead of using the line, "When the oppressors ask you about me," Allah uses, "When my servant asks you about me." Even when the human has done haram, Allah refers to the human as "my servant." Normally in the Qur'an Allah refers to Himself as being plural, e.g., in Surah Kawther, "We have given you al-Kawthar." Allah uses the plural because of His greatness, therefore the more formal Arabic is used. However, this verse is the only verse in the Qur'an that uses singular when he mentions His creation. Seven times in one verse Allah (SWT) uses singular and not plural. Allah wanted to show that He is so close to us that even the high language he normally uses is unnecessary with du'a. In other words, we should never doubt Allah as He is the most Merciful.

Nevertheless, some still may ask as to why our du'as are still not answered. The first point as to why our du'as are not accepted can be answered by Imam Ali (AS). In Du'a Kumayl, he says, "O Allah, forgive me those sins which block my du'a from being answered." Sins committed by us must be forgiven, for in response to our du'as being answered by Allah, an unforgiven sin hinders its acceptance. Equally, if one stops relations with their near relatives their du'a will not be answered. Imam al-Sadiq (AS) used to have a cousin by the name of Hassan. This cousin of the Imam was known to be of strong build. It has been narrated that he fought with Abdullah against al-Mansoor al-Dawaneeqi. This cousin, Hassan, fought al-Mansoor without the Imam's orders and so became an enemy of the Imam to the extent where he even tried to kill our Imam. When the sixth Imam was dying, he let his servant Saleema know that he must pay a loan to Hassan. Saleema asked why the Imam would want to do this when he was betrayed by him? The Imam replied, "Do you want to be one of those people who Allah says in the Qur'an if they break the covenant with their families are punished on the Day of Judgement and their du'as are not answered because of this?"

Secondly, sometimes our du'as are not accepted because Allah's wisdom is more extensive than ours. We may be short-sighted whereas Allah sees things in the long term. Sometimes we don't accomplish things which we wish we had done, but then we find out it was for the best. Allah has a much greater wisdom than ours and so we should leave everything to Him. Therefore, one of Allah's names is "the Wise," or "al-Hakim." Thirdly, du'as are not answered if they do not begin with salutations to Muhammad and his Holy Progeny – Allahumma Salli 'Ala Muhammad Wa Alee Muhammad. Imam al-Sadiq (AS) says, "Every du'a has a veil on it, but when you recite salawat at the beginning of the du'a, the veil is removed."

There is also a narration that says the angels come forward and return back to Paradise where other angels see them and ask them what beautiful fragrance surrounds them. The reply is that this fragrance is from a gathering where the "fathaa'il," or "attributes," of the Ahlulbayt (AS) are being recited. The latter group of angels then go to this gathering to be blessed with this fragrance. And when they go, the Mu'mineen are not present but they still are fragrant as the salawats are retained there. The School of Ahlulbayt also believe that the reason why Prophet Ibrahim was named "Khalil," or the "Friend," of Allah was that he always used to recite salawat. When the verse was revealed saying, "O you who believe, send your greetings to Muhammad and his Family," when this verse was revealed, some people came to the Prophet and asked him if the greetings should only be given to him. The prophet replied, "No, the salawat [which is] only to me is "batraa," or incomplete. Whenever you hear my name, you say salawat on me and my family."

Fourthly, if you wish for your du'a to be accepted, one should pray for others before they pray for themselves. Once a man came to Prophet

Musa and told him how he always recites du'a but it is never accepted even though he is very sincere. The Prophet replied, "I do not know. You are a good man so let me ask my Lord." The Prophet then asked Allah as to why the man'ssdu'as are never accepted. Allah replied that the man was only reciting for himself. Another narration involves a man coming to Prophet Muhammad (PBUH) and asking for his du'a to be recited by the Prophet himself, and then the Prophet raised his hands in prayer. A few days later, the man returned and thanked the Prophet. As he got up to leave, he said, "Ya Allah, bless me and Muhammad, but no one else." The Prophet (PBUH) looked at him and said his du'a may not be accepted again as one of the etiquettes of du'a is to remember others before your own du'a. Hadith also reminds us to supplicate for our parents first, then ourselves. It is as if the parents have a similar relationship to us as Allah does with a child. Allah (SWT) created the child, and so did the parents, and so Allah is merciful towards them and protects them because they are the parents of the child. Allah doesn't ask back from the child, likewise with the parents.

The place where one is supplicating is the fifth point to consider in acceptance of your du'a. For example, places like Masjid al-Kufa, Masjid al-Nabawi, Masjid al-Haram, Karbala. Mutawakkil, the caliph, had a female dancer who used to perform for him. One day he had asked for her and they had told him she wasn't available. This was in the month of Sha'ban, when she had gone for hajj. However, Sha'ban is not the month for hajj pilgrimage. He then found out that this pilgrimage was a hajj to Imam Hussein (AS) in Karbala. She was secretly forced into dancing for Mutawakkil, but whenever she had anything to ask for she would go to Karbala. When she returned, Mutawakkil angrily asked her why she had gone there as Mutawakkil had tried to destroy the maqam in Karbala four times in his life. She replied, "O Mutawakkil, you have employed me as a dancer, but when I want to supplicate, I do not find a place nearer to Allah than the place where He said, 'God loves those who love Hussein.'" Also, Prophet Zakariya went to pray for Maryam in the mihrab where he secluded himself and carried out supplication to Allah.

A further reason as to why oursdu'as are not acknowledged is because Allah (SWT) loves seeing his servant ask. The Prophet (PBUH) used to say, "There is nothing more beloved to the Lord than when he sees his servant cry and ask." Sometimes Allah does not answer your prayer, not because you have done something wrong, but because he loves it when you read du'a to him. One day Prophet Ibrahim saw this man who was a known worshipper. This man used to worship in the woods. But one day he stopped worshipping, so the Prophet asked if he could see how he used to worship. The man replied, "O man, you cannot worship with me as I go across a river and you do not have the ability to cross the water. I do not know who you are and what you are capable of." Prophet Ibrahim asked him not to worry as he will try to walk with him. The Prophet walked with him across the water, but then the man said that he cannot pray with the Prophet as he had been praying for many years for this one thing. One day he had met a man in this place called Isma'il. "He said to me that he is the son of the Prophet Ibrahim. I prayed from that day until today to meet the Prophet Ibrahim, but I must have done something wrong as I still have not met him." "I am Prophet Ibrahim. The reason why Allah did not answer your du'a was not because you may have a sin, but he loved you when you were asking," the Prophet said when the man had finished his story.

A story narrated by Ayatullah al-Ha'iri, the creator of the Hawza in Qom, describes a plague in Sammara when he was a student there. His teacher at the time was Ayatullah Muhammad Taqi Shirazi and he had known that all of them were possibly going to die and had told all of them that if he was to issue a law, would they all follow it? If you do, then the next ten days each of you have to recite Ziyarat Ashura because this ziyarah is seen as the greatest to recite when you are going through a disease. Only the school of Ahlulbayt recited this as a community (and not the whole of Sammara) for ten days. When they did this the followers of the Ahlulbayt were not dying but the followers of other schools were dying one by one. Finally, every du'a has a time and place in which to be recited. There are some du'as that Allah has promised will be answered, such as when a mother grieves or cries for help.

Lecture 4

The Philosophy of Jihad in Islam

The concept of jihad is one which has a certain controversy, and therefore requires a thorough discussion; the media uses jihad within the context of words such as fundamentalist, radical and terrorist. Therefore we have to examine this word so the world can place it in the correct context. Media in general can shape the mindset of a community and when it continues to concentrate on a particular word with a particular usage then the community in turn focuses on the word in the same light. Jihad must be explained so people can see the different ways it has been used in the Qur'an and in the world of hadith so that misconceptions are removed. Within Islam we seek to see how jihad has been used in many contexts, and to understand both the minor and major jihad, as well as its relevance to the month of Ramadan.

The word "juhd" in Arabic means "to struggle," so here the human being struggles in every aspect of their life. When Allah (SWT) created the human being, the philosophy of this human is to struggle in whatever arena it is placed in. The opposite of struggling is detested in Islam, and is found to be someone who is lazy. Imam Musa al-Kadhim (AS) has said, "There are two impediments we should be aware of which can make us lose this world and the Hereafter – laziness and restlessness." The underlying character of this person is one who is not willing to struggle with that which Allah has given them. Allah (SWT) created us with senses which were to be used in struggling in the different areas of our lives.

These blessings are not only to be protected but to be used. If one door shuts on us, this does not mean that we should give up. On the contrary, the person who is idle falls into the hands of Satan. Hence, the English saying, "Idle thumbs make work for the devil." Even in Islamic history there were certain characters who, when they struggled, their struggle ended at a certain point. They were restless and did not follow through with the struggle. Abu Lahab was one of the greatest enemies of The Prophet (PBUH), although he was his uncle and he is the same man mentioned in the the Qur'anic verse, "Perish the hands of the Father of Flame! Perish he!"

Other personalities like Abu Jahal, Utba ibn Rabi'a and Umayyah ibn Khalaf struggled to fight The Prophet (PBUH). Abu Lahab, however, struggled to fight the Prophet until a certain point – until the Prophet had left Mecca for Medina. The battle of Badr took place in the second year after the Prophet's hijra to Medina. Abu Jahal, Utba and Umayyah decided that they would go to Badr to fight the Prophet. Abu Lahab, however, became too lazy to go fight. He paid al-Aas ibn Hashim to fight for him instead. In fact, al-Aas ibn Hashim didn't even return from the battle so he didn't live to take the payment from Abu Lahab. This shows how unsuccessful people like Abu Lahab are lazy.

Furthermore, one of the highest forms of jihad is "intellectual jihad," meaning that one of the highest positions you can reach in Islam is known as a "mujtahid." A mujtahid is one who is a scholar that has performed jihad in the sciences of knowledge. For example, Imam al-Kulayni who wrote al-Kafi, Man la yahdhuruhu al-faqih by Sheikh al-Saduq, al-Tahtheeb wal Istibsar by Sheikh al-Tousi, Sahih by Imam al-Bukhari, Sahih by Imam Muslim, Sunnan by Tirmithi and Nisai – these were not completed without a struggle. Another example to prove that jihad is not just in the battlefield can be seen in the example of the author of the book, Miftaah al-Uloom, which is used to analyse the twelve sciences of Arabic literature that are studied by students in the hawza. The author of the book was Seraj al-Deen al-Sakaki, who was a blacksmith. On one occasion he was asked to do a job for the king. The king approved of what al-Sakaki brought him and whilst he was standing someone had entered whereby the king and all his people ran to welcome the person. This person was a scholar, and al-Sakaki at first thought his struggle to make something for the king was much more than the scholar merely walking in. Al-Sakaki joined the Islamic seminary, or hawza, at thirty years of age, whilst all the other students were younger than him. One day at hawza he was asked to present on how a "dog becomes impure after tanning," but because of his nerves, instead of saying "my teacher said…," he said, "my dog said the teacher becomes impure after tanning." After this he thought he couldn't continue the struggle and wanted to leave hawza. As he was leaving, he saw a mountain with water coming off it striking a stone at the bottom. For many years the water has continued its struggle to break into the stone and after its struggle the stone has eroded. This influenced al-Sakaki to go through the struggle just like the water on that mountain, except through knowledge, and eventually he wrote Miftaah al-Uloom, a book which discusses the dozen sciences of Arabic literature, at 40 years of age.

The concept of jihad is looked at by many schools in Islam. For example, the school of Imam ibn Qayyim al-Jawziya. He is one of the highest scholars of the other schools in Islam. He divided jihad into four different areas – this included the jihad against the self, the jihad against satan, the jihad against the munafiqeen, or the kufaar, and lastly, the jihad against the people of bid'a or those who innovate. Likewise, in the School of Ahlulbayt, the concept of jihad is divided into two areas – jihad al-asghar, or minor jihad, and jihad al-akbar, or major jihad. Minor jihad is seen as the jihad of the battlefield, while major jihad is seen as the jihad of the self. This hadith comes from our Prophet (PBUH), who, when he returned from the battlefield with his companions, said, "We are going from the minor to the major jihad." When the Prophet was returning from battle, many expected that this was the major jihad. On the contrary, it was defined by him as the minor jihad.

Jihad al-asghar, or minor jihad, should not be taken lightly. It has many laws and conditions as it is one of the Furoo' al-Deen. According to the scholars of the Ahlulbayt, jihad al-asghar is wajib, or obligatory, on every Muslim. On the conditions that it is defensive, then the jihad can be called for from one of the just scholars. If it is an offensive war, then jihad al-asghar must be called for from an infallible Imam. Defensive wars include, for example, the battles of Badr, Khyber, Khandaq and Uhud. Jihad al-asghar is only vital because you are defending Muslims from injustice and oppression. In the Qur'an Allah (SWT) frowns upon those who are not ready to perform jihad al-asghar because that person recognises that his life is more important than the life of the religion of Islam. In Surah 9, verse 118, Allah (SWT) speaks of three Arabians who didn't go to jihad al-asghar with the Prophet. Allah is explicit here by initiating the verse with the number of people: "He turned in mercy also) to the three who were left behind; (they felt guilty) to a degree that the earth seemed constrained to them, for all its spaciousness, and their (very) souls seemed straightened to them. They perceived that there is no fleeing from Allah but to Himself. Then He turned to them that they might repent. For Allah is Oft-Returning, Most Merciful."

The Prophet (PBUH) was telling his companions to go to the Battle of Tabuk, one of the later battles and the only battle Imam Ali did not fight in as The Prophet (PBUH) wanted him to protect Medina from the Munafiqeen. The three mentioned in the verse were Bilal ibn Umayyah, Ka'ab ibn Malik and al-Marrara ibn Rabiee. They all created excuses to not go for jihad al-asghar. When the Muslims returned from Tabuk, Bilal, Ka'ab and Marrara found that no one would speak to them, even their wives found it difficult. The three of them reached a point where they felt guilty as "the earth constrained them." They prayed for forgiveness, but there was still not revelation on forgiveness. Each one of them then fled to a separate mountain crying for three days for forgiveness from Allah and hence Surah 9, verse 118, was revealed, "He turned to them that they might repent," meaning Allah had forgiven them. This meant that Allah (SWT) does not accept excuses to not go on jihad al-asghar.

The greatest characters in history were those who went on jihad al-asghar and sacrificed everything that they had for Islam. In the first thirty-three years of Imam Ali's life until the day The Prophet (PBUH) died – he performed every aspect of jihad al-asghar. He was the first to stand in Badr, Uhud, Khandaq and Khyber. Yet the irony is, that after The Prophet (PBUH) had died, Imam did not pick up his sword once for the next twenty-five years. It was as though Imam only wanted to do jihad al-asghar for the Prophet and no other caliphs that came after him. Until, upon becoming caliph, he defended Islam again. When Imam was caliph, jihad al-asghar was carried out in the battles of Jamal, Siffeen and Nahrawan.

Jihad al-akbar, or major jihad, was seen as the greater jihad of the self. The media focuses on Islam being the jihad of war; however, the greatest jihad is that of the struggle with yourself. Many philosophers ask how the jihad of the self is the greater jihad. The philosophers concluded the following: firstly, the jihad of the battlefield has only one enemy whereas the jihad of the self includes thousands of enemies. Secondly, in the jihad of the battlefield you fight your enemy, whereas the jihad of the self entails fighting friends and enemies. For example, Prophet Noah had a jihad with his son rather than a jihad on the battlefield. Because he was his son it was more difficult as he was his family rather than an enemy. One day the companions were with The Prophet (PBUH) when they saw a man lifting a rock. The companions were awed by this man's strength. The Prophet (PBUH) replied to them, "Someone who is even stronger than this man is one who can control his desires and purify their soul." The Prophet (PBUH) also has stated in the famous hadith, "He who knows himself knows his Lord."

When the Qur'an talks about self it is so that it can be a barometer in human behaviour. If one wants to know how pure their self is, then they must look at their reaction to areas such as wajibat and haram. Wajibat, or obligatory areas, include prayer. For example, the self of someone who, as soon as he hears the athaan, straight away prays. Then you have an area such as haram. For example, music. One person straight away stops listening compared to a person who believes it's a small sin so it's not a big deal. So one can test their jihad of the self with that which is allowed and that which is not allowed. In the Qur'an Allah (SWT) divided the self into three levels: nafs al-amaara, nafs al-lawama and nafs al-mutma'ina. The first, which is nafs al-amaara, is that level whereby you convince yourself that that which is haram is halal and sinning becomes easy. When Zulaykha was trying to tempt Prophet Yusuf, the Prophet said, "I am not going to make any excuses for myself because if I don't perform the proper jihad of the self, my self will be inclined towards sinning."

Thus, nafs al-amaara is the station of the self of someone who commits a sin without feeling guilty at all. Two incidents in the Qur'an show that someone can convince themselves that what is bad is good. The first incident is when Prophet Yusuf's brothers threw him in the well. The wording in the Qur'an shows how low their selves were and how their jihad was non-existent. When they came to their father Prophet Ya'qub with Yusuf's bloody shirt, Ya'qub tells them, "Your selves have deceived you in your act." So an act like throwing their blood brother into a well means that their selves are so low that it allowed them to suggest such an act to them. Likewise with the children of Israel. The same event occurred with the self being deceived in the incident of al-Saamari. When the children of Israel crossed the Red Sea, they came towards the area where Prophet Musa had to go and collect the commandments. The Prophet was up for thirty nights. Allah (SWT) then told him that he would be kept here for an extra ten nights. During these ten nights there was a man amongst the children of Israel named al-Saamari. Al-Saamari noticed that they were waiting for Musa who had been late; he took some dust from the horse of Jibra'il and placed it on a statue of a calf. This statue produced noise, and the children of Israel were influenced to worship this statue, when only a few days earlier Allah had opened the Red Sea for them. When Prophet Musa came back to Harun, he asked him why the children of Israel had gone towards a statue. Harun replied, "It is not my fault. I tried to keep them on the path towards Allah." Al-Saamari then admitted, "My self suggested to me something which deceived me. I decided to use their weakness to worship the calf." Thus al-Saamari admitted that his self did not go through jihad and was instead in the state of nafs al-amara whereby it made him sin without guilt.

When Imam Ali (AS) had come from the Battle of Jamal, he was giving a talk to the people of Basra. A man was seated who was writing what the Imam was saying. When Imam had asked who he was, they told him this was Hassan al-Basri. Imam then declared, "O people, there is a Saamari for every nation. Hassan al-Basri is the Saamari of this nation. There is a difference between al-Saamari and Hassan al-Basri. Al-Saamari would never let anyone approach him, whereas al-Basri tells people to approach him so that he may explain how Ali ibn Abu Talib is wrong." This highlights that there is one who deceives others selves so that they may sin without regret, like nafs al-amaara.

The second type of self is nafs al-lawaama. The Qur'an says, "I swear by the Day of Resurrection. Nay! I swear by the reproaching soul (nafs al-lawaama)." Nafs al-lawaama is defined by psychologists as the moral conscious of the human being. You may commit a sin, however you feel guilty afterwards. Nafs al-lawaama always follows the human in relation to what should and shouldn't be done throughout the day. But with nafs al-amaara, there is no relationship with one's self. A famous incident occurred with Muhammad ibn Shahab al-Zuhri, who was one of the governors of Bani Umayyah during the time of the fourth Imam. Ibn Shahab al-Zuhri and Imam Zain al-Abideen were both near the Ka'aba when al-Zuhri started screaming. This led to many individuals near the Ka'aba to approach him. Al-Zuhri's parents explained to them that he had a problem that wasn't improving even when he was close to the Ka'aba. They called upon the fourth Imam to help him. Al-Zuhri then confessed to the Imam, "I ordered the killing of one of my people and now my self (nafs) has not stopped calling me out and reproaching me." Al-Zuhri started to continuously cry when Imam said, "I am not worried about your crying and your conscience. I am more worried about your despair of the Mercy of Allah (SWT). The fact that your self is alive and telling you to feel guilty about the ordering of a murder, then this is fine compared to those who do not feel guilt at all. Go to the relatives and pay them the blood money." Al-Zuhri told the Imam that he had attempted to pay them but they had rejected it. So the Imam told him to just leave the money at their door. The fourth Imam, in this situation, was more concerned that the jihad of this man was functioning.

The highest self in Islam is nafs al-mutma'ina. This is when you know your self is linked to Allah (SWT). For example, innRamadan you don't break your fast because you want to end the hunger, but rather you break it so that you are strengthened to worship Allah (SWT). Nafs al-mutma'ina is when the person thinks of Allah before the act, during the act and after the act.

On the tenth of Muharam there were three personalities who were talking to themselves even though their selves were on different levels. The first of them was Hurr ibn Yazid al-Riyahi. He was at the station of nafs al-lawaama, and his self was telling him he would be guilty if he were to kill the son of Fatima al-Zahra (AS). He famously quoted, " I have to make a decision with myself between Heaven and Hell." The self that was speaking to him so much made him go towards Imam Hussein (AS). The second personality was Abu Fadhel al-Abbas, he had reached the station of nafs al-mutma'ina, and twice he spoke to himself, "Oh soul, don't drink this cold water because after drinking it there is nothing but humiliation when Imam Hussein (AS) dies." The next time he spoke to himself, he said, "Oh self, don't be scared from the kufaar. Think about what the Rahman has awaiting for you and think about your service towards Muhammad." The third person didn't need his self to talk to him; Allah was talking to him. "O pure soul which is mutma'ina, come back towards your Lord in a state where your Lord is pleased with you and where you are pleased with your Lord." The Imam performed his jihad al-asghar in a great way and his jihad al-akbar was performed in the best of ways.

Lecture 5

The Islamic Concept of Brotherhood

The concept of brotherhood is pivotal in society whereby unity, optimism and equality can occur as a basis for brotherhood. A community which lacks brotherhood is one that lacks direction, is not united, is open to chaos, and pessimism is clearly evident. In contemporary society, communities are centered on individuals and do not unite as a team. Thus they lack success. All great religious leaders, philosophers and scholars have concentrated on the trait of brotherhood.

One example is Prophet Jesus (AS) who has a beautiful line that is narrated in many Christian circles, *"Worship God with prayer, passion and intelligence and love others as well as you love yourself."* Prophet Jesus wanted to build an ethos of loving others as much as one loves themselves because humans tend to love themselves and do not display that same type of love to others. Likewise, Martin Luther King, in many of his statements, would concentrate on the concept of brotherhood in seeking to reform American society; the Black Rights Civil Rights movement, which was headed by Martin Luther King, is still studied today. Amongst his statements, he said, *"I have a dream that one day on the red hills of Georgia the sons of former slaves will sit with the sons of former slave owners at the table of brotherhood."* "The table of brotherhood" is metaphorical, so as to say here that one day everyone may be equal in society. Similarly, another of his beautiful quotes includes, *"We have learnt to swim the sea like fishes and fly the air like birds, but have not learnt to live together like brothers."* Sometimes you try and get two brothers in a community to sit together and it becomes almost impossible. We have learnt all other sciences but we have neglected the simple science of humanity. Malcolm X saw the idea of brotherhood in a different light, he states, *"I believe in the brotherhood of man, all men, but I don't believe in brotherhood with anybody who doesn't want brotherhood with me. I believe in treating people right, but I'm not going to waste my time trying to treat somebody right who doesn't know how to return the treatment."*

The concept of brotherhood in Islam is that, when we are in unison, we are unbreakable. If I was to give you one stick and tell you to break it, you will be able to break it easily. But if I give you a hundred sticks, it would make it difficult for you to break them all; this is why the following phrase is relevant here: "A bundle of sticks are unbreakable." In Islam we believe in brotherhood whereby unity can occur to build a society successfully, especially with many of those coming to a foreign country from their home countries and still building a united community. They all came from different ships but now they live in the same boat. The examination of brotherhood includes the questions of what was the vision of brotherhood of the empires that surrounded Islam (the Greeks, Romans and Arabians), what is the first right of your blood brother, and what is the brother in humanity and what is the brother in Islam.

Whenever you want to view the beauty of Islam, compare it with the empires that surrounded the message of The Prophet (PBUH) so you can see the effects of the message. The three main empires included the Greek, the Roman and the Arabian. The Greek Empire initiated the concept of government and society by Plato, Aristotle and Socrates. Plato brought about the *Republic* and Aristotle brought about theories of how society can prosper. Aristotle used to have a conception about the members of a community. He said, *"Some people were born to rule, whereas others are born to serve."* This type of conception will not build any form of brotherhood because, if I believe I am superior to my brother because I come from a high class family, it can cause disunity. If I am born into a slave family, then I will think that I will never be in a high position in society. Therefore this brings about an inferiority complex whereby people will never be able to believe in equality.

Within the Roman Empire you found inequality in their formation of society. The Roman Empire was divided into six classes; the highest was the free Roman citizen, then you had the free Latin-speaking citizen and the final four classes were the slaves in Rome. The only one of these six classes who had the right to free national health was the free Roman citizen; the other five had no rights to health service. They used to treat slaves like animals. When they put the slaves in cargo they would place them with animals as they believed the two had no souls.

Likewise in Arabia there was no conception of equality and brotherhood. They had two types of slaves, "Mowla Itaqa" and "Mowla Taba'a." The word "Mowla" in Arabic has twenty-three different meanings; amongst the meanings is "slave." The two classes of slave in Arabia could never be anything but inferior to the normal Arab. "Mowla Itaqa" was a slave who was caught in war, while "Mowla Taba'a" was someone who had been kicked out of a tribe and became lower in status. For example, Bilal belonged to the tribe of Umayyah ibn Khalaf, but was kicked out, and so he became lower class. Ammar ibn Yasir belonged to the tribe of Bani Makhzum. With such a class system in Arabia there was no such thing as brotherhood until The Prophet (PBUH) came into the picture.

When The Prophet (PBUH) came, he reformed brotherhood on three levels: blood brother, brother in humanity and brother in Islam. The first type of brotherhood in Islam is where you have to respect your blood brother. This is because the first crime in humanity was between Habeel and Qabeel from Adam and Eve. The community was only made up of four personalities, but Prophet Adam was told by Allah (SWT) that before you pass away you must appoint your successor. Adam appointed Habeel on behalf of Allah (SWT). Qabeel became jealous and quarrelled with Habeel. Adam went to Allah (SWT) to ask what he could do to stop this; Allah (SWT) requested that they both offer a sacrifice and see which one is accepted. Habeel gave the best of his flock, whereas Qabeel gave withered corn so Allah (SWT) accepted Habeel. This led to an even greater jealousy from Qabeel's side to the extent where he decided to kill him. Habeel told Qabeel that if he did kill him, then he wouldn't kill him too, as he feared Allah (SWT). Qabeel killed Habeel, and it took a bird to teach him how to bury his brother. So the first right of brotherhood in Islam is your blood brother because he is meant to be your strength, and by respecting your brother you are respecting your mother who looked after you both. Many Muslim communities today don't even maintain relationships with their blood relatives. Imams al-Hassan and al-Hussein were the essence of brotherhood. The Prophet (PBUH) describes them thus: *"They are the masters of the youth of Paradise."* Their brotherhood was so strong because they thought of Allah (SWT) in every act they carried out. There is a famous story of an old man performing wudhu'. When young Hassan and Hussein came by, they saw him performing wudhu' improperly. The brothers spoke to him and said, *"Oh man, we want to perform wudhu'. Can you please say which one of us is performing it the correct way?"* The old man then proclaimed that it was his wudhu' that needed to be corrected.

The second right of brothers in Islam is your brother in humanity, and this is a vital form of brotherhood. We live in a cosmopolitan world with people from different religions and cultures. When Islam came forward to say the second right is humanity, it is because the aim is to say there's no harm in becoming a brother of someone even though their ideology may differ. The Prophet (PBUH) and Imam Ali (AS) believed in developing relations with humanity. As Amir al-Mu'mineen says in one of his legendary quotes, *"If someone is not your brother in faith, they are your equal in humanity."* This means that if someone has a principle, and they act upon it in a way that is better than the Muslims, then that person is closer to you than sometimes your own Muslim brother. There are some Prophetic hadiths that prove this, such as, *"An ignorant person who is generous is more beloved to Allah (SWT) than a worshipper who is stingy."* Allah (SWT) is concerned about the humanitarian principles a person has and not your ideology.

Once, when The Prophet (PBUH) had seen Adee ibn Hatim, he said, *"I have respect for you because of your father Hatim al-Taee. Hatim has a universal generosity."* Hatim al-Taee was a Christian that defined generosity; The Prophet (PBUH) would always mention his name when he would preach of generosity. Hatim al-Taee's wife narrates that one day her and her children were at home during a severe famine in Arabia. They had nothing to eat at home and at night Hatim heard a woman crying out for him and saying that her children were howling from hunger. Hatim had nothing to give her but one horse; he slaughtered his horse and woke up his family too. He welcomed the woman and her children into his family's home and let them eat whilst he sat down without eating. He said, "It gives me pleasure to serve Allah (SWT) and see everyone happy." The Prophet (PBUH) used to also say, "A just non-Muslim leader is greater than a tyrannical Muslim leader."

In Islamic history there were some tyrants who call themselves Muslim but were in fact evil, such as Walid ibn Yazid, Hajjaj ibn Yusuf al-Thaqafi and Abdel Malik ibn Marwan. The just non-Muslim leader looks after the citizens of the state, ensuring their security, even when the Muslim tyrant does not. When The Prophet (PBUH) faced the most difficult part of his Prophethood, he told his companions to go to a Christian priest named Najashi in Abyssinia as he was just and much purer than the tyrannical Arab leaders. When Ja'far al-Tayyar, the brother of Imam Ali (AS) went there, he had the intention of being the brother of a Christian who also says, "There is no God but Allah." Najashi gave them sanctuary until the seventh year of Hijra, the time of the Battle of Khyber. After that, when saw the akhlaaq of Ja'far, he decided to become a Muslim. When Najashi became a Muslim, he read the nikkah of The Prophet (PBUH) when he married Um Habiba, the daughter of Abu Sufyan.

A Greek Christian man once came to Imam Ali (AS) and asked if he could follow him everywhere he went. He sat with him one day when he heard Imam talk of brotherhood. One person had asked Imam about the rights of the brothers in faith. Imam answered, "Your rights to your brothers in faith is that you fulfil their needs, redress their grievances, love them with friendship and you help their wealth if they are in need of it." The Greek Christian man said that he wanted to convert to the religion of Islam because in four lines you have explained the meaning of brotherhood, and they were universal principles that belong to the whole of humanity.

The third aspect of brotherhood is the brotherhood between Muslims; the Qur'an describes this in its unique Arabic grammar. In Surah 49, verse 10, Allah says, "Verily (Innama), the Believers are but a single Brotherhood (Ukhwa). So make peace and reconciliation between your two brothers and fear Allah that ye may receive Mercy." The unique Arabic grammar used here is with the words "innama" and "ukhwa." Whenever the word "innama" is used in the beginning of a verse, it is known as "innama al-hasr," which means squeezing a particular attribute upon a particular group of people. For example, in the verse which says, "Verily (Innama), your Wali (Protector or Helper) is Allah, His Messenger, and the believers, those who perform al-salat (iqamat al-salat), and give zakat, and they bow down (submit themselves with obedience to Allah in prayer)." This verse started with "innama," proving that the guardianship is pressed upon Allah's Messengers and those who give zakat whilst praying. Likewise in verse 49:10, "innama" is used to squeeze the attribute of "believing" upon a group of people who are brothers. The attribute of "ukhwa" is normally used in Arabic for blood brothers, but this verse is relative to all believers, thus all believers in Islam are like blood brothers. Furthermore, if Allah had said "ukhwan" it would have meant friends. Allah (SWT) used "ukhwa" to say that your brother in faith has a greater right over you than your own blood brother has on you. If you want no one to hurt your blood brother, ensure that your brother in Islam is not harmed.

Moreover, The Prophet (PBUH) was once asked what was the best act in Islam. The Prophet replied, "The best acts in Islam are three; being just even if it is against yourself, helping your brothers with material help and with co-operation, finally remembering Allah (SWT) in all circumstances." Helping your brother with wealth and co-operation is the best of iman as said by the Prophet. The Prophet (PBUH) further states, "When you are making brotherhood with your brother in iman, your rizq is increased by Allah (SWT)." This hadith goes on to say that every act of worship in Islam is an act to bring the Mu'minoon, or Believers, together – for example, individual prayer and the congregational prayer, whereby the latter contains more reward. This greater reward comes from the fact that it brings people shoulder to shoulder with each other. Muslims also pray in front of the "mihrab." Mihrab means you are engaging in "harb," or war with satan. Thus you need brothers alongside you when you are at war.

Another type of worship is fasting. In a mandatory fast you cannot eat when someone offers you food, however in the "mustahab" fast it is recommended that you eat if someone offers you food. Allah (SWT) didn't want us to reject a Muslim brother in the mustahab fast, so that we may have iftar together. A third example is with du'a. Du'a is accepted when you ask for others before you ask for yourself, and this again strengthens brotherhood. A fourth example is hajj, whereby Muslims all wear white cloths so that we are all equal in brotherhood.

This is why, in Mecca and Medina, The Prophet (PBUH) formed two brotherhoods. On the twelfth of Ramadan, in the second year of Hijrah, The Prophet (PBUH) had come to Mecca with the Muhajiroon (the Immigrants). He then went to Medina to meet the Ansar (the Helpers). The Prophet (PBUH), in order to reduce any friction between them, decided that they all should become brothers and have rights over one another as believers. For example, he brought Abu Bakr and Kharija ibn Zuhair al-Khazraji to join in brotherhood, and Umar ibn Khattab and Aytan ibn Malik, and Uthman ibn Affan and Aws ibn Thabit, and Abdel Rahman ibn Auf and Sa'ad ibn Rabia to join in brotherhood. Sa'ad ibn

Rabia thought brotherhood was so powerful he told Abdel Rahman that he could have some of his wives. The Muslims would even inherit from each other as they were brothers. When The Prophet (PBUH) had brought them together, he turned to Imam Ali (AS) and told him that he was his brother. This is why The Prophet (PBUH) declared about Ali, "You are to me what Harun was to Musa." They were blood brothers but the Prophet wanted to show that their relationship was higher than that of a cousin. This can be seen in the Prophet's narration, "Only Allah (SWT) and Ali know me, only me and Ali know Allah (SWT), and only Allah and me know Ali."

49:10 continues, "So make peace and reconciliation between your two brothers; and fear Allah, that ye may receive Mercy." There are those who don't speak to each other, be it brothers in blood or Islam. Imam Ali (AS) stated in his wasiya before he died, "Make sure you reconcile the people, for reconciliation of brothers is greater than fasting or prayer." If you want your prayer or fast to be accepted, insure that you reconcile with your brothers as Imam has said. One day Mufathil ibn Umar al-Kufi, one of the companions of the sixth Imam, was walking past Abu Hanifah, who had a major problem with his son-in-law over inheritance. Mufathil took Abu Hanifah and Abu Hanifah's son-in-law to reconcile them; he gave 400 dirhams each to both of them. Then he said to them, "It is not me who has reconciled you; it is Ja'far al-Sadiq. My imam told me that whenever you see two brothers fighting each other, reconcile them, for The Prophet (PBUH) has said reconciliation is better than giving two dinar in charity."

Thus, in the Muslim world, it is vital that we don't have disunity. For example, if I follow the School of Ja'far al-Sadiq (AS) and my brother may follow the School of Imam Ahmed ibn Hanbal, there shouldn't be disunity because we follow different schools of fiqh. They both have reached conclusions and they both lie under the banner of Only One God that is Allah and Only One Messenger that is Muhammad (PBUH). We should invite other brothers to our mosques; every mosque is the house of Allah (SWT). Muslims divided means that Muslims will be unsuccessful.

On the tenth of Muharram the only reason why seventy-two companions died and are remembered by over three hundred million today was because they were blood brothers, brothers in humanity or brothers in faith. In terms of brothers in humanity Wahab al-Kalbi originally was a Christian but the akhlaaq of Imam Hussein (AS) made him come to

Karbala. Then you had brothers in faith, like the personalities of Habib ibn Muthahir, Muslim ibn Awsaja, John the Abyssinian, Hurr ibn Yazid al-Riyahi, who were all from different backgrounds but their religion kept them as one firm wall. Lastly, you had blood brothers. Abu Fadhel al-Abbas, who from a young age protected Imam Hussein (AS) from any harm, he was his flag bearer. When Imam saw Abu Fadhel on the grounds of Karbala, this was the only time in his life whereby he called the Imam "akhi," my brother. Imam replied through poetry, "O my brother, the apple of my eye, my backbone, you advised your brother until Allah will take you to the pool of Kawther, O moon that is shining." Were it not for the brotherhood on the tenth of Muharram, Imam would have never said, "My companions are the best of companions."

Lecture 6

The Power of Salat al-Layl

The Night Prayer, or Salat al-Layl, is viewed as one of the secrets of worship in Islam and is viewed by all Schools in Islam as being one of the greatest acts of worship as well as one of the areas in which to reach the highest spiritual levels. The human being aims to achieve health both on a physical and spiritual level. In the same way that we want our bodies to be healthy, we seek to have souls that are healthy. This is as a result of the recognition of physical and spiritual diseases. Allah (SWT) mentions in the Qur'an in Chapter 91, "And by the soul and Him who made it perfect, then inspired it with knowledge of evil and piety. He has succeeded who purifies it." Allah (SWT) tells us that the soul has been shown both the good and the bad way, and the aim is for the human is to purify the soul to be successful. Imam Ali (AS) also states, "He who knows himself (or his soul) knows his Lord."

The soul goes through many stages. For example, in the station of al-nafs al-sawaama, or the conscious self, after you have committed a sin you feel a sense of guilt. The person who is at the station of al-nafs al-amaara is one who doesn't feel guilty after committing a sin. A person also can reach a stage where everything he sees is Allah (SWT), and this is al-nafs al-mutma'ina. Salat al-Layl is seen as one of the doors which opens the purification of the soul. The Holy Prophet (PBUH) is narrated to have said, "The honour and the greatness of a believer is in Salat al-Layl."

Further than this, Imam Ali (AS) defines his followers according to Salat al-Layl, "Our Shi'a are those who pray fifty-one rukaats a day." For many of us, the five daily prayers conclude with seventeen daily rukaats, but the other thirty-four rukaats must be taken on board. Eleven of the thirty-four rukaats are in Salat al-Layl, while the final twenty-three rukaats are in Salat al-Nawafel – the additional prayers we have with every prayer. Therefore, Salat al-Layl is part of the prayers that are used to define the followers of the Ahlulbayt. In the examination of Salat al-Layl, the effects of it must be noted to not just benefit this world but also the next world. This is why in the Qur'an it says, "Wealth and children are the zeena of this life." The Prophet (PBUH) says, "Wealth and children are the zeena of this life, but Salat al-Layl is the zeena of the Akhira, or the Hereafter."

Salat al-Layl is mentioned in the Holy Qur'an in Chapter 73, "O you who wraps himself up, arise to pray the night except for a little, half of it or subtract from it or add to it and recite the Qur'an with measured recitation. Indeed, we will cast upon you a heavy word. Indeed, the hours of the night are more intense for worship and more suitable for words." This verse addresses The Prophet (PBUH), who used to stay up the whole night in prayer. Allah (SWT) addressed the Prophet, telling him that He knows the Prophet loves Him, but he doesn't have to stay up the whole night in prostration. Instead of this, it reminds the person to stay up half of the night or less than this or a bit more. "Indeed, the hours of the night are more intense for worship and more suitable for words." This part of the verse suggests that staying up at night has a special value. In Surah 51, verse 17, again Allah (SWT) refers us to Salat al-Layl and its importance. He speaks about the companions of the Prophet – "A little part of the night did they sleep and in the morning they would always do istighfar (asking Allah for forgiveness)."

Another group of verses which will be examined here is Surah 17, verses 78 and 79, in the Qur'an. These verses all talk of prayer generally but Salat al-Layl in particular. "Establish prayer at the decline of the sun [from its meridian] until the darkness of the night and [also] the Qur'an of dawn. Indeed, the recitation of dawn is ever witnessed. And from [part of] the night, pray; it would be an additional prayer for you and it will upgrade you to a level where you are at a praised station, or maqam mahmood." Why does Allah (SWT) begin a verse about prayer with "Aqim as-Salaat?" What does "Aqim" mean or "Yuqemoon as-Salaat"? What is the meaning when Allah says "Qur'an al-Fajr," "Ghasaq al-Layl," "Duluk ash-Shams?"

How did Allah define for us what Dhuhr, Maghrib and Fajr is? What does Allah mean in this verse when he tells the Prophet to "stay up in the night, for this will upgrade you to a level where you are at a praiseworthy position status?" What is this praiseworthy position or "al-Maqam al-Mahmood" and how does Salat al-Layl make you reach it?

Firstly, when Allah generally speaks of prayer, He always says "Establish prayer, Aqim as-Salaat" or its derivatives. For example, "Yuqemoon as-Salaat," or you find Allah (SWT) saying, "And establish prayer at the two ends of the day and at the approach of the night". Another verse which uses its derivative is, "The people who, if We give them control in the land, would keep the prayer established and pay charity and enjoin virtue and forbid from evil; and for Allah only is the result of all works." Allah (SWT) uses the word "aqim" with prayer for a specific reason; never in the Qur'an does it just say "pray," rather it says "aqim," or "establish prayers." There are two opinions as to why "establish" is used. The first of these is that it means to make sure you know the fiqh of the prayer that you are praying. One should know the jurisprudence behind the prayer in order to carry it out properly. It is a shame if the followers of the Ahlulbayt are making mistakes whilst they are praying; sometimes there is a lack of understanding of fiqh. There is a hadith that categorises prayer in two types – one whereby Allah accepts your prayer and a second whereby it is rejected. The latter is when those do not understand the fiqh of the prayer. For example, when we pray, some do not say "Allahu Akbar" in the standing position after saying, "Sami Allahu liman Hamida," but do takbeer on their way down to prostration. A second example of a mistake is those who go in sujood, or prostration, and do not sit down all the way but come up half-way.

The second meaning of "aqim," or "establish prayer," is that which the Ahlulbayt find stronger, whereby Allah wants us to find prayer as the springboard for our actions in society. Prayer, and the actions outside prayer, should not contradict each other; rather they should be in tandem. In Surah al-Fatiha, which is recited in prayer, we state, "Ya Allah, guide me on the path of that which You have blessed, not the path of those who are cursed or astray." However, there is no point in saying this if our actions outside prayer mean that we do not wish to be guided. When a person understands the words they are reciting then their actions should mirror their words. In some situations there are those who wear the hijab whilst they are praying in the idea that Allah is watching them worship, however as soon as prayer ends, the hijab is taken off. This shows a lack of understanding that Allah is watching them everywhere they go. Our actions should show a sign of our guidance towards Allah everywhere in our daily lives.

There is a hadith about the female and the "kafan" – the white cloth with which the human is wrapped in burial. The hadith states that the angels say, "What is the point of this kafan at death, when there was no covering when they were alive?" One day Imam Ali (AS) was asked, "How do we know if our prayer has been accepted?" Imam replied, "Look at your actions from the time of Dhuhr to Maghrib if you want to know if Dhuhr was accepted (for example)." Amir al-Mu'mineen's companions would always be viewed by others as to how they behave outside their prayers because the people believed that these companions would act in reflection to how greatly they prayed with Imam. This relates to what it says in the Qur'an, "Prayer protects you from evil and indecency." If someone thinks that their prayer is not protecting them from evil and indecency then there must be some sort of wrong behaviour being carried outside prayer.

Imam Ali (AS) used to say of Malik al-Ashtar, "Malik is to me, like I was to The Prophet (PBUH)." One day Malik was going through the markets of Kufa. People knew Malik by his prayer but they wanted to see if Malik was just praying it as a way of ritual. The Arabs were selling their food when one of the date sellers started throwing date stones at Malik. Another man came to the person who was throwing dates and told him that the man who he was abusing is Malik, the commander of Ali ibn Abu Talib in the Battle of Siffin. This man decided to go after Malik in the mosque and found him praying there, so he waited. When Malik finished his prayer, the man apologised and told Malik that he didn't know that it was him. Malik replied, "Do not worry. I came to pray two rukaats so Allah may forgive you." Thus, when Allah (SWT) began the verse with "aqim," he wanted us to know our fiqh and allow our prayer to be the basis of how we behave in public.

This verse provides the timings of our prayer, and there are those who accuse the followers of the Ahlulbayt of praying only three prayers, so this verse will be examined in response. "Establish your prayers to the decline of the sun ("dulook al-shams") until the darkness of the night ("ghasaq al-layl)," and [also] the Qur'an of dawn ("Holy Qur'an al-fajr")." "Dulook al-shams" in Arabic is when the sun is so intense that you turn your eyes from it. This was categorised as Dhuhr by Allah. Then Allah wanted to say until Maghrib, so he said "ghasaq al-layl." In Arabic this means when there is darkness in the sky. If Allah wanted it to be when the sky had a hint of redness, then He would have said "shafaq al-layl." Therefore, when it is dark, it is Maghrib. Also, there are no verses in the Qur'an which show prayer to be a five time daily ritual. Instead the Qur'an gave us three periods of prayer. The three periods were "dulook il shams," which meant Dhuhr, "ghasaq al-layl," which is Maghrib and "Holy Qur'an al-fajr," which is Fajr. This is why, in the School of Ahlulbayt, we pray five prayers divided into three periods as the Qur'an states. Likewise, we say you have an option either to combine them or split them into five prayers. Even in the fiqh books of our Sunni brothers, Malik, Shafi'ee and Ahmed ibn Hanbal all say that you can combine prayer when you are travelling. Abu Hanifah says you can combine prayer only in Muzdalifah in hajj. In the School of Ahlulbayt we believe there are times where you can combine, as the Prophet did, and separate, as the Prophet did.

The verse then continues, "Indeed, the recitation of dawn is ever witnessed. And from part of the night, pray; it would be an additional prayer for you and this will upgrade you to a level where you are at a praised station, or maqam mahmood." This part of the verse is concerned with Salat al-Layl. This prayer has a philosophy, a jurisprudence, benefits and conditions that must be understood to appreciate its treasure. The followers of Imam Ali must take Salat al-Layl on board as stated in his hadith that a follower prays fifty-one rukaats a day. Firstly, the philosophy behind Salat al-Layl is that human beings seek to find opposites in their lives, the more you grasp the opposites the more you uncover the secrets of Allah. Allah created everything in pairs and everything in opposites. We seek to understand the opposites – for example, life and death. Similar to what it says in the Qur'an, "We created for you life and death so that we may find which one of you has got the best deeds."

Allah wanted us to open our souls and grasp the meanings of these opposites. For example, the more we grasp life, the more we understand death. Likewise when you understand death more, you prepare your lifestyle according to what you want to reach from your understanding. This is why we are always told to "pray as if it were our last prayer" because if we knew that our death would occur soon, then we would pray much better in this life because we would have understood the two opposites of life and death. A second example of opposites is male and female; Allah wanted us to grasp an understanding of each other, so the male must understand that the female needs comfort, respect and understanding. At the same time, the female must understand that the male needs trust and the feeling that he is cherished. A third example of opposites are the moon and the sun. Our lifestyle must be adjusted to fit the understanding of Allah's relationship with the sun and the moon. Imam al-Sadiq (AS) was once asked by someone to show him God. Imam replied that he should look at the sun. As soon as he looked up at the sun, he moved his eyes away. The Imam then said, "If you cannot bear to see the created, how do you expect to see the Creator?" The final example of opposites is day and night. Allah created them both so that we may understand their significance and what we must do in each of them. Surah al-Naba' in the Qur'an states, "And [He] made the night a cover. And [He] made the day for seeking livelihood."

The Qur'an and the Ahlulbayt tell us that the purpose of the human is to divide his life between his family, work and Allah (SWT) in the day. One day a group of people came to the sixth Imam and asked him about the duties of the day. "O Imam, we are here to ask you about our brother, he fasts the whole day and prays the whole of the night. But we pay everything for him." Imam said, "Islam has not come for these types of people. The daytime wasn't created for you to be praying the whole time, part of your time is to earn, part of the daytime is to sit with your family and part of the time is to worship Allah." Ahlulbayt understood that it wasn't shameful for a person to work, but rather it was beneficial. Once a man walked past Imam al-Baqir (AS) and saw him ploughing in the fields. He came up to the Imam who was sweating from the labour and said to him, "Imam, what are you doing? Let us do the work for you." "Why? It isn't shameful that I work. This is no problem because if I die in this state, then I would die whilst worshipping Allah (SWT)," the Imam answered.

Then in the night time, it was understood that it was a time for rest – except for four types of people who do not rest at night. These included those who seek knowledge. Sayyed Muhammad Baqir al-Sadr used to sleep only three hours in the night, and when he used to gain knowledge he lived in a period of poverty, so he would take his books and sit close to the lampposts in Najaf. The great followers of the Ahlulbayt do not waste their time sleeping many hours; there is not much time when there is an Imam out there waiting for his soldiers. Allama al-Hilli was a great scholar who defended the Ahlulbayt. When he found they were attacked by ink, he wouldn't sleep except for a few hours in the night. This was because al-Hilli couldn't stand sleeping while the Ahlulbayt were being attacked. Once a scholar from another sect challenged the Ahlulbayt in a book and stated how none of them deserved to be caliphs. The author of this book gave the book to al-Hilli for one night only. He had copied most of it so that he could reply to the author, then he fell asleep for a couple of hours. When he woke up, he was devastated as he thought he had no time, but then saw all the book had been copied for him. He knew it was completed by Imam Mahdi (AS). Knowledge gained at night can be on fiqh, hadith, history, philosophy and poetry. The follower of the Ahlulbayt does not sleep the whole night. The follower of the Ahlulbayt must have answers to everything, especially if someone asks them about the Holy Progeny; there is no need for you to ask Mawlana or a religious speaker for a question that someone asked you. Every follower of Ahlulbayt is a Mawlana themselves, the moment we grasp this is the moment Imam Mahdi (AS) will reappear.

The second group of people who do not sleep in the night are those who do not sleep because they think about the affairs of the Muslims around the world. This is why the Prophet (PBUH) has said, "The one who wakes up in the morning and does not care about the affairs of the Muslims around the world, then he is not a Muslim." All those in poverty, dying in disasters and wars need our help. A good Muslim is one who is constantly sending e-mails, letters, and articles to newspapers and donations to other Muslims that are suffering.

The third group of people who do not sleep at night are those who come out and serve the orphans and poor when no one is looking. When Imam Hassan (AS) had just buried Amir al-Mu'mineen (AS) and Hassan returned back home, he saw an old man crying. This old man said he was crying as every night there was a man that fed him and for three nights he has not come. Imam Hassan (AS) began to cry as he knew this was his father; Imam Ali had hid this even from his own son. InnRamadan especially you should never leave food behind, with no regard of those who are poor.

The fourth group of people are those who pray Salat al-Layl, because they have mastered the power of the night. Our Holy Prophet says, "Jibra'il advised me so much about staying up for Salat al-Layl that I thought the virtuous of my Ummah will never go to sleep." The Prophet (PBUH) has another hadith that says, "The two rukaats in the night I pray for Salat al-Layl are more beloved to me than this world and everything within it." A third hadith by the Prophet states, "Three things make a believer happy; when you meet your brother, when you break your fast and Salat al-Layl." Imam al-Sadiq also has said, "Salat al-Layl is the kaffarah of our sins." This is why Allah (SWT) wanted to explain Salat al-Layl to his Prophet. He told Him, "I say to my angels when I see someone praying Salat al-Layl...I say to my angels, 'Look at my servant, he speaks to Me in the night. Go and place noor (light) in his heart. He calls to me while the false ones are sleeping and the heedless ones are playing.'" Allah has also promised to the Prophet, "[For] those who pray Salat al-Layl, I send nine rows of angels behind him. Each row is the distance between the heaven and the earth." Imam al-Sadiq says, "My Shi'a will never miss Salatul Witr."

Salat al-Layl is eleven rukaats. Four prayers of two rukaats is eight rukaats. Then Salat al-Shafi' is two rukaats. In the first rukaat you recite Surah al-Naas, in the second rukaat you read Surah al-Falaq. Lastly, Salat al-Witr is one rukaat. This involves Surah al-Fatiha, three times Surah al-Tawheed, then Surah al-Falaq, then Surah al-Naas, then you raise your hands in qunoot to read seven times, "Hathal maqamu al-Aithi bika min al-Naar". This translates to, "This is the position of the one who seeks refuge from your Hellfire." This is because we can reach Paradise, not just because of Allah's justice, but also because of His Mercy. If it was only justice, then no one would reach Paradise. Imam Ali (AS) said, "It is better for me to be in a mosque praying to God than Paradise, because in a mosque Allah is pleased with me, but in Paradise I am pleased with myself."

After this, you say three hundred times "al-afwa,"– forgiveness. Following this, you say "Astaghfurallaha Rabbi wa atoobu Ilayk", "I seek forgiveness and I turn in repentance to you" one hundred times. Lastly, in qunoot you say, "Allahum ighfir lil mumineen wal muminaat"O Allah, please forgive the believing men and women" whilst remembering forty people either alive or dead so that God may forgive their sins. Remember, in du'a, your du'a is accepted when you think about others before yourself. Imam al-Sadiq says, "My Shi'a are those who recite Witr." If we have excuses for the former ten rukaats, then we can at least pray the one rukaat of Witr daily. Salat al-Layl is any time between midnight and Fajr.

The early Muslims were so certain about the power of Salat al-Layl that they used to oppose their caliphs with the prayer. Al-Mu'tasim al-Abbasi, an Abbasid caliph, went with his horses to fight the Turks. When his army would march, everyone would separate. One day when he was marching there was a man praying. Al-Mu'tasim ordered that he be removed or that he remove himself, but the man wouldn't move. When the man finished praying prayer, he said that he would not move and would instead fight him using his Salat al-Layl.

The benefits of Salat al-Layl have been narrated to provide rizq (wealth) to the human being. The Ahlulbayt also say it removes punishment of the grave. It also is the lamp that lights your grave in the darkness. Tawoos al-Yamani, one of the companions of the Ahlulbayt, was near the Ka'aba when he saw Imam Zain al-Abideen crying whilst he was praying. He heard the Imam asking Allah to be merciful to him as he has wronged Him. He then narrates that all of a sudden the Imam collapsed to the floor and said to him, "What is wrong, Imam? You are the son of Fatima and Ali. Surely, if you cry, then what do we do?" The Imam answered him, "O Tawoos, on the Day of Judgement it doesn't matter which family you came from. You may be an Abyssinian slave or a Quraishi master, in the eyes of Allah, it is only your taqwa that helps you."

Salat al-Layl on its own is not enough, because Umar ibn Saad himself prayed Salat al-Layl. Some people curse him when they don't even pray Salat al-Layl themselves. Umar ibn Saad used to have two traits about him. He would not wear shoes that had soles that touched all the ground beneath him. Instead he would walk with shoes that had four nails. He was scared that he would trample on the ants, so he would put four nails so not everything would be hit. He used to pray Salat al-Layl, but the problem was, that outside the prayer he wasn't acting in a way that reflected this. One day Amir al-Mu'mineen was walking with his companion Kumayl when they heard a man praying Salat al-Layl whilst he was crying. Kumayl looked at Imam and told him he was impressed how, whilst everyone was asleep, this man was crying in prayer. Imam replied, "One day Kumayl I will show you who this man really is." When the Battle of Nahrawan was finished, there was a man's head which was on a spear. Imam Ali reminded Kumayl that he was the same man that was praying Salat al-Layl, except he never understood his position.

The verse then states, "And from [part of] the night, pray. It would be an additional prayer for you. This will upgrade you to a level where you are at a praised station, or maqam mahmood." In Arabic this is, "Wamina allayli fatahajjad bihi." This means to be sincere whilst you are praying, for example, with emotions. It then says, "It would be an additional prayer for you," or "naafila." It is as if Allah was telling the Prophet that the reason He is telling him to pray Salat al-Layl is because…everyone else, I have told them to pray seventeen rukaats a day because that is their capability. The Prophet praying Salat al-Layl would be upgraded to a higher position by praying more rukaats. This prayer was mandatory for the Prophet. This is why Allah had promised him that if he prays it, Allah will upgrade him to a "maqam mahmood." This is such a lofty position that whoever the Prophet would like to do shafa'at for, Allah will allow him. This shows you that Salat al-Layl is one of the ways you can do shafa'at for your family on the Day of Judgement.

Ayatullah Najafi al-Marashi, may Allah bless his soul, went on the ziyarah of the son of Muhammad, the son of Imam al-Hadi (AS), on the way to Sammara. He says that the heat had overcome him on the journey and he fainted. When he had woken up, he saw a man in front of him. This man called him by his name al-Marashi, and offered to take him to Muhammad ibn Hadi (AS). Al-Marashi was confused as to how he had known his name and had known his destination. The man looked at al-Marashi and stated, "I would like to give you a piece of advice to give our followers. Tell our followers there are certain acts they should never miss:

1. They should all wear a ring on their right hand with the names of the Ma'soomeen written on it.
2. They should never neglect our ziyarah.
3. They should always recite Qur'an.
4. 4- Let them learn Ziyarat Ashura.
5. Let them learn Khutba al-Shaqshaqiya of Imam Ali in Nahj al-Balagha.
6. Let them learn the Khutba of my grandmother when she spoke out for Fadak.
7. Tell our ulama/scholars of Ahlulbayt not just to preach Salat al-Layl but to practice [it] as well.

When Ayatullah al-Marashi realised who was speaking to him, as this man used the word "our ulama" and "grandmother," he was preparing to say, "O Imam Mahdi (AS)," but the man had disappeared. Therefore the twelfth Imam advises his followers to pray Salat al-Layl as well. Allah (SWT) also says through the Prophet, "If a man sleeps with an intention of praying Salat al-Layl then even his sleep, I will reward it because of his intention (niyyah)."

Lecture 7

Rizq: God's Sustenance in Islam

The discussion of rizq is a fundamental one as it affects the life of each and every human being as well as every creation of Allah (SWT). Every human being aims to find out the foundations of rizq and seeks to understand how to search for rizq, of that which is ordained by God, and is that which has to be sought after. Sometimes you hear the phrase, "May Allah increase your rizq," but what is the deep-rooted meaning of the word rizq? Normally we associate it with the narrow definition of wealth, whereas the actual definition is broader and is part of the governing structure of Allah (SWT).

The word rizq is translated in English as "sustenance" and this gives us the idea that there must be a sustainer who shares out this sustenance. There are many sustainers, such as our parents, and this includes the period when we were in our mother's womb. Likewise our father was our sustainer when we became older. Governments, or the country that we live in, can also sustain its population. Yet the highest of sustainers and the origin of all sustainers is Allah (SWT). Hence, one of the ninety-nine names of Allah (SWT) is "al-razaaq," i.e., the one who sustains. Amir al-Mu'mineen in his famous munajat, the whispered prayers, says, "My master, O my master, you are the Sustainer and I am the sustained. Who is there for the sustained except the Sustainer?" Here the Imam highlights that, although there are intermediate sustainers, the ultimate sustainer is Allah (SWT).

Surah 11, verse 6, Allah (SWT) states, "There is no moving creature on earth but its sustenance depends on Allah. He knows the time and place of its definite abode and its temporary deposit. All is in a clear Record."

This means that Allah gives sustenance to all of his creations in the bacteria, plant, animal and human kingdom. Two Prophets of God understood this definition of sustenance whereby they understood that those creations we cannot perceive are sustained by Allah. The first Prophet was Prophet Sulayman (AS) whereby his story is described in Surah a-Naml. Naml is translated as "ant." Prophet Sulayman was given a miracle to communicate with animals, and the Jinn and also the wind was under his service. One day Prophet Sulayman was speaking to the ants. He saw an ant that left his hand to start walking towards the frog at the entrance of the lake. The ant entered the mouth of the frog and the frog swam in the river. The frog returned and this time opened his mouth to release the ant. Prophet Sulayman was bewildered at this; he picked up the ant and asked what had happened. The ant answered, "Allah (SWT) has ordered me everyday to go in the mouth of that frog, the frog swims to the bottom of the river to a worm. I take with me a piece of sustenance which is then carried by the frog and then carried to the worm at the bottom. When the worm is given sustenance, it says, "How grateful I am to a Lord who sustains His creation even though they are at the bottom of a river.'"

Likewise, Prophet Musa (AS) was taught of Allah's rizq to every creation. Before the Prophet was going to die, he wondered who would look after his daughter at his departure. Angel Jibra'il then came towards Prophet Musa and asked that he come with him to the Red Sea. Jibra'il asked that Musa strike the Red Sea like he had done once before, when Musa struck it he found a rock which was at the lowest place in the sea. He lifted the rock to find a creature, so he asked Jibra'il what the significance of this was. Jibra'il responded, "O Musa, your Lord is willing to look after the sustenance of a small creature at the bottom of the rock at the bottom of the sea and you are wondering who will look after the sustenance of your daughter?"

As with verse 11:6, Allah states that He is the sustainer of every single creation. Philosophers that examine rizq propose two questions, the first is social and the second is economical. The social question is the following: if Allah (SWT) looks after the rizq of everyone, then what's the need for one to work? This question can build a society that either earns a living or one which stays at home without a job. This was looked upon by Imam al-Sadiq (AS). The Imam used to have a companion named Umar ibn Muslim that frequently visited him. For a certain period of time, Umar had not seen the Imam so the Imam asked about him from his companion Ali ibn Abdel-Aziz. Ali explained to the Imam that Umar now believed that Allah will protect his sustenance and hence he stayed at home to worship. Imam al-Sadiq (AS) instantly remembered an incident that occurred during the time of his grandfather, the Holy Prophet (PBUH), when Surah 65, verse 3, was revealed, "God will make a way (out of difficulty) for one who has fear of Him and will provide him with sustenance in a way that he will not even notice. God is Sufficient for the needs of whoever trusts in Him. He has full access to whatever He wants. He has prescribed a due measure for everything."

Many Muslims at the time of this revelation believed that if they feared Allah then this simply meant that they will achieve this sustenance mentioned – "in a way that they will not even notice." They decided that they would stay at home, and in the daytime they would fast and at night they would pray, whilst Allah will look after their rizq. The Prophet (PBUH) explained to them that the meaning of this verse is not that one fears Allah while they are restless. It is only when someone fears Allah, and uses the faculties of intellect and senses that Allah has given them to struggle in the environment they live in…after that Allah will then protect their rizq. Allah (SWT) has given us an intellect and the role of this intellect is to allow us understand different concepts in order to to apply them in different fields. Islam did not want to build a society that did nothing; this is why The Prophet (PBUH) has said, "There are seventy stages of worship and the best of these is earning a living lawfully."

The second economical question was the following: if Allah (SWT) looked after the creation's rizq, then why are there rich people and poor people in the world? Some say God's system of governance is of an economic inequality whereby the rich are getting richer and poverty is increasing. Islam has answered this question in three stages. The first stage is the response of Imam Ali (AS) when he asserted, "The only reason why there are poor people in the world is because of the extravagance of the rich." George Bernard Shaw has a beautiful metaphor related to this point. He had a physical appearance whereby he had a lot of hair on one side of his head and was bald on the other side. He was asked once to explain inequality, and he replied by saying it was due to his hair. He said,

"Good production, bad distribution." Thus, Allah (SWT) does provide us with sustenance, but with the greed of the rich, this meant that the distribution is not shared out. This is why Islam brought about the concept of "sadaqa," "zakat," and "khums" in order to try and bring equilibrium between the wealthy and the poor.

The second response to the economical question in Islam is that being rich does not equal happiness. Many in the world are rich but they seem to have more problems than the poor. One day the Holy Prophet Muhammad (PBUH) was travelling with his companions when they reached a valley in Medina, and The Prophet (PBUH) approached a man who was milking a camel in the area. The Prophet (PBUH) asked if they could drink some of the milk as they had been thirsty while travelling, but the man said no as the milk would be used for the breakfast and dinner of his tribe. The Prophet (PBUH) turned around and raised his hands in prayer, "Ya Allah, increase him in wealth and in children." The Prophet (PBUH) continued walking and reached another man who was milking a camel. This time when the Prophet had asked him, the man replied take as much milk you desire and here are some sheep for your travel. The Prophet (PBUH) prayed to Allah the following, "Ya Allah, give him what is sufficient of wealth and what is sufficient of children." The companions later asked why the Prophet asked for more to be given to the man who didn't share his milk and asked for what is sufficient with the latter man who gave. The Prophet (PBUH) answered, "That which is sufficient may bring you closer to Allah (SWT) because sometimes having more wealth and children provides you with greater tests."

The third response to the economical question is that when Allah (SWT) does not provide rizq to some people, there is a reason which mere humans do not understand. Prophet Musa (AS) was walking one day past a town. He saw an old man lying on the ground with no food and was not wearing any clothes. Prophet Musa felt sorry for him and asked the old man for help. The man replied that he would like the Prophet to pray to Allah to increase his rizq. The Prophet then went to Mount Sinai to pray to Allah for an increase in sustenance for that old man. A few days later the Prophet came past a crowd and a crowd member explained to the Prophet how the old man was rich now and started drinking wine. The old man began causing trouble with others and killed a man while he was intoxicated, thus the crowd had come to punish him. The Prophet turned to Allah and cried out to him, "Ya Allah, you are the All-wise."

This is relative to Surah 42, verse 7, "Had God given abundant sustenance to His servants, they would have certainly rebelled on earth, but He sends them a known measure of sustenance as He wills. He is All-aware of His servants and watches over them all." There are those unfortunately who, instead of thanking Allah (SWT) while they are given wealth, they go against Him, as their temptations increase. This is reminiscent of the father-son conversation between Imam Ali (AS) and Imam Hassan (AS) whereby the Imam divides rizq in our life and says, "Know my son that sustenance (rizq) is of two types, a rizq which you seek and a rizq which seeks you." The latter type whereby rizq seeks you means that Allah (SWT) has already written for you how much rizq he will give you. But how it reaches us, depends on how we earn it, either through halal ways or haram ways. The following story explains this well. Imam Ali (AS) used to leave his horse outside and pay someone to look after it while he used to go into Kufa to pray. One day, Imam returned from prayer to find his horse with no saddle. The Imam thought to himself he would have given two dirhams to the man who took his saddle, but nonetheless he needed to purchase another saddle. When the Imam went to the market he found his saddle that had been taken from him. The Imam asked the price for it and the man replied that he brought it for two dirhams. Thus, Allah (SWT) had written for that person to obtain two dirhams, but how he obtained it was in a haram way. The sixth Imam says that "the rizq that seeks you, seeks you in the same way as death does." We cannot run away from death, comparatively rizq comes to you whether you request it or not.

The former type of rizq the Imam mentions to his son Hassan is the one you have to go after, thus there is no shame if one works outside the house. The Ahlulbayt detested a person who remained idle and lazy because Allah (SWT) would like us to struggle at our work in the daytime in the environment we live in. The Prophet (PBUH) used to say that it is one of the greatest jihads to work. In al-Kafi there is a hadith which narrates a story about Muhammad ibn Munkader, who lived in the time of the fifth and sixth Imam. One day Muhammad ibn Munkader was walking on one of the hottest days in Medina. He saw Muhammad ibn Ali al-Baqir working in the valley. Muhammad ibn Munkader couldn't believe how al-Baqir was working the same amount of labour as the two slaves with him. Muhammad ibn Munkader went to advise the fifth Imam that if the angel of death would come now to al-Baqir it would take him at a time where he was running after dunya. Imam replied, "I am not ashamed if the angel of death comes now because I will die worshipping Allah (SWT). I will make sure my family is not in need of anybody. Ibn Munkader, I would rather my soul be taken away now when I am serving Allah and my family, than when I am committing a sin away from Allah."

Here, in this way, Imam al-Baqir (AS) showed what his grandfather The Prophet (PBUH) did one day. Prophet Muhammad (PBUH) came one day to Sa'ad al-Ansari to ask where he had been. Sa'ad said he had been ploughing the ground so he that may earn for his family. The Prophet (PBUH) kissed the hand of Sa'ad and said, "These hands will not touch the fire of Jahanam." As long as you earn through halal means, your hands will not touch the Hellfire. Therefore, you find that the second type of rizq is the rizq you have to go and search for. This can be seen in the du'a of Salatul Isha where we recite, "Ya Allah (SWT), I do not know where my rizq resides. I search for it from the lines of the bottom of my heart. I search for it in country after country, but I am like those wanderers who continue to wonder where their rizq is. I do not know if it is in the heavens, on the earth, in the sea, in the land, or in that which is dry or in whose hands it is, but one thing I do know, the knowledge of my rizq is with you and the alleyways and shortcuts are with you, the ease to how I can reach it is with you. Ya Allah, make it easy for me to find." When we recite this du'a we are searching for the rizq but only Allah (SWT) knows where it resides, and He is The Greatest of Creators, al-Razaaq. Therefore He can help us. This is why the best of actions is to give away your rizq once you get it.

In Surah al-Baqara it says, "Alif, Lam, Mim. This is the Book about which there is no doubt, a guidance for those conscious of Allah – Who believe in the unseen, establish prayer, and spend out of what We have provided for them." The "Muttaqeen," or those who are conscious, include those who spend out of what We have provided them. A truly pious person spreads their rizq as they believe the same Lord that gives me is the same Lord that can give me again. The stingy person, however, is the one who doubts Allah (SWT). Abu Hanifah performed one of the greatest acts of his life when he saw the way Bani Umayyah treated Ahlulbayt. Abu Hanifah knew that Zaid, the son of fourth Imam, was being treated badly by Hisham ibn Abdel Malik. Abu Hanifah gave ten thousand dinars to Zaid. He gave him this because he said that Zaid should use it to fight Bani Umayyah for they're destroying the message of The Prophet (PBUH). Because of this, they placed Abu Hanifah in prison. Thus this man was given rizq and he gave it away. Moreover, the Ahlulbayt state ways in which rizq can be blocked. Imam narrates that "the one who neglects his prayer, his rizq is blocked."

It is important to note that to make rizq is not only money, rather it is having children, good health and freedom of speech. Abu Dharr al-Ghafari spoke out against Mu'awiyah ibn Abu Sufyan as he was building green palaces; Abu Dharr told Mu'awiyah that the caliphs before him were just. Abu Dharr's freedom of speech was a rizq from Allah (SWT). However, with all these types of rizq, Allah (SWT) tells us to not spoil our family too much with rizq. In the time of the Bani Abbasid caliphs, one caliph used to hire a personal tutor for his child. The tutor was late on the first day. Food was brought late to him and when the boy had made a mistake, he would tell him not to repeat it again. When the caliph found out, the tutor told him, "I only taught your son a lesson about life, one day your son will become caliph. I came late because I wanted to show him the feeling of waiting when someone is inside. His food was late because I wanted him to feel some of the pain of those starving. Then I wanted him to taste the meaning of punishment so he knows that he doesn't take it lightly when he becomes caliph, thus he won't behead humans like he would animals." He taught the caliph that his child is a blessing from Allah (SWT) and that one should not allow their child to be spoilt.

Rizq can either be sought after or it can come to you in this life, except for one group of people that have continuous rizq until the Day of Judgement. These are the martyrs who died in the way of Allah (SWT). In the Qur'an Allah says, "Do not count those who die in the way of Allah as being dead, no, rather they remain alive, still receiving rizq from Allah (SWT)." Even though their bodies died, their souls remain with us, and secondly, their message is echoed forever. For example, Imam Hussein (AS) may have died on the tenth of Muharram, yet his name continues to be called out by millions today and his message remains strong against oppression. Allah (SWT) wanted to give Imam rizq in this lifetime and in the world of Barzakh.

Lecture 8

Lessons from the Biography of the Holy Prophet

The Holy Prophet of Islam occupies a prominent position within the religion of Islam and is revered as the greatest personality within the religion. He is a man whose life has to be examined in depth for there are many lessons to be learnt and indeed many examples to be derived. And he is indeed a man whose biography has been unfortunately very much undervalued and indeed very much underestimated. Therefore it is vital that we discuss his biography from the day that he was born until the day he died in order that we are able to, firstly, take as many practical lessons from his life and apply them in our own lives; and secondly, remove any misconceptions that surround his biography, for there was a period in Medieval Europe when he was seen as being the devil incarnate or as being the false Messiah, the Antichrist. Therefore, there is a need for us to examine his biography so that we present him in his true light - as a mercy for mankind and a moral exemplar for everyone.

The Holy Prophet (PBUH) was born in the year 570, known as the "Year of the Elephant." The Arabs did not have a calendar dating system as such. They would look at what was the most important event in that particular year and then name the year after that event. For example, if there was a famous personality who died, they would name the year after that personality. Or if there was a war that took place, they would name the year after that war. The year within which the Prophet (s) was born was called "Am ul-Feel," the Year of the Elephant. This was because of an incident that took place involving an army of elephants.

At that time in Arabia there were people who would visit the Ka'aba. In Yemen there was a church that was built by an Ethiopian man by the name of Abraha. [Bear in mind the words "Ethiopian," because Abraha's niece was Bilal al-Habashi's mother. When Abraha's niece was caught as a prisoner, she got married within one of the Arabian tribes and gave birth to a son by the name of Bilal. Hence, when Bilal is said to be of the people of Habash, it is because of his mother's uncle being Abraha, who was an Ethiopian, yet was the governor of Yemen.]

Abraha had always been envious of the fact that there were people who would visit the Ka'aba rather than his church in Yemen. He attempted to send emissaries and ambassadors to go towards the Ka'aba and tell the Arabs, *"Leave your place of worship because your place has been polluted. Originally you were people of Abraham, but now you worship idols. It is better that all of you come to my church in Yemen and make my church the main center of the area."* When he noticed that his emissaries were not successful, the narrations tell us that he decided it was better for him to take his army and march to the Ka'aba with an army of elephants. Hence, within the religion of Islam there is a chapter called "Surat ul-Feel," which is chapter 105 of the Quran. The chapter begins, *"Have you not seen how your Lord dealt with the People of the Elephant?"* because, although Abraha arrived in Mecca with elephants, he had brought only a few elephants with him; as we know, elephants are of a size where there only needs to be a few for them to capture your attention. When he came towards Arabia with these elephants, there were people who were unquestionably scared. That is why the main person who thwarted his plans was Abdul Muttalib, the grandfather of the Prophet (PBUH).

Abdul Muttalib told the people to hide in the desert hills. So they went to hide there in the desert hills and then Abdul Muttalib was chosen by the people to meet Abraha. Notice from the beginning of the biography of the Prophet (PBUH) we see that the line of Abraham through Isma'il is still looking after the birthplace of Isma'il. Earlier on, we said that in Genesis, chapter 17, verse 18-20, says that "God promised Abraham that in the line of Isma'il there will be twelve princes who are part of a fruitful generation..."

Abdul Muttalib entered Abraha's tent. Abraha was sitting down. When Abdul Muttalib entered the tent, Abraha looked at him. He saw quite an imposing figure; he told him to sit down and then said to him, *"What is it that you want?"* Abdul Muttalib said, *"I want my camels."* Abraha said, *"Sorry?"* Abdul Muttalib said, *"I want my camels. You took my camels. I want my camels returned back to me."* Abraha looked at him and said, *"Do you know when you entered my tent I had a lot of respect for you, but now I have lost all that respect."* Abdul Muttalib said, *"Why?"* Abraha said, *"When you entered my tent, I thought this is a man who will want to protect his 'black cube,' known as the Ka'aba, but instead all you want is the camels?"* Abdul Muttalib said, *"That house has a Lord of its own to protect it; and I am the protector of my lot of camels. I want my two hundred camels given back to me!"* Abraha said, *"Get out! Get out! There is no agreement between us."* Abdul Muttalib came back a second time to persuade him; again Abraha wouldn't agree. Abraha decided that he would take his elephant (most of the other narrations indicate another six or seven elephants) and march towards the Ka'aba. They marched towards the Ka'aba and the Quran put it quite beautifully when it said, *"Have you not seen how your Lord dealt with the People of the Elephant? Did He not ruin their plan? And He sent against them flocks of birds, striking them with stones and petrified clay. And thus He reduced them to rotten chaff."*

What did Allah do? He ensured that *"you plan and I plan, but I am the greatest of planners."* These elephants were ready to achieve victory. The narrations state very clearly that some birds pelted them with stones until the opposition army was defeated. In other words, the Arabs had not began the Hijra calendar in the year in which the Prophet (PBUH) had been born. We know the Hijra calendar began after the Prophet (PBUH) migrated from Mecca to Madina. So from that time on they named their years 1 AH, 2 AH, 3 AH and 4 AH and so on, but before that they named their years according to the major incidents which happened in them.

There is a difference in the date of the Prophet's birth within the various schools in Islam. Our brothers in other schools celebrate his birth on the 12th of Rabi ul-Awwal whereas we celebrate his birth on the 17th of Rabi ul-Awwal. It is vital that this is not a cause of friction between us. Why? Ayatollah Montazeri (may Allah bless his soul) used to stress on this week as being a week of unity between Muslims because all of us share a common denominator, and that is the life of our Prophet (PBUH). Therefore, it should be the case where our leaders and congregations go to the mosques of our brothers on the 12th of Rabi ul-Awwal and celebrate with them, and our brothers are welcomed into our mosques to celebrate with us on the 17th. Thus, there is a difference of opinion, and in the historical research you will find, barring Sheikh al-Kulayni, most of the others will say that he was born on the 17th of Rabi ul-Awwal.

The Prophet (PBUH)'s first few years of life were not easy. Imagine that your father passes away in first few years of your life; according to some narrations, it was only a few months into his life. Since his father Abdullah passed away, the Prophet (PBUH) therefore was born an orphan; hence the Quran says, *"Did we not find you an orphan?"* His mother Aminah did what most Arabs did with their babies at the time. If you were of the noble aristocracy of Mecca, what would you do with your baby? Eight days after the birth of their babies, the Meccan aristocrats would take them to the desert to be suckled and breast-fed by a wet nurse. Someone may ask, *"Why couldn't his mother suckle him? Why did she have to take him to the desert?"*

There were a number of reasons the Arabs, and especially the aristocrats, would take their babies to raised in the desert. The reasons why the Arab aristocrats would send their infants to be raised in the desert are very important to understand because they have a major role to play on the upbringing and the psyche of the Prophet (PBUH).

The first reason is that it allows you to grow up in an environment where you are independent and a free thinker for the first few years of your life. In the desert there aren't buildings or forests surrounding you, nor are there lots of humans and shops, or markets and trade. It is open in the desert. You can sit there and look at the creation and reflect upon your creation and your meaning and role in life. The Arabs who would send their babies to have their first eight or ten years in the desert would want that baby to be living in a world where they would grow up as a child who is not told *what* to think, but is rather shown *how* to think.

The second reason was because Mecca's climate was not a healthy climate for children both in terms of what they saw and what they breathed. Imagine you are a child growing up in an environment where you see baby girls being buried alive? Is that a good start to your life? Or you see people performing tawaf (circumambulation) of the Ka'aba naked. The Arabs used to go around the Ka'aba naked because they said, *"God created us free so there is no need for clothes; clothes are impure. Let's go and circumambulate His house like how He created us,"* completely naked. The Prophet (PBUH)'s mother wanted him to grow up in the desert so he would not see this.

The third reason was that Mecca's wind and climate was hot and unhealthy. There were pests and epidemics. So his mother made sure that he was sent there.

Most narrations say that there were two women who breast-fed the Prophet (PBUH), and Abdul Muttalib chose both of them. The first lady to have breast-fed the Prophet (PBUH) was Suwaiba, the servant of his uncle Abu Lahab. Before Muhammad (PBUH) announced his prophethood, Abu Lahab used to love the Prophet (PBUH) because he was his younger brother's son. So first Aminah asked Abdul Muttalib who should breastfeed their son and he said, "Suwaiba." Suwaiba also suckled Hamza because the Prophet (PBUH) and Hamza's ages were very similar. That is why when the Prophet (PBUH) was one day told to marry Hamza's daughter, he said, "*We cannot because we suckled from the same wet nurse.*"

The other lady who Abdul Muttalib chose was Halima Sa'adiyya. Halima Sa'adiyya was a pious God-fearing lady. Halima Sa'adiyya herself would say, "I saw vast riches and goodness affect my life the moment I started to suckle the Prophet (PBUH)."

Some narrations in Islamic history try and tell us that *when the Prophet (PBUH) was with Halima as a two-year-old, "he remembered" he was sitting down one day; two men came, opened his chest, gave him a "heart transplant" because there was the black dot of Shaytan (Satan) on his heart, so they put a new heart in and Muhammad was pure after that day.* We of course differ with this idea because even if someone has the dot of Shaytan, it is not on their physical heart. The dot on the heart is metaphorically referring to being on one's "nafs" (self or ego) therefore a change of the heart is not needed.

On the contrary, the Prophet (PBUH) was born with this purity. He did not need people to open him up, perform an operation, and then move on. The Quran says, "Have We not expanded for you your breast (which was able to take in knowledge)?" Therefore, some narrations say that Halima saw this happening to the Prophet (PBUH), but we differ with this completely. Halima twice went back to Aminah, the mother of the Prophet (PBUH), and said to her, *"Do you want to take him back to Mecca?"* Aminah twice replied back to her saying, *"O Halima, keep him there because I see diseases and epidemics which will affect him."*

Some people ask the question, *"If God loves Muhammad so much, why let him have such a difficult beginning as an orphan?"* - meaning why did not God allow him to have a natural beginning like everyone else and have a father and a mother? When the Imam was asked this question, he replied, *"God wanted to ensure nobody protected and brought up Muhammad but Himself."* He wanted to ensure that the Prophet (PBUH) would not show obedience to anybody, even from his early life, except Himself. Sometimes your parents may sway you one way or the other. Even though his parents were loyal believers in the message, God wanted to be the One who oversaw his development. Therefore you find that his father died when he was young, then his mother died, and then his grandfather Abdul Muttalib looked after him.

His grandfather died within a couple of years, so his uncle Abu Talib brought him up. His uncle Abu Talib acts as a backbone not only to him, but also to the message of the religion of Islam. Abu Talib preferred his nephew even above his sons. His wife Fatima bint Asad was exactly the same. When the Prophet (PBUH) buried Fatima bint Asad, he said, *"This is my mother. This is the lady who preferred me above her sons. This is the lady who used to clothe me and wash me and look after me and she is the one who nourished me."*

So notice these were the two who looked after him, and that is why there is a certain question that is asked: *"What do we know about him before the age of forty?"* In a few moments we will examine his life after the age of forty, but if you were to ask many Muslims, *"Tell us about your Prophet before the age of forty,"* many would be unaware of his biography. Notice that before the age of forty, when Abu Talib was bringing him up, the Prophet (PBUH) would latch on to him everywhere he went to the extent that Abu Talib himself narrates, *"One day I was about to leave for Syria on a commercial expedition. The young Muhammad was only twelve, and he latched on to me as I was leaving. When he latched on to me, it hurt me that my nephew was an orphan, so I said to myself, 'Let me take him with me.'"*

The narration states that he took him towards Syria. On the way towards Syria they walked passed a monastery. The monk saw these people coming. They said to him, *"We are coming here to reside for the night."*

The monk looked at him and said to Abu Talib, *"All of you can come and are welcome to eat what you want to eat, but Abu Talib, I want to ask you a question."* Abu Talib said, *"What is it?"* He said, *"You know that young man walking alongside you? Bring him along with you tomorrow as well."* Abu Talib said, *"Very well, I will bring him tomorrow."* The next day when Abu Talib came, the monk looked at him and said, *"Where is the young man?"* Abu Talib said,

"My nephew?" The monk said, *"Yes."* Abu Talib said, *"He's just over there."* The monk said, *"Call him towards me."* And this is one of our proofs within Islamic theology that he was already inspired with the knowledge of God and the knowledge of his mission. It is not the case that he became a Prophet at the age of forty and was now told to announce his prophethood. He knew about his prophethood beforehand because that monk came to him when he was the age of twelve and said to him, *"In the name of Allat and Uzza…"*

As soon as the Prophet (PBUH) heard this, he said to him, *"Do not mention those names in front of me. Those are the most detested names to me."* They were the names of the idols of Qureish. Then the monk said, *"I want to give you some sadaqa."* The Prophet (PBUH) said, *"We do not accept sadaqa."* The monk then said to him, *"Can I see the mark between your shoulders?"* He allowed him to see the mark between his shoulders and then he looked at Abu Talib and said, *"Abu Talib, if you did not know already, then know that this young man is the Prophet whom Jesus spoke about, and whom Moses spoke about, and beware of the enemies that he is going to face."* Abu Talib said, *"How did you know?"* He said, *"When you were walking and Muhammad was next to you, I saw every tree bow down after Muhammad passed by."*

Even after the age of twelve the Prophet (PBUH) had this innate love for justice and the removal of oppression. One of the greatest incidents that happened in his youth was at the age of twenty, and years later he would always refer back to this. At the age of twenty he joined a group called "Hilf ul-Fudhool." What was this?

In Arabia many people would come to the markets. They came from outside the market area and would bring their goods as well, and the people of Arabia would buy them. One of these people came from the Banu Zabid tribe (or some say Banu Zubayd) to sell some of his goods to Aas ibn Wa'il, the father of Amr ibn Aas. When he sold these goods, he said to Aas, *"Give me my money."* Aas replied back to him, saying, *"What money?"* He said, *"You've just taken my goods and I want my money back."* Aas said, *"There's no money for you and you are a stranger in our land. You are not going to get your money back and I am one of the aristocrats of Arabia so you might as well forget about it."*

This person was so enraged that he went on one of the mountains of Arabia and said, *"O people of Arabia! I have come as a stranger to your land and I have been involved in a business transaction. None of you have sought to help me when this man has taken my right. At least one of you speak up!"* A twenty year old man named Muhammad spoke up for him. He got up and said, *"It is unjust for us to be like this with a person who is a guest in our location; and secondly, how can we be unjust when the goods have been sold in a business transaction? Let's form a league which looks after the rights of business employees and let us form a league which protects transactions within the Arabian state."* How old was he? Only twenty, and there was still no announcement of his prophethood; but from that young age the first sign that people noticed was that he was a man who spoke out against injustice.

In 2012, how many of us speak out against injustice, whether it be injustice against Muslims or non-Muslims? Our Prophet (PBUH) did not look at that man and say, *"Well, that man is not a Muslim so I am not going to speak up for his right."* Whenever we see any oppression anywhere in the world, we must speak out against that oppression because our Prophet (PBUH) taught us this even from the time of his youth. This is the first lesson that we can take from him.

Not only did he achieve this at the age of twenty, later on he achieved two attributes which the Arabs would honor him for. They gave him the title, "as-Sadiq" (the Truthful) and "al-Amin" (the Trustworthy). Notice that the Arabs did not know that he was a Prophet nor did they receive any book from him, but they were concerned with his ethics as a human being.

When a flood affected the Ka'aba and it was damaged, they needed to put the Hajr al-Aswad (the black stone) back into the Ka'aba after repairs were made. The Arabs fought with each other about who would put the Hajr al-Aswad back in its position. One tribe said, *"We should put it back."* Another said, *"We should put it back."* A third said, *"We should put it back!"* They said, *"Okay, let's do this. The man who walks into this meeting next will be the one who chooses which tribe puts it back."* As soon as he walked in, they did not say, *"Muhammad has walked in."* They said, *"As-Sadiq…al-Amin has walked in!"* The focus wasn't on the name; the focus was on the morals of the man.

Today in Islam there is too much focus on names and not morals. When he began his prophethood, or even before he began, he did not just come in front of the people and say, *"People! I am a Prophet. Follow me!"* You need to have those attributes where, for forty years, no one can find a black dot on you.

Yet do you know what we do as humans? If you give us a white piece of paper and there is a black dot in the middle and you ask us, *"What is on that paper?,"* we will say, *"A black dot."* None of us will focus on the white, will we? We love to focus on the dots. Even if there is so much white about someone's character, all we can remember is the black dot; whereas the Prophet (PBUH) did not allow them to point at one black dot - he was Sadiq and Amin.

Therefore, when he came to announce his prophethood, he said, *"Did you not call me as-Sadiq? Did you not call me al-Amin? When the Hajr ul-Aswad was to be placed in the Ka'aba, was I not the one who said, 'O you four tribes, do not fight each other. One of you hold one part of the cloth, another hold a second, a third hold the third, and the fourth hold the fourth part of the cloth; all four of you carry the Hajr ul-Aswad and I will pick it up from you and I will place it inside.'"*

When he announced his prophethood at the age of forty, the question arises, *what was the aim of his prophethood?* The aim was nothing more than allowing mankind to meditate and reflect on their existence, in order that, after meditation and reflection, mankind not only had respect for themselves but they had respect for other creations of God as well. That's it.

We made our Prophet (PBUH)'s religion complicated, whereas his mission from the beginning was a mission that was simple. Arabians were in Jahiliyya (Age of Ignorance). If any society is stagnant, it means that it is a society that does not reflect; and when the human does not reflect, then he is the cause of a virus in his society. When the Prophet (PBUH) began his mission, did he begin his mission by saying, *"All of you, pray namaz right now!"*? Did he say, *"All of you, it is Shahr Ramadan…Fast! Fast!" "All of you, keep a beard!"* or *"All of you, wear hijab!"*?

He began first by saying, *"Mankind, reflect on your existence. Have an hour of reflection, it is greater than seventy years of worship."* Today's Islam is too dogmatic. It is too focused on *halal ,haram halal, haram,, wajib,, makrooh,, halal, ,haram.* Is this what the Prophet (PBUH) brought to mankind?

The first part of the Prophet (PBUH)'s mission was to emphasize that a true human being is one who is reflecting on his role in this world. The moment he reflects, everything else will fall into place. The Muslims of today focus on the jigsaw pieces and have forgotten the puzzle.

Miqdad, a close companion of the Prophet (PBUH), says, *"In those early days in Islam I heard the Prophet through one hadith saying, 'An hour of reflection is greater than a year of worship'; Then I heard Ibn Abbas say that the Prophet said, 'An hour of reflection is greater than seven years of worship'; Then I heard another companion say that the Prophet said, 'An hour of reflection is greater than seventy years of worship.' So I decided that I was going to go to the Prophet and ask him, how is it that in one hadith you are telling the people an hour of reflection is greater than a year of worship; then in a second you are saying it is greater than seven years of worship; then in a third you are saying it is greater than seventy years of worship?"*

When he asked the Prophet (PBUH), the Prophet (PBUH) said, *"Miqdad, come with me. Let's ask the first person."* They asked the first person, *"How do you reflect?"* He said, *"I look at the creations of the heavens and the earth and I think to myself that these could not have come by an accident."* The Prophet (PBUH) said, *"His one hour of reflection is greater than a year of worship."* Then they went to the second and said to him, *"How do you reflect?"* He said, *"I think about the Day of Judgment and the questions I am going to be asked, about what I did in public, and what I did in private."* The Prophet (PBUH) said, *"His one hour of worship is greater than seven years of worship."* Then they went to the third and asked, *"How do you reflect?"* He said, *"I am going to be very frank with you, I think about the hellfire and I get scared."* The Prophet (PBUH) said, *"His one hour of reflection is greater than seventy years of worship."* Why? Because the moment you think about the hellfire it will make you change your ways quite quickly.

Thus the Prophet (PBUH) began first by saying, *"One hour of reflection in this religion is greater than seventy years of dry worship."* You can fast and pray, and fast and pray, and fast and pray, but if you fast for thirty days in the year and for the other three hundred and thirty-five days you are not reflecting on your life, on your role, on your meaning, on your objectives, then you have not understood the true message of the religion of Islam. On the other hand, the moment you reflect on your creation that you were one day insignificant, you weren't worth mentioning, you came from something that when you look at it you are disgusted, then you may look at those around you and say, *"If I am so low, then why am I so arrogant to those who are around me?"*

That is why, when the Prophet (PBUH) first began his mission at the age of forty, he asked people to reflect on their existence.

Then he brought their attention to the disease of racism in their society. Why? Because he knew that when the human reflects upon things, he will never be a racist. *Am I better than another just because I am a certain color?*

No. We are both sons of Adam created from dust. Thus in the first part of his prophethood he spoke out against any type of racism. How did Bilal come to Islam? Bilal came to Islam when he saw Ammar ibn Yasir captured one day. When Ammar was captured, the early aristocrats of the Qureish looked at Ammar and said, *"O Ammar, are you the one who is trying to come forward and say that Muhammad's religion is the one we should follow?"* Ammar said, *"Yes."* He said, *"Explain to me Muhammad's religion."* Ammar said, *"The Prophet talks of one God and that God is Merciful to His creation. He has given them free will and has a Day of Judgment where He will judge us, but He will not judge us on our race. He will judge us according to our consciousness of His presence."* Bilal was standing there. Bilal was then still a slave. At that moment, one of the members of the Qureish said to Bilal, *"Bilal torture Ammar."* Bilal said *"No."* He said, *"What? Bilal! You black slave, torture Ammar!"* Bilal said, *"No."* He said, *"How dare you, Bilal! We brought you up. Torture him!"* Bilal said, *"I have never heard of a message where a man with my skin complexion is protected, where a man of my skin color is honored."* Notice here that when Bilal came towards Islam, it was because there was the avenue of reflection by the Prophet (PBUH). He allowed the religion to be intellectually spread, not emotionally.

In Madina when the Prophet (PBUH) said, *"I want someone to call for prayer,"* the people came forward and asked the Prophet (PBUH) whom he would assign to call for prayer. The Prophet (PBUH) said, *"Bilal, go up and give the adhan."* Therefore the Prophet (PBUH) destroyed racism from the beginning. He preached the fact that not only should we respect people from different races, but we must also learn to respect people of different religions. In the early years of his prophethood, his companions were being tortured, so he said to Ja'far ibn Abu Talib, *"Ja'far, go to Abyssinia. Leave with the companions."* Ja'far said, *"Where shall we go?"* The Prophet (PBUH) said, *"Ja'far, go to Abyssinia because you will meet a Christian priest."* Notice the message. On the first level he wants to remove racism, then encourage respect towards other human beings, and then to other religions, because if their principles are the same as ours then they are closer to us than people of our religion who are hypocrites without our principles. Thus Ja'far went to Abyssinia and met the Christian priest. Amr ibn Aas was alongside Ja'far. When Ja'far came, the Abyssinian priest asked, *"Who are these people?"* Ja'far replied by saying, *"We are people who believe in all the prophets and the final prophet of God, who spoke about Jesus, son of Mary."*

When the priest heard this, he said, *"What does your book say about Jesus, son of Mary?"* He said, *"Our Book says that Jesus, son of Mary, was born from a virgin birth and a chapter is named after his mother Maryam."*

The Prophet (PBUH) could have said, *"But he is a Christian and he believes in the crucifixion of Christ and we do not believe in that."* On the contrary, the Prophet (PBUH) said, *"He is a believer in God and there are more similarities between us than there are differences."* Look at the attitude the Muslims have today. They do not look at a human being as a fellow member of humanity rather they look at them as disbelievers.

Thus the early message of Islam was: no racism and respect people of other religions because those people have principles that we preach and understand. Thus, because of this, Ja'far was able to stay in Abyssinia and build the early Muslim community in Africa.

In the early years of Mecca the Prophet (PBUH) preached not only respect of other human beings and other religions but also the respect of the other gender. The Prophet (PBUH) was noticing that female infants were being buried alive; these people had no morals. Even someone like Umar ibn Khattab himself narrates, *"In the days of Jahiliyya before Islam came, we used to bury our daughters alive. There are two things, one of which makes me cry and the other makes me laugh. The one that makes me laugh is that we used to worship a god made out of dates. During our worship, when nobody was looking, we would take a date and eat it. By the end of our worship that god was dead. That used to make me laugh. The area that used to make me cry was when I buried my daughter alive. My daughter held onto my beard as I was burying her. But I got the spade and I hit her and I buried her alive."*

Thus, the Prophet (PBUH) made them first reflect on their existence, then he made them respect fellow nations and not be racists, then he let them be tolerant towards other religions, and then he led them to respect the role of the woman in society. He knew that if women were given rights there would be great nations. He established that first, women were not to be buried alive; then women were to inherit and not be inherited; and dowries were to belong to women. In the days of Arabian Jahiliyya, the dowry went to the father of the girl, not the girl. Then he said, *"Heaven lies underneath the feet of the mother."* One day a young Jewish man who became a Muslim came to the Prophet (PBUH) and said, *"O Prophet, my mother is Jewish but I am a Muslim. How do I treat her now that I have become a Muslim?"* The Prophet (PBUH) said, *"You treat her better than you used to treat her before."*

He went home and started to do all the chores; his mother looked at him and said, *"Ever since you became a Muslim, you behave like this. Why?"* He said, *"My Prophet tells me that heaven lies underneath your feet."* She said, *"If this is what the Prophet (PBUH) preaches, then I want to join the religion of this Prophet."*

As a result of his moral system, even his enemies would respect him... so much so that many of them would keep their trusts with him. He lived in Mecca for thirteen years and then he migrated to Madina and lived there for ten years. On the night that he left Mecca, he left Ali ibn Abi Talib behind to sleep in his bed. Was this the only role of Ali ibn Abi Talib (as)? No. Ali ibn Abi Talib (as) had a second role. *"O Ali, after you have left my bed, the next day return the trusts of my enemies that they entrusted with me."*

Imagine the enemies of Qureish saying to the Prophet (PBUH), *"We do not believe in you, we hate you, you are crazy...do you mind looking after this gold necklace for us?"* Because it was an ethical trait where *even though the person is his enemy he as a Prophet (PBUH) of God has not come to make enemies. If he can show that he is trustworthy, then let his enemies deposit [their belongings] with him.* Thus, after living in Mecca for thirteen years, he moved on to Madina.

At the age of 53, when he went to Madina, they fought him in battles. Many people say, *"Muhammad spread his religion by the sword."* The reality is that those battles were defensive battles and not offensive battles. Were they defensive battles which only protected Muslims? No. The Quran says in chapter 22, verse 39-40, *"And had repelled not God some people by others, verily had the monasteries been pulled down and the churches and the synagogues and the mosques in which God's name is much mentioned."*

I ask you, that if this Prophet (PBUH) came to spread his religion by the sword, why is the Quran talking about churches and synagogues? Islam was trying to say that when we are defending ourselves in Madina we are looking to defend every single area of worship that says *"There is only one God."* It is not just for the Muslims. The Quran says, in chapter 3, verse 64, *"Say, 'O People of the Book! Come to a word common between us and you that we worship none but God and shall not associate anything with Him and some of us take not others for lords other than God."*

After those early battles, you even notice his focus on the message of education. After the Battle of Badr, when he takes prisoners, his companions said to him, *"Let's kill them."* He said, *"No. Let's treat them well and make a proposition to them."* They said, *"What?"* He said, *"We will ransom them if they *teach ten of our people how to read and write."* From the beginning the message in Madina was focused on education: *"Seek knowledge from the cradle to the grave...Read until the final moments of your life...The value of a believer is their knowledge, their wisdom."* Thus the Prophet (PBUH) introduced the idea of reading and writing among the Muslims because he knew that these skills were the basis of a great society.

Then, after establishing himself as the head of the state in Madina, he formed a constitution called "The Constitution of Madina." This constitution gave the Jews the freedom to worship in their synagogues and the Christians to worship in their churches, alongside the Muslims who would worship in their mosques. He emphasized that there was nothing wrong with having a society with multi-religious dimensions.

And even after that, in Madina, when the Prophet (PBUH) was ordered by His Lord to go back to Mecca, which he had not visited ever since he was expelled...when he returned to Mecca, his companions said, *"Let's go back and fight those Meccans!"* He said, *"No, we will conduct a peace treaty with them."* They said, *"What do you mean by a peace treaty? Surely it is our chance to destroy these people's lives, to finish them like they tortured us."* The Prophet (PBUH) said, "No. Let us have a peace treaty and allow them to be opened up to the mercy of the religion of Islam." When the Prophet (PBUH) entered Mecca victorious, he taught us another ethical lesson of forgiveness. Many Muslims find it hard to forgive today. People find it hard to forgive a person who wrongs them, or a person who they see committing a wrong. You tell them, "But the years have gone by. Maybe the person has changed or repented." But they refuse, whereas their Prophet (PBUH) was the most forgiving of men.

When Mecca was conquered, there were two people who approached the Prophet (PBUH) and he forgave them. The first of them was Wahshi, the man who mutilated the body of his uncle Hamza to the extent that Hind, the mother of Mu'awiyah, cut so many pieces of Hamza's body that she made a necklace for herself. This Wahshi ripped Hamza's chest apart. When Mecca was conquered, Wahshi, Abu Sufyan, Hind and people like Habbar ibn Aswad, thought to themselves, *"We are never going to be forgiven by Muhammad; Muhammad is going to enter Mecca and is going to execute us for what we did."* Wahshi and Habbar said, *"But we hear Muhammad is a man of Mercy and that his religion is merciful and forgiving. He came to perfect the akhlaq of man."* So they said, "Let us go and approach him." Wahshi went to him and said, "O

Prophet of God, forgive me. I was in the days of ignorance. I did not know about the message of Islam. I heard rumors about you but they were not true. Prophet (PBUH) of God, forgive me for what has happened." And the reply was, *"O Wahshi, you are forgiven. Now leave this area."* Then Habbar ibn Aswad came forward. One of the Prophet (PBUH)'s stepdaughters was pregnant. She was going towards Madina. Habbar wanted her to miscarry, so on her way to Madina, he came and scared her in such a way that she ended up miscarrying her child. When the Prophet (PBUH) heard this, he was saddened. So when Habbar came to the Prophet (PBUH) after the conquest of Mecca, he said, *"O Prophet of God, I am the cause of the miscarriage of your grandchild. I scared her in a way that led her to miscarry, but I was ignorant and they deceived me about your behavior and your character. When I see you now, I see a man of morals. Please allow me to be forgiven."* We must ask ourselves, as Muslims today, how forgiving are we of our brothers, sisters, aunts, uncles, grandparents and cousins? The Prophet (PBUH) told him, *"You are forgiven by Allah. Do not worry over what you have done."*

The Prophet (PBUH) knew that the basis of a great community is all of these ethics of tolerance, patience and forgiveness. We must take our morals from him. Some of us have to be patient in our marriages; some of us have to be patient with our children. He too had to be patient with his marriages and his children. He had married a lady by the name of Shamba. Narrations say that this lady was the daughter of Amr al-Ghaffariyya. When she saw the Prophet's son Ibrahim die, she said, *"You know, if you were a Prophet of God, God would not have made your son die; I'm leaving you!"* and she left. Do you know how much patience you need to have when you are married to someone and they speak like that to you? But the Prophet (PBUH) was patient.

He had another wife by the name of Malika. Once she heard someone say that, *"Muhammad is the cause of your father's death."* She took all her possessions and left. Sometimes in life we complain about what we have to face, but our Prophet (PBUH) had to face more than us. He used to say, *"Patience is to faith like the head is to the body."* There can be no body without a head and there can be no faith without patience. Even he had to see a lot of his children die. His son Ibrahim died, his son Qasim died, even his son Abdullah died. Some of us today ask, *"Why did our children die? Why did my friend's child die?"* When we say, "The Prophet (PBUH) is an example," it is because everything that we face, the Prophet (PBUH) faced in his life as well.

That is why, before he died, he did what any great leader would do. He made it clear to his people that *"even though I am dying, I will first ensure that I will leave behind guidance for you."* He left behind guidance on the Day of Ghadeer when he raised the hand of Ali and made it clear to the people that *"I will never leave this world without ensuring that there is a guide for you who continues to protect the message in the way I gave you the message."*

But his final act was a true act of charity. In Islam, causing a fellow human being to smile is an act of charity. When his daughter Fatima came towards him when he was dying, there is a narration that states that first she cried and then she smiled. In this one act, the Prophet (PBUH) was showing us that, from the beginning of his life until the end, ethics and morality was the message of his biography. When Fatima turned around and they asked her, *"Fatima, you cried and then smiled?"* She said, *"I cried because he told me that he was about to pass away; but then I smiled because he told me that I would be the first from his family to join him."* Notice from the beginning until the end he was a man who brought a smile onto the lives of humanity, and left with a smile, and that is why until today it is not only Islam that respects him but others as well.

Guru Nanak, the founder of the Sikh religion, believed that *"Muhammad was an agent of Brahman."* Some Christian priests have been quoted as saying, *"Although we do not believe in the Prophet, he was a moral exemplar to mankind."* And there are no better words than the words of Gandhi when he said, *"It is impossible that millions are attracted to this man because of his sword. No, it was not his sword. It was his pledges which he kept and his simplicity in his life and his devotion to his family and friends that made this man the man that he was."* Gandhi then said, *"I was saddened when the second volume of his biography ended because I wish I had learnt more about this man, a man whom there is none like, Muhammad."*

May Allah's Peace, Mercy and Blessings be upon him and his purified family.

Lecture 9

The Disease of Backbiting

The discussion of "gheeba," "nameema," and "buhtan," or backbiting – telling tales and making false accusations – is a discussion that requires a thorough analysis in order to cover three of the worst spiritual diseases. These spiritual diseases cause the destruction of many communities today, as well as disunity between communities. This backbiting in turn has brought a lack of confidence, not only with themselves, but with people around them. It prevents harmony in a community, and so the lives of many people have been destroyed because of the false accusations, or due to revelations of past acts that they have preferred to conceal. Around the Islamic world today, there are many who have left their communities because of scandals and false accusations that people have made. Therefore, backbiting in a community brings about pessimism as people fear who they discuss their affairs with. A strong community is one whereby people trust one another, thus there is a need for brothers to work together, and sisters likewise, to prevent backbiting. The listener of backbiting is also as bad as the backbiter themselves. On one occasion, a person came to our fourth Imam and said that someone had been speaking behind the Imam's back. The fourth Imam told him that he was part of the crime because someone had shot an arrow, but he made sure that the arrow reached Imam. Therefore, an examination of this topic can be used to purify our community.

The first area that must be examined is the power of the tongue of the human being. The tongue is one of the blessings of Allah (SWT), but it can also be one of the most destructive weapons that the human being possesses. There is an interesting anecdote in the life of Luqman, where we find that one day his master had said to him to go sacrifice a sheep for him and provide him with the two best parts of the sheep. Luqman brought the heart and tongue of the sheep. Two weeks later the master asked Luqman again to do the same, but bring the worst parts of the sheep. Luqman brought the heart and tongue again. The master questioned this. Luqman answered his master by saying, *"The best parts of the body when purified are the heart and tongue, whereas the worst parts of the creation when left alone are the heart and tongue."* Thus our tongue, if purified, is a blessing but if left to sin, it can be devastating. Hence, in Surah 30, verse 22, Allah (SWT) states, "And among His Signs is the creation of the heavens and the earth, and the variations in your tongues and your colours. Verily in that are Signs for those who know." Amongst the signs of Allah are the differences in tongues and colours – this means that the beauty of different languages is a sign of Allah. You go around the world and you find the many languages which remain in what is now a very small world.

Furthermore, you find Prophet Musa (AS) talking about the power of the tongue, as mentioned in the Qur'an, "Ya Allah, loosen the knots from my tongue." It is vital for us as humans to be eloquent with our tongues, especially in the professional world. The Qur'an again mentions the tongue in Chapter 55, "Al-Rahman. It is He Who has taught the Qur'an. He has created man. He has taught him speech (and intelligence)." This shows that the beauty of mankind lies in expression and speech. This is why Amir al-Mu'mineen talks about the tongue in a beautiful expression, "The tongue of the human being…its weight is so light, yet its devastation is so powerful." Hence we notice that the tongue is a vital instrument that needs to be purified and must not be let loose. Imam Ali (AS) also states, "I am surprised and amazed when I look at the human being. He speaks through a piece of meat and he sees through a piece of fat and he hears through some bones." The saying here is to let people know that it isn't the intricacy of the weight of the senses, but the intricacy is in how we use it.

Hajjaj ibn Yusuf al-Thaqafi, when he used to give the khutba of Salat al-Jumu'ah…a famous incident occurs which shows us that the tongue can be used in a proper manner and a devastating manner. When Hajjaj was giving the khutba, as per usual his speech extended the time of prayer (in the same way as Ziyad ibn Abeeh). One of the crowd members stood up and said, "For how much longer are you going to prevent us from praying

Salat al-Jumu'ah on time? Every week you extend your khutba." To this the people looked around and were amazed as to how this man stood against Hajjaj. Hajjaj looked at him and shouted, "How dare you stand up against me? No one stands up to me." The man who had challenged him left and went to do his own affairs. Hajjaj was willing to find this person and execute him. Hajjaj found where he was and entered the house when the family of the man were all sitting there. Hajjaj asked him if he was the same man that challenged him and he replied "yes." Hajjaj then asked him if he felt guilty and he replied "no." His parents pleaded to their son to claim that he was insane, but the man said, "I will not say that I am insane because my duty with my tongue is to enjoin the good and to forbid the evil. This man extends his khutba and doesn't allow us to pray. I will never remain silent whilst he gives the khutba." Hajjaj was stunned by this and answered him, "You are a brave man. Normally I end someone's life when they speak out against me but because of your bravery I want to release you and reward you with money. Someone as eloquent as you are has to be rewarded."

An example of the tongue being used in a wrong way is lying – this is one of the worst ways you can use your tongue. Hadith tell us that there is a door of evil, and the key to this door is lying. The religion of Islam sends a curse upon the liars; this is why there is a narration by Asmaa bint Tumays whereby she narrates that on the day The Prophet (PBUH) married A'isha, Asmaa was nearby A'isha when they had entered the house of the Prophet. They had gone in to see not much food there except for a bowl of milk. The Prophet (PBUH) drank from this bowl of milk and then he gave it to A'isha but A'isha refused to have some. Asmaa asked A'isha to not be arrogant as this was from the mouth of the Prophet. The Prophet had then offered the milk to his companions, but they either answered with, "I am not hungry" or "I am not thirsty." The Prophet told them all to not associate hunger with lying. Even this is counted as a lie if the person is really hungry and pretends they are not.

Another method in which the tongue is employed in an unhealthy way is when a person acts as a clown. For example, Mutawakkil used to have a clown who was employed for the sole purpose to ridicule Ali ibn Abu Talib (AS). Muntasir, the son of Mutawakkil, once came in to see this clown. Muntasir came to his father and told him, "We may not agree with Ali ibn Abu Talib but there is one thing we cannot deny, and that is that he was a man with a truthful tongue. You are now employing clowns to represent Ali. This is not acceptable." Mutawakkil answered him by saying, "Ali and his line are our enemies, and we will continue to ridicule them one by one." This, however, may have led to his death, as Mutawakkil was killed by his own son. Muntasir hated his father's actions against Ali so he used the Turks to come kill his father. Therefore you find until today certain people use their tongues to act as clowns and ridicule others. Imam Zain al-Abideen (AS) states, "Let your tongue acts as politeness and accustom your tongue towards goodness. Make your tongues too noble to say words of obscenity."

A third way is when the tongue is misused by cursing. This is why the Qur'an responded to the cursers of the early Muslims. "When you come abuse the idols of the idol worshippers, they will turn around and abuse your Lord and your Prophet." The early Muslims would use abusive language against the idols that were worshipped. The Prophet (PBUH) let these people know that abuse is not part of the religion of Islam. A further method of misuse of the tongue in Islam is arguing with one another. A believer can never claim to have reached full faith if they are still arguing with each other. Humans today constantly try to put each other down and fight back using their tongue. When you come towards backbiting in Arabic – "gheeba" – this is when you reveal the traits or history of another person which they wanted concealed. "Nameema" is when a person takes this trait or history of someone else and adds extra information to it, i.e., adding spice to the gossip. Surah 49, verse 12, displays backbiting in a very graphic manner, "O ye who believe! Avoid suspicion as much (as possible), for suspicion in some cases is a sin. And spy not on each other behind their backs. Would any of you like to eat the flesh of his dead brother? Nay, ye would abhor it...But fear Allah. For Allah is Oft-Returning, Most Merciful."

The examination of this verse about "gheeba" provides us with seven points, the first of which is why is this verse so graphic? This verse is very graphically showing a prophecy, meaning you are told how you would act on the Day of Judgement in relation to the way you were with your brothers on this earth. This verse transfigures an action. Your action of gheeba, or backbiting, in this world is transfigured into you eating dead meat on Judgement Day. This is why The Prophet (PBUH), when he was on the night of Mi'raj, and when he came across people who were eating dead flesh, Allah told the Prophet that these were the people that used to backbite people in Dunya.

What is the commonality of eating human flesh in history? Eating human flesh is something very detested in human history. This is why, when you view Islamic history, you find very rare cases of people who have eaten dead bodies. One case was in the battle of Uhud, whereby after the battle Abu Sufyan returned home to his wife Hind who was sitting alone. She asked him how he had done in the battlefield and he told her that they had been defeated by the army of Muhammad. He then told her how her brothers and father were killed by Ali ibn Abu Talib. She then angrily answered that she wanted Ali dead in revenge. She told Abu Sufyan that she wanted a man who could throw a spear with the best of targets. She found a man named Wahshi and asked if he would kill Muhammad or Ali. He told her the former was difficult to target and the latter was like a wolf in battle. Then she told Wahshi to kill Hamza, the uncle of the Prophet. After he had killed Hamza, Hind reached an even lower point by entering the battlefield to chew the liver of Hamza. By the mercy of Allah, Hind couldn't digest the liver and she vomited it all out. History has shown us that eating dead bodies is repulsive. Likewise Allah wanted to show us that gheeba, or backbiting, is equally detestable. Why did Allah (SWT) compare "gheeba" to eating our dead brother's flesh? Allah (SWT) wanted to show that eating your brother's flesh takes place whilst he is dead, thus he is not able to defend himself. Likewise, with backbiting, your brother is absent so he cannot defend himself.

How are both these traits related to diseases? When someone eats a dead body, their own body becomes physically full of a disease. Likewise when you carry out gheeba you carry a spiritual disease. Eating a dead body is an accumulation of acids, poisonous gases and blood being ingested into your own body. How can this disease lead to being a social outcast? If you have a physical or spiritual disease, you are likely to be left alone as people are worried that this disease is contagious and they may catch it. If you are constantly infected from eating a dead body and if you constantly backbite someone, people will eventually abandon you as you become the centre of diseases. How are the two traits related to their conditions? There are certain times where you are allowed to eat a human body and likewise there are certain times where backbiting is permissible. The former is in a situation whereby I am in a desert and there is nothing else for me to eat apart from dead human flesh to survive. There are some cases where gheeba is allowed and even wajib. This will be examined later.

How have the two compared overtime and how is this important?

Eating a dead body has increasingly been found to be the lowest of the low, however, increasingly backbiting has been found in society. Therefore, if you want to see how your community is progressing then just look at the way backbiting has risen. If they treat gheeba as something normal, then they are the lowest of the low, just as how the world has seen eating a dead body as low.

Some of the hadith that have been narrated about gheeba show the extent of its power. The Prophet (PBUH) has said that Allah (SWT) has told him, "Gheeba is worse than adultery. I am willing to forgive those committing adultery but backbiting I can never forgive. A person who commits gheeba must be forgiven by the person he backbited on." In another hadith The Prophet (PBUH) narrates, "The worst type of income is when a person earns his income with one dirham of interest. Interest is worse than adultery. The worst type of interest is when a person backbites his brother." In a third hadith by the Prophet, he says, "Gheeba affects the religion of a person faster than leprosy affects a human body." Leprosy is one of those diseases which require a miracle to be cured; this is why Prophet Jesus' miracle was to cure the blind and the leper. When one continuously speaks negatively about others, it becomes something of the norm for them and infects their whole body. A further beautiful hadith by the Holy Prophet (PBUH) is, "Gheeba affects the person's religion and it removes the person's good deeds faster than fire does away with wood." Similar to this, a hadith narrates that when a person comes on Judgement Day with their good deeds, while another comes with their bad deeds. It then occurs to them that their deeds have been switched over, all because the former had carried out gheeba on the second person.

Unfortunately, some carry out gheeba because they believe they are religiously superior to someone else. Another reason whereby gheeba is carried out is when people think that they are economically superior to others. A third type of gheeba is when we believe our physical appearance is superior to everyone else and we begin to put others down. One day A'isha was with The Prophet (PBUH) when she mocked Um Salama because of her short height. In some other narrations they say Saffiyah was mocked. The Prophet (PBUH) told her that the gheeba she was doing is greater than the waves of the ocean and that these things should not be said by the wives of the Prophet.

In addition, there are three types of gheeba: absolute, implied and apparent. Absolute gheeba is when a person reveals a trait of someone which they had wanted to be concealed. Implied gheeba is when a person carries out gheeba but attempts to justify it whilst they are saying it. For example, "I don't mean for it to be gheeba, however that person is stupid." Secondly, in implied gheeba, you mock someone with body or facial expressions. Thirdly, in implied gheeba, you pray for it to not be a gheeba, such as saying, "Ya Allah, don't make this a gheeba, but that person is really stupid." Apparent gheeba is when you discuss the life of someone, even though everyone knows about it, you constantly discuss it. Ahlulbayt differ in this. Some hadith tell us that it is fine as long as such types are discussed in a way in which you want to help the person. However, if it is discussed with the intention to mock the person, then this is not allowed. Thus, the standard definition of gheeba is when you discuss the action of someone which they wanted to be concealed. Nameema, as mentioned before, is when you work vigilantly to add spice to something and ensure the gheeba is spread within the community. Hence, nameema is known as "scandal" or the "telling of tales," and results in the destruction of marriages and causes a reduction in social activities, etc. This is why nameema is seen as one of the worst diseases in Islam and Allah describes this in the Qur'an, "Woe (Waylun) to every (kind of) scandal-monger and-backbiter." Waylun in Arabic means the deepest pits of Hell, so Allah wanted to say this deepest pit in Hellfire is reserved for those who make scandals ("nameema") and those who backbite ("gheeba").

One day, when Prophet Musa (AS) was living with the children of Israel, there was a drought – so the Prophet prayed to Allah (SWT), but Allah told the Prophet that there was one person who was causing scandals for the people, thus this was the reason for the drought. The Prophet told the children of Israel that this one person causing scandal was causing this drought so collectively they all must ask for forgiveness. A few days later the rain had come and Allah told the Prophet that they were blessed with rain because that one person came to ask for forgiveness. Unfortunately, today in each community there is more than one member who carries out scandals and backbiting. The Qur'an states that, Fitna is worse than murder, in the verse: "And kill them wherever you find them, and drive them out from whence they drove you out, and persecution is severer than slaughter, and do not fight with them at the Sacred Mosque until they fight with you in it, but if they do fight you, then slay them; such is the recompense of the unbelievers." (2:191). So when a person causes a scandal that spreads in society, it doesn't just affect one person, it affects families, tribes and a religion.

Moreover, a narration has been given about a scandal which included one of the masters of the children of Israel. This master found a slave in the house of his neighbour and asked this neighbour if the slave was healthy and fit so that he could buy the slave. The neighbour answered that he was healthy and fit, however one thing about him was that he tended to cause scandals. The master bought the slave despite this, and on the first day the slave told the master's wife that the master wanted to marry a second wife. He then convinced the wife to cut the master's hair as this would stop others being attracted to him. When the master had come home, the slave had told him that he overheard his wife plotting to kill him. When it came to bedtime, the wife wanted to take the knife out to cut his hair, while at the same time the master was vigilant because of what the slave had told him earlier. Because the master believed the slave, he defended himself by killing his wife first. The family of the wife killed him in revenge, and likewise his family retaliated by killing the whole tribe of the wife. All of these murders occurred because of one person and their scandal.

The Qur'an, in 33:30, talks to the wives of the Prophet by saying, "O wives of the Prophet, whoever comes out with you with an open indecency Allah will punish you with double the punishment." Here Allah (SWT) was warning the wives of the Prophet that, irrespective of who they are, even if only one of them comes out with a scandal they will be punished double. This is why, when the Battle of Jamal happened, it was as a result of the fitna of one person who acted with two others against Ali ibn Abu Talib (AS). Imam Ali was caliph for four and a half years. Throughout this time they never let him rest once because there was always a new scandal being fabricated. One day a man came to Imam Ali and said to him that when Abu Bakr and Umar were caliphs there were no wars, but when Imam was caliph there were many wars. Imam responded to the man by saying, "At their time they dealt with people like me, whereas in my time I deal with people like you."

In the battle of Jamal, Imam knew that the scandal was against him and they had come to kill him. They believed that he was the cause of Uthman's death. Before the battle, Imam had come to Talha crying and told him, "O Abu Muhammad, do you not remember the days me and you grew up together? Or the times where we fought together to defend Islam? Now you come to kill me in battle? Ask Allah for forgiveness. We are causing a fitna that will involve the killing of thousands of Muslims." But Talha persisted in the scandal. "You are the cause of Uthman's death and you are protecting the killers. We will kill you," he said. Then Zubayr came out and Imam came out. Again Imam said, "Do you not remember one day you said that you will always be with me? The Prophet (PBUH) has also told you that one day you will leave Ali and not be on his side and you replied to him that you will never leave me. How can you leave me now?" Zubayr could not handle this, so he ran out of the battle. Then A'isha, the Mother of the Believers, came out. Imam spoke out. "A'isha, we will find the killers of Uthman and we will bring justice to justice, but we should not bring thousands of Muslims and kill each other because of a scandal which is false." A'isha replied, "You are defending the killers of Uthman, and they are in your army. Either you give them to us or we kill you and your army."

This is the type of people that Imam had to deal with, yet when A'isha was sitting on her camel in the carriage, Imam knew that this scandal would end if she would come off the camel. So Imam told Malik al-Ashtar to cut the feet of the camel. Then he said to another companion to go and pick her up when she falls. When she had fallen, A'isha became angry and said that the companion must not touch her as he is not mahram to her. However the companion that held her said he was Muhammad ibn Abu Bakr, her brother. Imam had done this deliberately as he knew the only person that was able to hold her was her brother in his army. Therefore we find that scandals caused the death of over thirty thousand Muslims because of the fitna against Amir al-Mu'mineen.

The final examination comes to the exceptions whereby gheeba is wajib (mandatory). In fiqh, there is something called "bab al-tazahum." This principle is called the "order of importance." This means that sometimes in our lives we have to judge the order of importance. For example, someone is drowning and to reach this person I have to cross a land which has been usurped, or ghasbi. Normally I cannot go across this land, but it is a situation of life and death, thus it is wajib for me to save someone drowning. In regards to gheeba being allowed due to "the order of importance," this can involve situations like marriage. If it comes to proposals, and the family is asking about the person their son or daughter is marrying, it is wajib for me to do gheeba if I know of something – such as in the past they have been physically abusive. This is because the order of importance dictates that, in the long term, if the husband abuses that girl and you had not said anything, that is haram. The second area where gheeba is allowed is against an oppressor, because this can stop oppression and save the lives of many people. This is what the Ahlulbayt stressed; you are allowed to talk of an oppressor in order to raise justice. Bahlool was a man who always spoke out against oppression no matter who and what the situation was. According to the following hadith by the Prophet, "If the faith of Ali ibn Abu Talib was put on one side of the scale, and the faith of the whole of humanity was put on the other side, Ali's faith would always rise." One day this hadith was exchanged with someone else's name and Bahlool saw this as oppressive so he stood up against anyone that said the transformed hadith to him with, "I do not agree with this form of the hadith, there must have been something wrong with the scales." The idea in the School of Ahlulbayt is that gheeba is allowed against oppression, either in your tongue, or with your heart, or with your weapon.

One day Prophet Musa came to Allah and said, "Ya Allah, everyone talks behind my back and they make false accusations about me. Ya Allah, will you not stop those people?" Allah (SWT) answered, "Oh Musa, I have not given myself that honour. I am Lord and they always attack me and some don't even believe in me. Have I ever stopped them?" Therefore, we learn here that even if our community talks about us, this doesn't give us an excuse to run away, rather it should be a reason to enjoin the good and forbid the evil as well as purifying ourselves before we purify others. In the end, it is important to understand that the listener of gheeba is worse than the person doing gheeba themselves. This is why The Prophet (PBUH) has said, "If a person listens to gheeba and he defends his brother in faith when the gheeba is happening, Allah removes a thousand sins of that person. But if a person listens to the gheeba and continues without defending his brother, Allah adds seventy sins to that person."

Lecture 10

The Biography of Lady Khadijah

The biography of Lady Khadijah is a fundamental one as she is an influential character in Islam and a role model for men and women. Her life acts as an example for us; she was seen as the greatest wife of The Prophet (PBUH) as she was the first to believe in his Message, and she was the first Mother of the Believers. She was also the first to pray behind The Prophet (PBUH), she was the first to hear the voice of the revelation when it came to The Prophet (PBUH), and she was the only wife of the Prophet that didn't lead a life co-existing with another wife. Whilst Khadijah was married to the Holy Prophet, he didn't marry anyone else. The Holy Prophet has stated, *"There are four women in Paradise, Aasiyah bint Muzahim, Maryam bint Imran, Khadijah bint Khuwaylid and Fatima al-Zahra."* The integral feature of these four women is the fact that they sincerely gave all they had for the religion of Islam. Therefore, when we come to examine the biography of Khadijah bint Khuwaylid, the aim is to not only look at historical sources but to apply as many examples from her life in our own life. In the same way in which Khadijah lived in a period of ignorance, got married, and faced trials in life, we may face these too in our lives today.

The analysis of Khadijah's life takes two stages. The first stage addresses historical differences which can be seen regarding her age, her marriages before The Prophet (PBUH) and how many children she gave The Prophet (PBUH). The second stage of the analysis is to view her as the greatest businesswoman in Arabia, how she was named the Princess of the Quraysh, how she was called "Tahera" in a society ravaged by ignorance, and her marriage to The Prophet (PBUH), as well as how her wealth caused the spread of Islam.

The historical issues concerning Khadijah's life have become so amplified therefore they require analysis. The first issue concerns her age and the belief that she was forty and the Prophet was twenty-five when they had married. Unlike many of the other figures in Islamic history, Khadijah's exact date of birth is not known by any historian, thus we cannot estimate her age. For someone like Imam Hussein (AS), we know that he was born on the third of Sha'ban in the fourth year of Hijra and he died on the tenth of Muharram in the sixty-first year of Hijra, thus he died at fifty-six. Whereas with Khadijah there are no details of her birth date. Moreover, if we say that Khadijah married The Prophet (PBUH) when she was forty and he was twenty-five, this means she gave birth when she was sixty. This is because Fatima al-Zahra (AS) was born five years after The Prophet (PBUH)'s Prophethood. He was forty when he was a Prophet, thus making Khadijahh sixty. But this is a bit questionable as to how she could give birth at sixty.

Secondly, the issue of Khadijah being a virgin or not when she married The Prophet (PBUH) can be addressed here. There is an opinion in some schools of Islam that Khadijah had already been married on two occasions before she married The Prophet (PBUH). Some say that she married Abu Hala who was from Bani Adi. Supposedly, Khadijah gave him Hind, Taher and Hala. When he died, she married, according to certain narrations, Atiq ibn Aa'ith, with doubts on whether or not she gave him any children. He died too, and then she married the Prophet. On the contrary, this is not true because Khadijah was getting proposals from the whole of Arabia, so it seems doubtful that she would accept someone from Bani Adi and Banu Makhzum. She was getting Arabian princes like Abu Sufyan, Walid ibn Mugheera, and Abu Jahal proposing to her, thus this is a false claim that she married into lower class tribes. The School of Ahlulbayt thus believe that The Prophet (PBUH) married Khadijah when she was a virgin.

The third misconception is about the children Khadijah gave The Prophet (PBUH); some schools believe she had six children while others argue that she had three children. The first was Qasim, then Abdullah, and lastly, Fatima. Qasim and Abdullah died in their infancy, while Fatima remained alive. The other three who are claimed to be their children are three other daughters, Zaynab, Um Kulthum and Ruqaya. Zaynab was originally married to Abil Aas ibn Rabi'. Abil Aas originally did not believe in God. Then he fought The Prophet (PBUH) in Badr which led to his capture by the Muslims. This led Zaynab to come to the Prophet and ask if the necklace her stepmother Khadijah gave her could be given for Abil Aas' release, and the Prophet accepted. Um Kulthum and Ruqaya were married to Utba and Utaiba, the sons of Abu Lahab, but when Abu Lahab found out about his nephew's Message he ordered his sons to divorce them. Then Ruqaya married Uthman ibn Affan, the third caliph. When she died, he married Um Kulthum, which led to him being named "Thul Nourain," the one who married two lights. It has been argued that they were the stepdaughters of The Prophet (PBUH). Khadijah had a sister who had she sought to help. Her name was Hala, and she it is argued had three daughters Zaynab, Um Kulthum and Ruqaya. Khadijah then took them into her care.

The historical questions now discussed, the biography of Khadijah can now be examined here. Khadijah was related to The Prophet (PBUH) from the fifth line of the family tree. Her full name was Khadijahh bint Khuwaylid bint Asad ibn Abdul-Uza ibn Qusay. The full name of the Prophet was Muhammad ibn Abdullah ibn Abdul Muttalib ibn Hashim ibn Abd Manaf ibn Qusay. Thus they are both descendants of Qusay. Khadijah's father's original name was Khalid, but the Arabs had a tendency of shortening the name to Khuwaylid, similar to Jabir and Juwaybir. Khadijah's family was prominent; Khuwaylid was the protector of the Ka'aba as well as Abdul Muttalib, the grandfather of The Prophet (PBUH). When Abraha wanted to demolish the Ka'aba with elephants, the two people that guarded the Ka'aba were Abdul Muttalib and Khuwaylid. Khadijah also had a cousin by the name of Waraqa ibn Nawfel, who was, like Khadijah, a "haneef." Haneef was the belief in One God and Ibrahim, the originator of Islam. Waraqa was one of the high priests of the religion of Christianity. Waraqa used to translate the Bible from Hebrew to Arabic. He was also one of those who were against the ignorant ruling of burying girls and would tell the Arabs, *"I will look after you, just look after your daughter. Do not bury her alive. I will help you financially."*

Everyone in Arabia used to know Waraqa was a man who was just, and who helped the oppressed. Waraqa never worshipped idols in his lifetime. The third prominent figure in Khadijah's family was her brother Usaid, who was known as one of the most just men in Arabia, and was known as "al-Adel," or the just. This was because he formed "hilf al-futhool," or "the league of justice," whereby Arabs would protect their visitors and not scam or transgress against them. This covenant was signed by the heads of Arabia, which included the young Prophet. Khuwaylid, as well as Khadijah's mother, Fatima, had died at a young age, thus the whole of their business was left to Khadijah and her siblings, Usaid, Hala and Awwam. Khadijah used this wealth wisely and initiated her own business whilst maintaining her modesty. Arabia used to go to business in winter and summer. During the former they would go to Yemen and in the latter they would send caravans to Syria. The Arabs would take their goods with them, and horses were exchanged for goods such as olives, oil, and handicrafts. Their caravans would be sent with a leader. This person had to be firstly skilled to travel in the desert in the night-time. The person would have to know about the areas where bandits can attack you, and they should be skilled in first-aid. Before Khadijah would send her caravans she would ensure the head of the caravan would accomplish these skills.

Khadijah was also known for looking after the needy and the orphans. Maysara, the head of her administration, has narrated that one day a lady knocked on the door during the night. This lady had a sack in her hands and said that she knew Khadijah would help her. When Khadijah had come, the lady opened the sack to reveal her newborn baby. The lady was terrified that if her husband would find out, he would kill the baby as it was a female. Thus Khadijah took it upon herself to look after this baby. On the one hand, you have Khadijah who was taking care of the needy whilst working, and on the other, you have the Prophet who was an orphan that was taken by his uncle to Syria. The Prophet's father had died at the age of seventeen when he had travelled to Syria and fallen ill. A few months later, Amina, the Prophet's mother, gave birth to him. A few years later, Amina died, so he was taken into the care of his grandfather Abdul Muttalib. When Abdul-Muttalib died, he was taken in by his uncle Abu Talib. When Abu Talib took the young twelve year old Prophet to Syria, The Prophet (PBUH) narrates that they once went past a monastery, and there was a monk by the name of "Buhayraa." Buhayraa invited Abu Talib and his tribe to his house for a feast the next day, ensuring the young Muhammad would come with him. The next day the monk went towards the Prophet and said, *"I ask you by the Allaat wa al-Uza'..."* The Prophet (PBUH) answered, *"Do not mention those names in front of me."* The monk went to the feet of The Prophet (PBUH) and kissed them. He turned to

Abu Talib and stated, *"This is the Prophet that Jesus said will come, firstly when I told him, 'I ask you by the idols of Quraysh,' he didn't want them mentioned. Secondly, when I saw his shoulder I saw that there is the mark of Prophethood. Thirdly, when you and Muhammad were coming in your caravan the trees they would bow down to him as he was passing."*

Therefore, the Prophet would accompany his uncle so that he may be taught the business trade, and Abu Talib has been narrated to have praised the Prophet's memory when he would teach him of the business. The Prophet (PBUH) would also be trained in the fairs of Mecca in the markets of Ujaz, Thul Mejaz and Mejana. In the four holy months, Rajab, Thul Qi'dah, Muharram and Thul Hijjah, the Arabs couldn't fight each other. The Prophet (PBUH) would go to these markets whereby he learnt poetry, heard conversations and became familiar with the markets. Meanwhile, Khadijah reached a stage where she was in need of someone to head her caravan, so she asked Maysara to research this. Maysara told her of Muhammad's prominent reputation, how his memory was outstanding, and he was called "al-sadiq al-ameen," or the truthful and the trustworthy. Khadijah said that in this way she would employ him and that she would double the commission for him on the basis that he would take her caravan and return with profit. Maysara accompanied The Prophet (PBUH) to see if his reputation was true. They left in the night and in a month's journey they reached Syria.

When they returned, The Prophet (PBUH) carried out "tawaf" while Maysara went to Khadijah. Maysara told her that he had never seen a professional like him. Everybody trusts him when he makes a deal, but there is something else that is special. When Muhammad finished his deals, he sat alone and spoke to someone as if he was speaking to a higher being. The Prophet (PBUH) performed a form of meditation with Allah (SWT), even before being a Prophet. Khadijah decided then that he would take the caravan for Yemen, and that she would triple his commission. Khadijah's friend Nafisah bint Munabi went to The Prophet (PBUH) and told him that he should get married to Khadijah. When The Prophet (PBUH) told Abu Talib, Abu Talib said that they would be honoured and he told his sister Saffiyah to go to take the proposal. Saffiyah was married to Khadijah's brother Awwam, so when Saffiyah asked her for this proposal Khadijah accepted. When Abu Talib heard the good news, he took his brothers Hamza and Abbas to Khadijah's house where they gave her presents. Then he gave The Prophet (PBUH) the cloak and staff of

Abdul Muttalib and placed a black turban on his head. Hence, the reason why sayyeds wear black turbans today. Abu Talib also gave him a ring with a green agate on it when they had gone to Khadijah's house; Abu Talib read the nikkah, which was the following, *"All praise to Allah the Creator of the heavens and the earth. All thanks to Allah for His Mercy, His Bounties and Blessings. He sent us in the world in the posterity of Ibrahim and Isma'il. He put us as those in charge of His House and the guardians of His Ka'aba, the sanctuary for all His creatures. My nephew Muhammad is the best of all of mankind, in his intelligence, wisdom, in the purity of his lineage, in the purity of his personal life and in the distinction of his family. He has the makings of the greatest man; I give my nephew Muhammad to Khadijah bint Khuwaylid for a mahar of four hundred gold coins."*

Then Khadijah's representative Waraqa ibn Nawfel said, *"We agree with all that you have said, Oh Abu Talib. You are saying the truth. We are the servants of Allah and we are proud to unite both families."* They had a walima for three days, just like we have a walima today. They broke all the stereotypes of Arabia because in Arabia a woman had to be equal to her husband in three and greater than him in one and the husband had to be greater than his wife in two. The woman had to be equal to her husband in wealth, age and in descent, yet greater than him in her looks. The husband had to be greater than his wife in wealth and height. Khadijah, however, was older and wealthier than him and she eventually married him.

When Khadijah and the Prophet married, Qasim and Abdullah died in infancy. The Prophet would take Khadijah with him three miles to the East of Mecca to the cave of Hira alongside his young cousin, Ali ibn Abu Talib. The Prophet taught them the importance of meditation. Yahya ibn Afeef, one of the companions, has narrated that the uncle of the Prophet, Abbas, invited him in the days of Jahiliya, and Abbas showed him three people praying together. Abbas told him that the one who was leading was his nephew Muhammad, and to the right of him was Ali, his other nephew, and behind them was Khadijah. The three of them were submitting to Allah's message before the Message, until on the night of Qadr when The Prophet (PBUH) was forty years old. The Prophet (PBUH) was in the cave of Hira when the revelation came down on him to "read." Some schools in Islam believe that The Prophet (PBUH) didn't know what to read at the time, so Jibra'il came down and pressed on his chest, which led to him saying, "Iqra bismi rabbika alathi khalaq," however this is just a myth. When the Prophet came home, he said he had just achieved the announcement of his Prophethood, Khadijah said, *"O son of my uncle, be cheerful in what Allah has given you, you were always good with the orphans and poor. You were always good with your neighbours. Allah will never forsake you. He will always protect you."* Khadijah was his backbone and always supported him. When he had gone back to the cave of Hira, the second revelation of Muddathir came, "O you who covers himself, arise and warn, and glorify your Lord." The Prophet (PBUH) told Khadijah that Allah (SWT) wanted him to arise with his mission; Khadijah encouraged him to arise to tell the whole world about his mission.

In the first three years, the Muslims had to be careful, as they were under persecution. After that, The Prophet (PBUH) preached his mission openly. In the fifth year of The Prophet (PBUH)'s task, Jibra'il came towards him and asked that he stay away from Khadijah for forty nights because Allah (SWT) wishes for a plan to proceed. This plan was the birth of his daughter Fatima al-Zahra (AS), and a birth involves two things. First, the foods which can result in the sperm, and two, the mood the couple are in at the time. Allah (SWT) wanted to ensure that the food and the psychological mood of the Prophet was the purest. Allah told Jibra'il to feed The Prophet (PBUH) from the fruits of Paradise and waited forty nights so it would make him psychologically in the mood. Allah ascended him into the heavens to eat an apple from Paradise and this was one of the few Mi'raj that The Prophet (PBUH) experienced. When The Prophet (PBUH) would come near Fatima, he would say, *"Whenever I yearn for Paradise, I smell Fatima al-Zahra because Fatima is a human virgin on earth."* The Prophet (PBUH) also has stated about Khadijah, *"I love Khadijah more than any other wife, she trusted me when everyone else doubted me. She gave me her wealth when no one else helped me. Lastly, she gave me a daughter like Fatima."* Khadijah would speak to Fatima when she was in her womb. She wouldn't tell The Prophet (PBUH). Then one day The Prophet (PBUH) heard her speaking to her. Then The Prophet (PBUH) said, *"Be proud of Fatima because from her line eleven Imams of Allah will be born and the final of them will bring justice on earth."*

After Fatima al-Zahra was born, Abu Jahal, Abu Lahab and Abu Sufyan made a major attack on The Prophet (PBUH). They made his companions leave Mecca and go to Africa. They had to migrate, but they needed money, so Khadijah's wealth provided this. This relates to The Prophet (PBUH)'s saying, *"Islam would not have spread if it were not for the sword of Ali and the wealth of Khadijah."* When Abu Jahal, Abu Lahab and Abu Sufyan saw that some of the companions had left, they said they would now enact economic sanctions on Muhammad. No one was able to deal with him or give food and drink to him. Abu Talib apologised to The Prophet (PBUH) about the way Abu Jahal, Abu Lahab and Abu Sufyan were treating him. Abu Talib asked that he stay in his valley, known as "shi'ib Abu Talib." The Prophet (PBUH) stayed there for three years, living on the leaves of the plants. People were dying in that valley due to food and drink shortages. Khadijah's money was the only thing that saved The Prophet (PBUH) in those three years. Abu Talib and Khadijah would sacrifice what they had for Islam; Khadijah would not sleep if The Prophet (PBUH) was awake nor would she sleep when he slept to ensure that no one would attack him. Likewise, Abu Talib ensured his son Ali would sleep in the bed of The Prophet (PBUH) so that the army of the Quraysh would capture Ali instead of The Prophet (PBUH). Eventually, after three years, Khadijah had become frail after she had given everything to her husband and for Islam. Allah called her one of the women of Paradise because of her sacrifices to her husband. Later wives of The Prophet (PBUH) would be jealous and ask for money, but Khadijah would give her money. When the three years ended, the Muslims returned to Mecca. Khadijah, however, suffered from a very high fever because of those three years of suffering. This was one of the hardest times of The Prophet (PBUH). He had to see Khadijah go through a period of poverty and poor health. Asmaa bint Umays has narrated that, in the moments before Khadijah passed away, she saw her crying. Asmaa reminded her of Allah's promise of Paradise. Khadijah replied, *"I don't cry because of my fear of death, I cry because normally when a daughter wants to get married her mother should be next to her to support her whereas when my daughter Fatima will get married, I am not going to be there alongside her."*

When The Prophet (PBUH) had to bury Khadijah, before he returned her to his Lord, he realised he could not even afford a kafan to wrap his wife in. Before Khadijah died, she said to The Prophet (PBUH), I want two tasks from you; first, I want your shroud to cover my body. When the Prophet brought that shroud, however, it only covered half of her body, which made the Holy Prophet cry and raise his hands to Allah in du'a. When Jibra'il came down, he came with five shrouds, which made the Prophet ask as to who they were for. Jibra'il answered, *"The first kafan is for Khadijah, the second kafan is for you when you pass away, the third is for your daughter Fatima, when her ribs will be broken. The fourth is for Ali ibn Abu Talib who will be stricken on his head and the fifth is for your grandson Imam al-Hassan who will be poisoned."* The Prophet then asked, *"Jibra'il, where is the shroud for my grandson Hussein?"* Jibra'il looked at the Prophet and said, *"There is no kafan for Hussein; he will be lying on the grounds of Karbala, martyred by your Ummah."*

Lecture 11

Charity, the Welfare of Humanity

Charity is a universal act, and an act which is discussed worldwide in many meetings, conferences and seminars. Charity affects every human being, as charity is a compound term, and therefore denotes the idea of the protection of the welfare of the community in which one lives. There is a responsibility for humans to protect the welfare of their family, friends, and relatives as well as the welfare of the community at large. Therefore, around the world today many charity organisations seek to eradicate poverty and allow everyone to live lives of prosperity, and in peaceful co-existence. The three types of establishment in every state should encourage giving charity in the community; these are the government, the clerics and the economics system of the state. The government has the role of looking after the needy and the charitable donations of the country, and as they are in charge of the treasury, this gives them an outlook on how funds are shared and pinpoints the weaknesses of the welfare of their community. On the first level, government bodies have systems to regulate the charity commissions so they can see who are the groups of people that are in need. On the second level, clerics must encourage charity and giving. It is vital for them to say to whom the charity is going to ensure accountability as well. Thirdly, the economic system seeks to bring equilibrium between the rich and poor or the different classes of a country. Charities which are revered as being those which constantly strive to provide for a better community, for example, Amnesty International and Oxfam, voluntarily work to eradicate poverty.

Charity is a vital component in the religion of Islam; Islam focuses on the idea of giving away from what one has so that others in the community can benefit. The examination of charity within Islam involves a number of stages:

1. Obligatory charity

2. Recommended charity

3. Charity of the night and day

4. Charity which continues after your death

Charity in translated in the Arabic language with the word "sadaqa," which gives the idea of maintaining the welfare of a community. Sadaqa is of two types; there is sadaqa which is wajib or obligatory, and a sadaqa which is mustahab or recommended. The obligatory sadaqa is known as "zakat." This is established in the "Furoo' al-Deen," or the "roots of the religion" of Islam. Zakat was first established in Medina by Prophet Muhammad (PBUH). When The Prophet (PBUH) had gone to Medina for the latter ten years of his life, his aim was to build an Islamic state. A social, political and economic system must make up any Islamic state. The economic aspect was built through zakat; this obligatory sadaqa can be seen from the revelation in 9:103, which says, "Take [O, Muhammad], from their wealth a charity (sadaqa) by which you purify them and cleanse them, and invoke [Allah's blessings] upon them. Indeed, your invocations are a reassurance for them. And Allah is Hearing and Knowing."

From the start of the verse you can see the intention of sadaqa, which is to "purify" mankind. The word sadaqa also comes from the Arabic word "sidq," which means to be truthful. Thus charity should be given truthfully and sincerely. An Islamic scholar narrates a parable of the truthfulness of sadaqa. One day a community member was stuck in the well. Many people decided that they would go help. One by one they had gone to the well to say, "Give me your hand," but the person in the well kept rejecting their aid. A wise man of the community decided he would eventually succeed. He came to the well and stated, "Take my hand." Immediately the person took his hand. The wise man described the difference between "give" and "take." How we question everyone when it comes to being asked to give but do not hesitate when it comes to taking.

When the verse says to "purify them and cleanse them, " this meant that giving charity takes away your sins and cleanses your soul. Moreover, the giving of sadaqa is that which purifies you whereby it gets you closer to Allah (SWT)…because the moment you recognise what Allah has given you, you are ready to give in His cause. The soul is enlightened when you are generous with what you have. This is why The Prophet (PBUH) established obligatory charity. Surah 9, verse 60, displays this: "Alms are for the poor and the needy, and those employed to administer the (funds); for those whose hearts have been (recently) reconciled (to Truth); for freeing captives and in debt; in the cause of Allah; and for the wayfarer. (Thus is it) ordained by Allah, and Allah is full of knowledge and wisdom." The Qur'an says that sadaqa is for the poor as well as the needy, such as those who are orphans and widows. Then the verse also mentions those who work in the administration of the Islamic state, those whose hearts are inclined towards the truth, which means those who are on the borderline to the truth, and who thus can be encouraged. The list continues with those who are captive, those in debt, and those who are lost in journeys. Thus the aim of charity in the Islamic state was to protect all the types of groups which are in need. The role of the treasury of the Islamic state is to ensure that people are looked after and that those in need do not feel that no one is concerned about them.

Zakat was instituted with the idea that all Muslims had to pay a certain amount of that which they own, for example, gold, camels, sheep, wheat, barley and raisin. The Prophet (PBUH) would ask the heads of the administration from different tribes to go collect this zakat. People were not forced to pay zakat by the Prophet, rather this was an obligation which they had towards Allah, just as prayer (prayer) and sawm (fasting) or the other Furoo' al-Deen are conditioned. There used to be a companion of The Prophet (PBUH) named Tha'laba al-Ansari, who was one of the companions who would pray behind The Prophet (PBUH) in every prayer. One day Tha'laba finished the prayer and asked the Prophet if he would pray for him to be rich. The Prophet (PBUH) told Tha'laba that what is sufficient is enough to worship Allah and is enough for a livelihood. This can be seen by the Prophet himself as he wasn't particularly wealthy. The next day Tha'laba asked the Prophet to pray for his wealth again, but the Prophet advised him again to be happy with what he had. Tha'laba was still not happy though, so he would ask the Prophet again until the Prophet prayed for his wealth. Tha'laba made a covenant that he would give from what he had if he was made rich by Allah.

When Tha'laba was made rich by Allah, he was rarely seen praying behind The Prophet (PBUH) until the time when Zakat was being instituted. When The Prophet (PBUH) had sent those to collect the zakat from Tha'laba, Tha'laba replied that he would need time to think about it. Then the collectors of zakat went to the village nearby in which the people persisted in giving the best of their stock to The Prophet (PBUH), even when they had been told to only give a certain amount of charity. Then Surah 9, verses 75 and 76, were revealed, "And among them are those who made a covenant with Allah, [saying], 'If He should give us from His bounty, we will surely spend in charity, and we will surely be among the righteous.' But when he gave them from His bounty, they were stingy with it and turned away while they refused." Thus, this verse was revealed about Tha'laba. Allah wanted people to be grateful towards what they had been given and in turn give a certain amount of it to those in need. The first, second and third caliph did not accept his charity as the intention behind the giving was not sincere. The aim of The Prophet (PBUH) initiating zakat was not to bring equality but to bring equilibrium between the rich and the poor. Equality does not necessarily mean justice. Allah (SWT) has a certain system of justice with everyone, and this system of justice is that not everyone achieves the same. The aim was that those who get more than others should think about giving back from that which they earn in order to provide equilibrium within the state.

However, there is a recommended or "mustahab" type of "sadaqa." Thus, if you do not carry it out it doesn't mean you have committed a sin. However it has a beautiful philosophy which is in recognition of one of the attributes of Allah being, "al-Mu'tee," or "the One who Gives." This is recited in the Munajat of Imam Ali (AS), the whispered prayers, where it says, "My Master, O my Master, you are the Giver and I am the one who begs. Who is here for the beggar except the Giver?" This means that Allah (SWT) does not have to share His Kingdom; however it is from His Mercy that He shares with His Creation. Even in Munajat Sha'ban, the whispered prayers of Sha'ban, we recite, "Oh You who gives the one who asks and the one who doesn't ask."

Allah (SWT) gives to those who ask, as well as those who don't ask, from Allah. This attribute of "al-Mu'dee" makes Him give to everyone, and this should be manifested in the soul of every Muslim. Our giving shouldn't be limited to only those who cry for help because there are those who need help but do not ask. The highest level of the soul is when the soul is willing not only to perform obligatory acts, but also recommended acts. The scholars of Islam also state that one of the lowest levels of taqwa is performing the wajib/obligatory deeds and one of the highest levels is performing the mustahab/recommended deeds. Throughout their lives, the Ahlulbayt would give the recommended form of charity, but they wouldn't look for any kind of reward except the pleasure of Allah (SWT).

The Ahlulbayt gave us particular conditions on the mustahab type of charity. Firstly, when mustahab is given, give away that which you love the most. Surah 3, verse 92, says, "Never will you attain the good [reward] until you spend in the way of Allah from that which you love. And whatever you spend – indeed, Allah is Knowing of it." Thus, giving charity from the belongings which we love is revered. This meant that we should give to people what we would like if we were ever in their position. Fatima al-Zahra (AS), the Lady of Light, on the night of her wedding day, originally had a dress that was patched up, but then she was given a dress that was beautiful. However, this didn't last for long as someone came to knock on Fatima's door. The woman knocking said that she was in need and came to the house of the family of The Prophet (PBUH) for aid. Fatima was about to give away her old dress when she remembered verse 3:92, so she decided to give away the beautiful new dress.

The second condition of mustahab charity is to give in secret, as this is looked upon with pleasure by Allah. The greatest personalities in history gave secretly; only after they passed away did people recognise how much they had given to the needy. The fifth Imam narrates that when his father died, and the Imam was performing his ghusul, he saw the marks of injury and bruising on his back. Then Imam al-Baqir found out about the bags his father would give in the night. Imam Zain al-Abideen (AS) was abused by his cousin; he was constantly told by him that he would give to everyone except his own cousin. Only when the fourth Imam had died did the cousin notice that for days on end he hadn't received charity from the person who would come to him. Imam al-Baqir (AS) then confessed to him that it was his cousin Zain al-Abideen who was giving him the charity.

The third condition regarding mustahab charity is that if you cannot give something, then notify someone else who can help, because Islam is all about brotherhood. For example, if someone comes up to you to build a mosque or a hospital and they ask for your help, if you cannot provide them with help then point them in the direction of someone who can.

One day The Prophet (PBUH) was sitting with his companions when they had just finished Salat al-Asr. Someone entered the mosque and spoke to The Prophet (PBUH). "O Prophet of Allah, I am someone who is poor and a wayfarer (lost in journey). I am a stranger. Help me." The Prophet (PBUH) answered him, "At this moment I cannot help you, but go to the house of my daughter Fatima. Bilal, please take him to the house of Fatima." When Fatima al-Zahra answered this man from behind the door, she said that she would look at what she had; she found some goatskin that Hassan and Hussein would sleep on. She gave this goatskin to the man. But the man exclaimed he wasn't sure what he would do with this goatskin. Fatima them gave him a necklace she was given as a wedding gift from the daughter of Hamza. When the man had gone to The Prophet (PBUH) and told him what Fatima had given him, The Prophet (PBUH) began to cry and at that moment he said, "Pray for Fatima." So the man raised his hands, "Ya Allah, give Fatima al-Zahra what you have not given to anyone." Ammar ibn Yasir had been seated during this and asked the man if he was willing to sell the necklace as he would be willing to buy it for three hundred dirhams. The man agreed and Ammar bought it, perfumed the necklace, and then told his slave, Sehem, to go to The Prophet (PBUH) with this necklace and he would also be freed. When Sehem took this to The Prophet (PBUH), the Prophet smiled and told him that he would be freed but only after he takes this necklace to Fatima. Sehem went to the house of Fatima to give her the necklace, then he smiled and said to her, "Look at what one piece of charity can do, a poor man can find his way, then he found some wealth, then a servant is freed and the owner of the original charity is reunited with what they gave."

The fourth condition of mustahab charity is to give something away even if you are going through a hard time. Surah 76, verse 8 and 9, refers to this, "And they give food in spite of love for it to the needy, the orphan, and the captive, [saying], 'We feed you only for the countenance of Allah. We wish not from you a reward nor gratitude.'" This verse was revealed about the Ahlulbayt. At the time Imams Hassan and Hussein (AS) were not feeling well so Amir al-Mu'minen had made a vow to fast, and they all fasted for three days. When they wanted to break the fast with some food, one narration states that Imam had borrowed 4.8 kg of barley from Shem'awn al-Khaybari the Jew. With this barley Fatima made five loaves of bread. On the first day a poor person came knocking, the second day an orphan and on the last day a captive. The Ahlulbayt would give away their food everyday "in spite of [their] love for it." Thus, they gave away food out of their love for the food because of their hunger, and they recognised that Allah loves those who give towards His Creation. Amir al-Mu'mineen later took his children to The Prophet (PBUH). The Prophet saw the children shivering out of starvation, and then the above verses were revealed. Thus, the sign of the greatest creations of Allah is to sacrifice what they had even if they themselves were going through hardships.

Furthermore, sadaqa itself has two benefits. The first is that Allah opens the door of forgiveness for you. Secondly, sadaqa removes "balaa'," trials and tribulations, or periods of hardship. The sadaqa of which you give everyday protects you as Ahlulbayt have promised through Allah (SWT) that those tribulations are removed. In the same way that a servant of Allah takes a step towards Allah, Allah removes any upcoming tribulations. Moreover, sadaqa is not only for this world. There is a sadaqa in Islam known as "Sadaqa Jariya, al-baqiyat al-salihaat." Sadaqa Jariya is the charity which you give that is not seen in the form of money, rather it is seen by a'maal or good deeds. An example of this is a good word you say to people. The Qur'an says in Surah 2, verse 263, "Kind speech and forgiveness are better than charity followed by injury. And Allah is Free of need and Forbearing."

Thus, even a kind word to someone is a form of sadaqa. Malik al-Ashtar sacrificed all that he did for Imam Ali (AS) because of Amir al-Mu'mineen's kind words. Imam's advice to Malik was seen as a sadaqa by Malik. Imam told him, "Malik, know that the people are of two types. They are either your brothers in faith or your equal in humanity." "Malik, have mercy upon the people you govern in the way that you want Allah to have Mercy upon you on the Day of Judgement." "Forgive the people as you want to be forgiven by Allah."

Sadaqa can be shown through good advice and kind words to people. Thereafter, Islam comes forward and says even a smile can be a form of sadaqa. A smile reaches the heart of a human being. The Prophet (PBUH) has said a third type of sadaqa is when you reconcile between members of a community. A fourth type of sadaqa, which doesn't involve wealth, is establishing justice in a community, for example when someone is being oppressed. Further on, the fourth Imam says a fifth type of sadaqa is to pick up something from the ground if you know someone may fall on it. This shows that sometimes wealth doesn't buy people's love but the heart does.

Imam Zain al-Abideen (AS) one day saw someone walking with his father. Imam would never get angry, however on this occasion his companions said his face was raging. The Imam stated, "How is the father carrying something and the son is walking without carrying anything?" The sadaqa of that son would be to carry what the father is carrying.

Sadaqa Jariya is described to us by the Ahlulbayt as being charity which continues after you have passed away. The Prophet (PBUH) narrates in a hadith, "There are three forms of Sadaqa Jariya. The first form is building a mosque, even if one brick is placed by you. The second form of Sadaqa Jariya is the knowledge you have given to people. The third form of Sadaqa Jariya is having a righteous son whom you leave behind." The knowledge imparted to people can be seen in the lessons and works of great scholars such as Imam al-Kulayni, Sheikh al-Saduq, Sheikh al-Tousi, Allama al-Majlisi, Allama al-Hilli and Sheikh al-Mufid. Also the scholars of other schools, Abu Hanifah, Imam Malik al-Shafi'ee, Imam Ahmed ibn Hanbal, Imam al-Tabari, Ibn al-Atheer, al-Balathuri. Their names are still remembered today as their knowledge continues as a sadaqa. Imam Ali (AS) says, "Whoever teaches you one letter of knowledge, it is as if they are your Master." The third form of Sadaqa Jariya is a son, who upholds your family name and upholds your message, for example, someone who leaves a book such as "Saheefa al-Sajjadiya" or "Risalat al-Huqooq" or establishes a du'a like "Makarim al-Akhlaaq" – a son who leaves a legacy that, when others view his legacy, they remember his father Imam Hussein AS). This son is Imam Zain al-Abideen (AS) who is a true role model in Islam.

Lecture 12

Envy and Jealousy

"Hasad," or envy, occupies a prominent position in Islamic thought; it is normally discussed under the heading of "ethics" because Islam is structured into three branches – theology, ethics and jurisprudence. Theology concentrates on our relationship with Allah and His attributes, jurisprudence deals with our relationship with ourselves, whereas ethics concentrates on our relationship with those who live in the same community and the same state as us. The Islamic ethical system provides us with guidelines on how to maintain relationships with people. The aim of this ethical system is to purify the human being from diseases which are either physical or spiritual. Physical disease may not be recognised from the outset, such as viruses or cancers that strike you silently and are diagnosed late. This leads the person to be treated so that they may continue with their lives and be happy. Likewise, the religion of Islam states that in the same way as there is physical disease, there are spiritual diseases as well, for example, hypocrisy, arrogance, greed and envy. In the same way that you are willing to go to unlimited lengths to cure the physical disease; there should also be a need to cure the spiritual disease.

In order to examine the spiritual disease of envy, the following questions will be considered – what is the difference between envy and jealousy? How do the world religions view envy? The most important topic in this discussion is: what is the positive type of envy and the negative type of envy? Is there such a thing as the evil eye or is it just a myth? How has envy destroyed communities? How can you prevent envy from reaching you? On the first level, many times we find the word envy to be synonymous with jealousy. However, according to psychologists the terms and behaviours differ as the jealous involves three whereas the envious involve two. In psychology, a jealous person is one who wishes to keep what they have and does not want anyone to intrude, whereas the envious wish to have what others have while wishing that attribute to be removed from them. When I say that jealous involves three, this means that, for example, in a relationship between you and your wife, and the wife fears an intruder, the wife wishes to keep what she has but is jealous of a third party. This can be seen in history, for example, with A'isha and The Prophet (PBUH). In Imam al-Bukhari there are many instances of her jealousy towards other wives. Imam al-Bukhari narrates two instances in his Sahih and Imam al-Balathuri narrates one instance. Bukhari narrates of how the Prophet would remember Khadijah. One day Hala, the sister of Khadijah, came to visit the Prophet. Before she entered she said, *"Oh Prophet (PBUH), I ask for your permission to enter."* In response to this the Prophet became sad because Khadijah would ask for permission in the same way, so the prophet called out, *"O Allah, in remembrance of Khadijah."* A'isha heard this and said, *"What's wrong with you? Why do you always remember that lady of the red gums who has passed away? Why do you remember her when Allah has given you better than her?"* The Prophet (PBUH) firmly replied, *"Allah has not given me better than her for she gave me a daughter like Fatima."*

Here you find that the jealousy of A'isha was of such an extent that she described Khadijah as having "red gums" because she was older than the Prophet. In another example in Bukhari it is narrated that A'isha was jealous of Saffiyah, the wife of the Prophet. A'isha would say, *"Saffiyah, make a bowl of food for The Prophet (PBUH)."* When Saffiyah would make a bowl of food, A'isha would be angry at the way The Prophet (PBUH) appreciated this, so once she pushed the bowl held by the maid so that it would fall. The Prophet (PBUH) then picked up the pieces of the bowl and A'isha apologised, asking him what she could do to make amends. The Prophet quoted, *"A bowl for a bowl and food for food."* This meant that the same bowl and food that Saffiyah had brought her, A'isha must do the same. Imam al-Balathuri narrates that A'isha herself admits she was jealous again of Mary the Copt, who was originally of the Copts of Egypt. She was jealous because Mary would wear beautiful ringlets, so that they would frighten her away from living with them, but then got jealous because she gave The Prophet (PBUH) a son named Ibrahim. A'isha did not give The Prophet (PBUH) any children so this must have made her jealous.

Also, sometimes you can see the biggest jealousy between scholars because some of the scholars feel that they are sitting on a perch that must not be knocked upon. When they feel that someone has knocked on that perch they become jealous of one another. Knowledge, however, is meant to bring you humility and not pride. A famous narration of al-Mu'tassim al-Abbasi, a caliph of Banu Abbas, talks about a couple of scholars in his court. He had once employed a certain scholar, and then a second scholar entered the court. The original scholar found al-Mu'tassim to be giving more attention to the latter. Al-Mu'tassim started to favour him and gave the second scholar a ministerial position. The first scholar became jealous, and one day after prayer invited him for lunch. He ensured that he would give him a dish filled with garlic. The second scholar was worried about returning to al-Mu'tassim but the first scholar encouraged him to go. The first scholar went to al-Mut'assim and told him, *"This new scholar has been saying that you have bad breath and you can see this when he will come to your courtroom."* When the new scholar came in, he placed a handkerchief on his mouth; al-Mu'tassim was convinced that what the original scholar had said was true. Al-Mu'tassim wrote a letter asking for the new scholar's execution, however the original scholar took this envelope from him thinking it was wealth. The original scholar was executed instead. The next day, the new scholar entered the courtroom; al-Mu'tassim asked how he was still alive when he had disliked his breath as someone had reported to him. The new scholar explained the story to him and al-Mu'tassim could not believe this jealousy between the scholars. Therefore, jealousy is different from envy in the sense that jealousy is a wish to keep what you have, whereas envy is a wish to have what the other has.

Moreover, in the world's religions today envy is seen as an attribute which is detested. For example, Buddha says, *"He who wishes to have peace of mind should not envy others."* Thus, if the aim of the human is to achieve peace of mind, and not constantly think about what others have, then do not be envious. Likewise, in the Bible, one of the seven greatest sins is envy, in the same way as lust and gluttony. This is why Paul, in his letter to the Corinthians, says, *"Love is kind. Love is patient and does not envy anyone."* This means that if you love someone you should not always try and keep up with others, i.e., there is no need to compare yourselves to others. Rather, humans should be grateful to what Allah (SWT) has already blessed them with. Even Imam Ja'far al-Sadiq (AS) states, *"If you want to achieve tranquility in life, stay away from envy."* Thus the aim of every religion is to ensure people are not constantly in despair, but rather to build personalities who are looking to live peacefully with others. One should be happy when someone succeeds and sad when someone is disappointed. The Imam also says, *"Envy devours faith in the same way as fire devours wood."* The famous hadith also declares, *"Iman (faith) and Hasad (envy) will never be in the same heart of a believer."* A believer is one who believes that there is no God but Allah (SWT) and He has sustained them with sufficient wealth, children, and knowledge with no need of envy towards others.

Hence, in Islam there is a positive type of envy and a negative type of envy, whereas in Christianity and other religions envy is viewed as only negative. The type of envy which is positive in Islam is called "al-ghibta," which is envy where you wish to have what others have without removing it from them. For example, if you see someone knowledgeable, positive envy would be to wish to reach that stage yourself without it being removed from the other person. Envy of the negative type would be to wish to be as knowledgeable as him and have his knowledge be removed. Another example of ghibta is when someone is wealthy, to say, "Inshallah Allah increases his wealth and gives me the same amount of wealth too." Islam is about brotherhood, so ghibta is when you are still happy for your brother. When the sixth Imam talks of Abu Fathlel Abbas, he says, *"Abu Fathlel Abbas's status in Paradise is something to have ghibta towards."* The envy which is positive is seen here, when you're happy for someone but wish the same for yourself. The sixth Imam also says, *"The believer exalts but does not envy."*

Mu'ala ibn Khunays, one of the companions of the sixth Imam, saw how Imam al-Sadiq was revered by the people as well as Allah (SWT). Mu'ala wanted to see what the Imam was doing that made him reach this position so he in turn could acquire the same happiness. He followed the Imam one day who had a bag of bread with him. Suddenly the bag dropped; Mu'ala went to help and picked up some bread. Mu'ala told the Imam he wanted to see the acts he performed. He saw the Imam putting a piece of bread next to each poor person on the roads; some were lying there asleep so the Imam wouldn't wake them up. Mu'ala asked, *"Imam, are these your followers?"* The Imam replied, *"No. O Mu'ala, know that there is a difference between the charity of the day and of the night. In one of them Allah's anger is eased and the exam on the Day of Judgement is made easier, and if you give charity in the day Allah increases your sustenance and lifespan."*

In this way, Mu'ala was able to learn from the Imam that charity may increase his sustenance and help him in the Hereafter. Mu'ala wasn't envious of the Imam in a negative way, rather he wanted to learn from him how to reach his level. A further form of positive envy is "tanafus," or competing with one another. The Qur'an says in Surah 83, verse 26, "The last of it is musk. So for this let the competitors compete." If you see someone in Islam who has done a gracious act, there is no harm in competing with them to achieve Allah's pleasure. For example, if you see someone making a donation to the mosque there is no harm in giving a bigger donation if my only intention is to please God. There is a narration in the Musnad of Ahmed ibn Hanbal of Abu Bakr and Umar, who tried to fight each other to please the Holy Prophet (PBUH). One day Umar ibn Khattab decided he would give charity and he knew Abu Bakr would do the same; hence he wanted to give a greater amount. Umar went to The Prophet (PBUH) and gave half of his wealth; Abu Bakr came and gave all of his wealth to the Prophet. In this way, Islam has said that there is a positive envy such as competing whilst having a pure intention to serve Allah.

On the other hand, negative envy is known as "hasad" in Arabic. Imam al-Khomeini, when discussing hasad, divides it into al-haasid and al-mahsoud, meaning the one who carries out negative envy and the one who is envied. Imam al-Khomeini then gives the attributes of the two types; he says the one who envies does so because of fear or pride. Imam Ali (AS) states, "Mankind, you were created from a drop of semen and you leave as a piece of dust. You do not know when you came and you do not know when you are going, so why walk around like you know everything?" Thus, when some people are arrogant this can lead to negative envy.

Imam al-Khomeini then says the one who is envied is envied because of internal and external characteristics. Internal characteristics are aspects like knowledge which are imprinted on the soul of the human being. Bel'am ibn Ba'uraa was jealous of Prophet Musa's knowledge, and because of this he went to extreme lengths to get the Pharaoh's attention. This was discussed in Surah 7, verse 176, "And if We had willed, we could have elevated him thereby, but he adhered [instead] to the earth and followed his own desire. So his example is like that of the dog – if you chase him, he pants, or if you leave him, he [still] pants. That is the example of the people who denied Our signs. So relate the stories so that perhaps they will give thought."

The external traits include good physical appearance, which can lead to jealousy and envy. When the human being sees someone who has great internal or external characteristics, some do not look at what Allah has blessed them with, rather they look at others in order to be envious towards them. The concept of "evil eyes" is discussed as if it's a cultural myth. However, in the Qur'an, hadith, and even within science, the evil eye is considered to be true. In the Holy Qur'an, Surah 68, verse 51, states, "And indeed, those who disbelieve would almost make you slip with their eyes when they hear the message, and they say, 'Indeed, he is mad.'" Thus envy can be carried out with the eyes because sometimes it is our first sense that views the person's enviable feature. In Nahj al-Balagha Imam Ali (AS) says, "The evil of the eye is something which is the truth." The Imam also agrees that the eye can have a magnetic force which can make someone else slip. There are some secrets of the human being which cannot be comprehensible, such as déjà vu, or a vibe you have with someone even though it's the first time you meet them and you feel that you know them really well. Likewise there is a magnetic force in the eye which you cannot see; evil eyes can destroy what they envy.

One day Asmaa bint Umays, the wife of Ja'far ibn Abu Talib, came to The Prophet (PBUH) claiming that there are those who have put the evil eye on their children, and asked if there was a charm or prayer she could do to remove this. The Holy Prophet (PBUH) answered, "If anything was going to precede Divine destiny then it would be the eye." The Prophet (PBUH) then told her a prayer to protect her children with. The Prophet (PBUH) would also pray for Imams Hassan and Hussein (AS) for protection against the evil eye, "Ya Allah, please remove from Hassan and Hussein the harm of the evil eye, the harm of death and the harm of the envious when they envy." Surah al-Falaq was revealed against those who are envious – "Say, 'I seek refuge in the Lord of daybreak, from the evil of that which He created, and from the evil of darkness when it settles, and from the evil of the blowers in knots, and from the evil of an envier when he envies." This evil thus comes from the evil of the creation, and from the darkness of the night. Also, the evil from those who blow on knots, as there used to be women in Arabia who would blow on knots to try and harm The Prophet (PBUH). Lastly, the verse states that it seeks refuge from the evil of the envious because this requires the help of Allah (SWT). Just like The Prophet (PBUH) would pray against envy reaching his Ahlulbayt, Prophet Ibrahim would pray about the envious who were against Ishaaq and Isma'il. One of the scholars of tafseer says that when Prophet Ya'qub sent his sons to go after Prophet Yusuf, he said to them, "Enter from different gates." This was said by Ya'qub because he didn't want the evil eye to attack them.

In addition, there are many historical accounts where envy was sought to destroy creation. In the beginning of our creation, the first act which was performed was an envious act when the angel said to the Lord of the Creations why they should prostrate to clay when they are made of fire. The hadith also says, "Negative envy is one of the traps of Satan." In the same way that Satan was envious towards Adam, he will try and cause envy between us. Imam Ali (AS) says that Satan obeyed Allah (SWT) for six thousand years or more, but that envy within meant that his worship was fickle.

The true believer has the positive type of envy rather than the negative. This was also seen with Prophet Yusuf's brothers who envied Yusuf for the attention he was receiving from their father. This is why Ya'qub told Yusuf to not say anything as he knew about their envy. They had so much envy that they were willing to kill their own brother. Sometimes, if you and a family remember have a fallout, do not think it could just be from your issues with each other but it could also be due to the evil eye. Likewise, sometimes cousins can be envious towards each other, for example in the story of Qaroon, the first cousin of Prophet Musa. Qaroon could not take that Musa was receiving a claim. Although Qaroon was the wealthiest in the community, he still couldn't understand how Musa would receive this claim. He asked an adulterer to admit that she had committed adultery with Musa so that his reputation would decline. Moreover, you can have envy between your own tribe and group. This is why Allah (SWT) says in the Qur'an that even the Jewish Arabs became jealous of what was given to The Prophet (PBUH). Abu Sufyan was also another person who was really envious of The Prophet (PBUH), he couldn't understand the success of The Prophet (PBUH). He told the Prophet's uncle Abbas, "Your nephew has acquired quite a kingdom." Abbas replied, "That's not a kingdom. That is Prophethood." The same Abu Sufyan would later on say, "Leadership should be in the hands of Banu Umayyah. Do not let go of it." The envy that Abu Sufyan showed was great even though they were of the same tribe, Quraysh.

In "al-Tahtheeb" of Sheikh al-Tousi, we find a hadith that comments on this envy. Imam al-Sadiq says, "The envy was towards us, the

Ahlulbayt, and how we were given the Book, wisdom and Khalafa." After The Prophet (PBUH) died, envy towards Ahlulbayt was intense, especially towards Imam Ali (AS). Imam had given everything towards Islam, yet people were still jealous about how he married Fatima al-Zahra (AS) and how on the Day of Mubahila The Prophet (PBUH) took him rather than the others. They were jealous that on the Day of Khaybar, Imam picked the wall of Khaybar, or how his father protected The Prophet (PBUH) for so long. So they took out this envy on his beloved Fatima al-Zahra (AS), who lost her life at the age of eighteen, whereby they oppressed her. Then they showed this envy in fabricating traditions against Ali ibn Abu Talib. When Ali died on the twenty-first of Ramadan (Laylat al-Qadr), when the people of Syria asked how the Imam had died, they didn't believe that he even prayed in the first place. Look at the level of envy and how they changed history. Ali originated prayer, being on the side of The Prophet (PBUH). Even after Imam had died, for years they would curse him on the minbar of Bani Umayyah. Even after the person has died, people still are envious of them.

We say to them, Ya Aba Hassan, let them do as they please, for you are still adored by millions around the world. There are some who took you so high that they worshipped you. There are others who took you as a caliph in Islam. Then there are others who knew your true value and your true worth. One day a student of the famous philosopher Ibn Sina came to him and said why he doesn't he say he is a Prophet of God. Ibn Sina replied, "I am not a Prophet neither will I reach such a level." On that same night Ibn Sina had asked for water from his student, but his student didn't respond. When it came to the athaan of Salat al-Fajr, they both went to pray. Ibn Sina looked at him and smiled, "Last night you asked me why I am not a Prophet of God. This morning I tried to wake you up for a cup of water but you didn't wake up. Then when you heard the Prophet and the son of Abu Talib's name in athaan you woke up. Therefore if Ali ibn Abu Talib is not a Prophet then how can I call myself a Prophet of God?"

Lecture 13

The Prohibition of Pork

The prohibition of pork is a fundamental discussion in Islamic Law and a discussion which requires a thorough analysis. As we know, each and every nation has its own eating habits. These eating habits have emerged either from years of cultural principles or years of religious guidance. Each culture has their own significant eating habits which they have sought to protect within their environment. As human beings we recognise that part of our make-up, and central to our existence, is that we have to eat in order to survive. Hence, when the Qur'an describes the Prophet as a human just like other people it does so by stating that the Prophet eats what you eat and walks where you walk. Human beings also recognise that they are what they eat; our nutrition has a great affect on our physical, psychological and social behaviour in general. People are more aware of their eating habits in contemporary society so that their health can be maintained and their existence prolonged. Likewise, the Qur'an says in 80:24, "Let mankind have a look at that which they are eating." This simple but effective verse allows us to reflect on what we consume, and if this has a positive or negative effect on our lives.

In regards to the different cultures, a wide spectrum of diets can be seen, such as the cannibals in Africa who are willing to eat human beings, or the Buddhist monks in Tibet who stay away from any type of meat. Some humans eat dogs and some avoid the consumption of any animal. Some Muslims eat all types of fish and others stay away from some types of fish. Thus, each community has their own eating habits and likewise the Muslim community is no different. It must be understood that when Muslims are placed in the situation of not eating certain foods, the response should clearly state that the same way other cultures or faiths have their own habits so do Muslims. There are certain things we are permitted to eat and other things which we must abstain from. The philosophy of the prohibition of pork is misunderstood in our community. Some follow the concept that if our peers eat pork there seems to be nothing detrimental in their lives.

Did Islam prohibit pork because it would kill the entire nation or affect the physique of every human? Or were there spiritual reasons as to why pork is prohibited?

1. Does our stomach have a right superior to us?
2. Are there times when pork is allowed to be consumed? If so, when?
3. What are the physical effects of pork that many medical journals have touched upon?
4. What are the spiritual reasons why we are not allowed to eat the pig? Is the animal associated with certain behaviours?
5. Why does the Qur'an narrate that Allah (SWT) may have changed certain humans into pigs and what lesson was there for the human being?
6. Who did Imam Hussein (AS) refer to on the tenth of Muharram that when he got killed, the Imam said, "Ya Allah, change his killers and humiliate them into pigs on the Day of Judgement?"

Firstly, does our stomach have a right over us? If one goes to any religion and sees what they have to say, they would not agree with this questioning. Only Imam Zain al-Abideen (AS) went into the depth of actually stating that even your stomach has a right over you in his work, "Risalat al-Huqooq." This work by the Imam is arguably one of the most important books after the Qur'an. The Imam states, "The right of your stomach is that you don't make it a container for that which is unlawful and that you don't belittle it in a way that you lose your manliness. You must restrain it at the time of hunger, not reaching a level of sluggishness." These beautiful words give us the first right where the stomach is "...not a container for unlawfulness," which the Imam refers to three different opinions – don't make your stomach a container for the food which you have bought with forbidden money. Some people get their food in haram ways. There are two types of sustenance – that which runs after you and that which you run after. The latter of which will reach you, Imam al-Sadiq (AS) says, will run after you more than your death does. But whether it reaches you in a legal or illegal way is a different question. For example, if one is employed in a job that is forbidden in the religion of Islam then that food which I eat becomes equally forbidden. Physically, the person will be strong, however spiritually you will be hollow because what you eat makes you what you are as a human being. It remains in your body for a certain period of time, and if you eat that which comes through pure means, then you find a blessing that comes from it. Forbidden money has no baraka in it – either it doesn't stay for a long period or brings issues.

Don't make it a container for that which is haram. Many cultural restaurants are assumed to being halal, however they sell haram meat or alcohol. One of the differences between our School of Thought and other Islamic Schools of Thought is when it comes to eating the meat of the People of the Book. In the School of the Ahlulbayt, we are not allowed to eat meat which is slaughtered by the People of the Book. On the other hand, other Schools of Thought believe, according to the verse which says, "Lawful for you is the ta'aam that is of Ahl al-Kitab." They believe that ta'aam is the meat of the Ahl al-Kitab, such as Jewish foods which are Kosher. Imam replied that ta'aam does not refer to meat; it means that which grows from the earth, therefore, there is no harm in taking herbs, vegetables and fruits from them. But meat from the People of the Book is unlawful. Also, watch out for the artificial flavours and emulsifiers in food. Certain sweets or drinks contain E numbers which contain certain animals that are not permissible to consume.

It is thus a vital responsibility that we must observe that which we consume. According to our Imam, our stomach is a trust from Allah (SWT). That is why, in the next line of the Imam, it states "…don't belittle it to lose your manliness." This refers to a person retaining his physique and his manliness. The religion of Islam is not just for the spiritual but it is for the physical also. This can be seen with the hadith from Prophet (PBUH) which says, "Make sure you know how to swim, make sure you learn how to ride a horse, make sure you learn archery." The Holy Prophet (PBUH) wanted your stamina to be looked after and protected. Imam Ali (AS) also stated, "Don't allow your stomachs to be graveyards for animals."

The third right the Imam touches upon is "restraining it in the time of hunger." For example, in the month of Ramadan, one should persevere in fast and not complain. If you can't reach the discipline to restrain the stomach, then you can't reach any discipline within this religion. So the first concept associated with the prohibition of pork is that the stomach has a right over you. However, the question leads to exceptions whereby pork is allowed, and there are different opinions put forward on this. Some believe it is fine to eat pork when you are in a business deal and you wish to conclude it. We reply to these people that Allah (SWT) is the Greatest of Sustainers, and the human being's sustenance is limited. If one instead goes towards Allah (SWT), Allah will open many doors for you. Unfortunately, some people compromise their following of Islamic law just so that they can make temporary earnings. There are even stories of those who eat "halal pork," so evidently the reasoning behind the prohibition is misunderstood. The pig itself is seen as impure. In fact the only time pork is permissible is in a life and death situation, meaning if one is stranded in the middle of nowhere with nothing to eat apart from pork then that is fine. Allah (SWT) values life above everything.

The reasons behind this prohibition are both physical and spiritual. The physical reason being that the pig has no neck and thus is not made for slaughtering. Also, the amount of uric acid that remains in the pig is unbelievable. This toxicity, if consumed, means that we are ingesting something which we as humans normally excrete. This can correlate with chronic digestive diseases. Furthermore, the highest level of fat in any animal is in the pig, and therefore this relates to high cholesterol levels and health issues. As well as this, the pig contains a wide variety of germs, and there are many medical reports on this matter. It was found that when pork is ingested, the digestive system of the human, and the digestive system's walls, which are normally used for protection, are destroyed. Different types of worms are also clearly seen just by heating the pig. The same worm which produces trichinosis, a parasitic disease, is particularly seen in pigs. That same worm lays ten to fifteen thousand eggs in the human body. Some journals went as far to say that even one kilogram of pork has over four hundred million eggs of this worm. This same worm affects the human's digestive system, resulting in gastrointestinal symptoms such as diarrhea. A recent report came out that one in six Americans has the trichina worm within their bodies. As stated previously, our stomachs have a right over us to consume that which is suitable. The Qur'an says in 80:24,

"Let man look at his food." Thus mankind must look at their food and question what they are eating, whether physically or spiritually.

In terms of the spiritual effects, the Bible has mentioned in the Book of Leviticus, "You do not eat the animals which are the splitters of the hoofs and the animals that do not chew cud and the animals that are formers of the clefts." The Bible here clearly shows that the pig is unlawful; unfortunately Christians have found it a norm to have pork. The Qur'an came and said, "He has only made unlawful for you that which is already dead, and the blood, and the meat of pig, and what was dedicated with to other than God." On the Internet, in the interpretation of the Arabic in 5:3, Rashad Khalifa states that which is prohibited is the meat of the pig and not the lard. However, in the Qur'an, if its states something is prohibited then the whole of it is unlawful because the Qur'an also emphasized the spiritual influences of things. Sometimes it is cautioned not to eat the food of a specific religion as it may have energy, or an aura, where they are willing to worship a God who is beside Allah…then that energy should be cautioned to not enter your soul.

The pig is the only animal in the animal kingdom that enjoys watching other pigs with its partner, in contrast to a lion for example who would not allow other lions to come close to the lioness. If the human being was to have too much of this pig, they will begin to be like it. In certain parts of the world there are people who say they enjoy watching other people with their partners without any concern for dignity. Moreover, the pig lacks the will to fight; even a squirrel is able to defend itself but a pig does not even defend itself as it is rather sluggish. If the pig lacks the will to fight, then it will lack the will to survive. So how will someone fight against injustice, oppression, crime and evil? If as a human you have no will power, then you lack that part of humanity that you need. The pig is so sluggish that it dislikes the sunlight, and if a human was to take this characteristic, they would not succeed. Other traits of a pig include it being a scavenger; it eats anything, even if its own dead child is in front of them, it will eat it. Some humans in the Far East eat stillborn children as a delicacy, and these same people eat pork. Likewise, a pig enjoys being in its own faeces, so one should not be surprised if humans reach this state too. Therefore, the prohibition of pork was brought about because of two reasons: the physical and the spiritual.

When the Imam was asked why then did Allah (SWT) create the pig, the Imam replied that Allah (SWT) on the first level wanted to remind mankind that the biggest humiliation that happened to mankind was when certain members of the children of Israel were turned into this animal. The Qur'an mentions how a few of these members were, as a punishment because of their arrogance to the message of Allah (SWT), turned into these animals. This was such a humiliation that after this they ceased to exist after a few days. Allah (SWT) allowed this to happen in some narrations because they doubted Jesus, the son of Mary, and even allowed it to happen to those who didn't perform the Sabbath with Moses. Thus this was a lesson about human arrogance and those who deviate away from the path of Allah (SWT), where there is no difference in his character from that of a pig. The only contrast between animals and humans is in reason or intellect. When a human being does not use their reason, they become the lowest of the low.

The Imams of the Ahlulbayt (AS) have many narrations where they state that there are certain people with certain characteristics whereby Allah (SWT) will not allow them to be raised as humans on the Day of Judgement. Imam al-Sadiq (AS) has stated that Allah (SWT) will raise the following people as pigs on the Day of Judgement: those involved in relationships that are illegitimate, i.e., constantly performing adulterous relationships (This is happening today with those who are carrying out adultery whilst they are married. Some Muslims go as far as having relations with those who are not People of the Book); those who listen to the music of the musicians (By simply looking at the words of these musicians one can understand why, and the videos made for their songs whereby women are degraded to being below the animals); thirdly, anyone registered in Bani Abbas and who helped their government (This is a limited focus, but it can be enlarged in general terms to include anyone who helps a tyrannical government). Imam Musa ibn Ja'far was imprisoned by his nephew Ali who took a bribe from Harun al-Rashid. Before Ali had taken the bribe the Imam had requested that he not be the cause of my children being orphans, however Ali ibn Isma'il did not listen and went to Harun accepting 4000 dirhams as his bribe. The angel of death came and took away the soul of this same Ali ibn Isma'il as he was leaving. Imam Musa stayed in the prison of Baghdad for over twenty years.

On the tenth of Muharram, a line delivered by Imam Hussein (AS) highlighted how much he was affected by the killing of one of his companions. On Ashura the Imam had lost many companions such as Hurr ibn Yazeed al-Riyahi, Muslim ibn Awsaja and Habib ibn Muthaher. But there was one companion in particular that, when Imam Hussein had seen him fall, he said, "Ya Allah, curse those people who have killed that companion of mine and raise them as pigs on the Day of Judgement as a humiliation." This companion was Zuhair ibn Qayn, and the Imam said this because he had a great love for him. Zuhair originally was not on the side of the Imam. He was returning back from hajj towards Kufa with his wife Dailam. The Imam had known that Zuhair was politically not with the Imam but had a pure heart. The Imam had sent a messenger to him and Dailam looked at Zuhair and said, "The son of Fatima calls for you and you still sit next to me? Go and answer his call. I ask for one thing. If there's ever a day where I am a prisoner, I ask that I be a prisoner with Zaynab." Zuhair wanted the Imam to reassure Zaynab that if he was killed and they chopped me a thousand times and they raised me again and chopped me into thousand pieces, it would be my honour to die for you.

Lecture 14

The Prohibition of Alcohol

4:43 – "O you who believe, do not attempt to pray while you are in a state of drunkenness."

One of the most important discussions in Islamic jurisprudence concerns the discussion of the prohibition of alcohol. This topic requires an in-depth analysis as it is a discussion that relates to our everyday life. Since time immemorial alcohol has been a part and parcel of the lives of many human beings. When one examines one of the greatest empires in history we would find that many of the emperors, for instance, in the Greek, Persian, Roman and Arabian Empires, would celebrate and drink alcohol. The alcohol industry is one of the biggest industries in the world in terms of how popular it is. You will find an advertisement in virtually every media outlet related to a particular alcohol product. People believe that a social atmosphere is only enjoyable with the presence of alcohol. Even if they cannot remember what happened that night, alcohol is still pivotal.

The Holy Qur'an is not just a book of history rather it is also a book that disciplines the human being in terms of their consumption. Thus this is an important topic to discuss in order to respond to those who ask why alcohol is prohibited in the religion of Islam. Some people ask about the subject because they receive a variety of answers. For instance, they may receive the answer that alcohol is allowed in moderation. Some Muslims may even respond that alcohol is allowed as long as the person has a pure heart and believes in Allah (SWT). Then you go to another Muslim who believes it is completely prohibited. Unfortunately today Muslims seem to be uncertain about the exact prohibition of alcohol, whereas the Qur'an shows a step by step prohibition that took place which can provide us with valid answers on this topic.

This discussion will involve the following questions: what was the philosophy behind the prohibition of alcohol? Why didn't the Prophet (PBUH) prohibit alcohol outright? Why was it in steps? In the great Islamic caliphate were there personalities who were known for their drinking habits? How did Islamic society seek to stop them? What did the emperor of Syria do with alcohol in relation to the grandson of the Prophet's head? The philosophy behind the prohibition involves firstly a spiritual reasoning. Islam as a religion aims to elevate the human being to the highest levels spiritually with the power of the faculty of reason not being inhibited. As humans we own four faculties that define our soul; the power of reason, the power of anger, the power of imagination and the power of desire. As a Muslim these four faculties must be purified in order to purify our soul and when our reason is paternal to the other three, the human can be higher than the angels. This means that reason guides anger, imagination and desire. On the other hand, if anger, imagination and desire guide reason the human being can become lower than an animal. Therefore, the religion of Islam wanted to stress that reason cannot be inhibited by anything, otherwise spiritually one cannot reach their maximum. In regards to alcohol, Islam wanted to say that if the human wants to reach the highest level of spirituality, then alcohol must not be permitted in the midst of your society as alcohol inhibits reason. Imam al-Sadiq (AS) states: "Every house has a door, and every door has a lock, and every lock has a key, and the key to many sins is alcohol."

Undoubtedly if one looks at the lowest of spiritual personalities you find that alcohol has become epidemic in their lives. When an atheist came to speak with our fifth Imam, Imam al-Baqir (AS)...this highlights how one should always seek to interact with every member of the community. The atheist asked why Islam prohibits alcohol. The Imam gave a reason along these lines, saying, "Islam doesn't allow alcohol because alcohol inhibits reason and will make a human being miss their prayers or commit adultery." Surprisingly, in the Book of Proverbs the Bible states, "Do not associate with the people of alcohol" – although there is a contradiction here with the biblical discussion of the Prophet's lives. In the story of Prophet Noah in the Bible, Noah is a drunkard in the vineyards. So this naturally leads to the question as to how Allah (SWT) can ask us to follow a man who cannot protect his reason and spirituality. The Bible here contradicts itself by saying the Prophet was a drunk, however one shouldn't be associated with the people of alcohol. This provides evidence against those who believe that the Qur'an is a copy of the Bible, as the Qur'an believes that Prophet Noah (AS) didn't commit any sins while the Bible believes that, because he was a sinner, one could relate to him more. Thus, the first reason that Islam prohibited alcohol was for spiritual reasons.

As for the second reason, Islam prohibited it on physical grounds. The physical effects of alcohol are still being studied, be it the effect on the production of white blood cells or effects on the liver or the kidney or on the brain and even the effects on the inhibition of the senses of the human being. The inhibition of senses means that this can affect your life or the life of the others, for instance, drinking and driving accidents can kill a human or a society at large. Islam is as strict on alcohol as this can lead to the loss of the life of a human being; when this happens, the loss of a family member is irreplaceable.

Some believe that alcohol helps the heart condition of a human being, however this is a fallacy, and it is a fallacy mentioned by Imam al-Sadiq (AS). When Ibn Abi Yazur came to Imam al-Sadiq, he said to him, "O Imam, whenever I have pain I want to drink alcohol. I have heard alcohol is good for my pain." The Imam then replied, "Beware of alcohol because for it is one of the arrows of Satan. If you are strong enough to alleviate the pain by staying away from drinking alcohol, Allah (SWT) will ensure the pain will be removed from you anyway." Ibn Abi Yazur narrates that when he was going back to Kufa the pain returned and his family had offered him some alcohol, but he said whilst I was able to stay away from alcohol not only was I able to withstand the pain, the pain became weaker and weaker by the day. The Imam thus had highlighted that the theory of alcohol being good for your health is simply due to a placebo effect. It is your brain telling you to just consume that which numbs you, however, it also means it doesn't cure you and degrades your soul as well.

On the third level, the prohibition was for social reasons. Islamic Law covers five areas in the life of the human being: property, honour, intellect, life and religion. If alcohol is allowed as a social norm in society then the legal system will not be able to protect these areas. For example, if I own a property whilst alcohol is a norm then I have no right against alcoholic vandals that trash the property. The legal system will not provide defence for the community that is destroyed. Islamic Law wanted to say socially that the protection of your property comes through the prohibition of alcohol. Secondly, it is the protection of your honour, for example, in terms of rape. In Britain, there were discussions in providing more drinking acts, such as "Beware of those that drink and drive" and "Beware of rape." Then there was a recent legislation for the provision of twenty-four hour bars. Islam came and said that socially alcohol was prohibited to ensure the legal system protected the community.

This is why the Holy Prophet (PBUH) came to Arabian society with the recognition of alcohol being a social danger in terms of peer pressure. The prohibition came in steps as alcohol was such a norm in Arabia where people drank as their peers equally did. Even today many of the Islamic jurisprudents will say that you may enter a restaurant that serves alcohol, however you cannot have the alcohol served at your table. The reason for this is initially sitting down you may drink juices but progressively sitting with someone that drinks alcohol at the same table can influence you to do the same. Thus when Islam came to prohibit alcohol, it recognised peer pressure which would not stop them and the Prophet (PBUH) took three steps to reach there. This provides advice that if someone wants to change something embedded in a community it will be successful in stages. Tarafa, an Arabian poet at the time, shows how alcohol was such a norm in his poetry, "I would not want to live in this world were it not for three things: number one, that on a gloomy day when I am unhappy I can get a woman to satisfy me, number two, if anyone offends me I take the law in my hands to finish them and number three, when I want alcohol it will be next to me."

The Prophet (PBUH) came with a three-step reform. The first step did not say it was forbidden straight away: "O you who believe, do not attempt to pray while you are in a state of drunkenness" (4:43). Imam al Nisai narrates that this verse was revealed about Abdel Rahman ibn Auf who was once leading prayer with the new Muslims and recited Surah al-Kafiroon which starts off with, "Say, 'O Disbelievers, I do not worship those who you worship." Abdel Rahman was so drunk that he recited instead, "Say 'O Disbelievers, I worship that which you worship." The Qur'an, in response to this, revealed 4:43, as this is the first guidance whereby you can drink but not during the time of prayer.

A misconception regarding verse 4:43 is that it was revealed about

Imam Ali (AS); this is unbelievable as this narration comes from Ataa ibn Saaib and Ahmed ibn Hanbal states that this Ataa ibn Saaib cannot be relied upon at all. Further than this, this was narrated in Tirmithi's work. Imam al Nasai's says it is Abdel Rahman ibn Auf and Bukhari and Muslim do not even comment on the issue. Therefore there is a contradiction within the issue itself. The second verse revealed about alcohol was in 2:219: "They ask you about gambling and alcohol. Say, 'In them there are advantages and there are disadvantages but the disadvantages outweigh the advantages.'" This was revealed for the rational minds, as the drawbacks of alcohol are greater than the benefits, i.e., rape, murder, domestic violence, the killing of children and drunk driving, etc. The Arabic of the verse uses the word "Khamr". This means not only wine but it also means "that which covers." Thus Allah (SWT) used this to say, "They ask you about that which covers the reasoning of the human being." Khamr can mean any intoxicant that inhibits your reasoning, i.e., drugs. So the Qur'an beautifully gathered every intoxicant together here. Then the final verse came as a confirmation towards the prohibition of alcohol in 5:90, "O you who believe, indeed the intoxicants, gambling and the divination of stones and arrows are impurities from the acts of Satan, so avoid it that you may be successful." The lists here in this verse are impurities from Satan. The word used here for impurities is "Rijs" and this same word is used in the 33:33 verse of tathir/purity. This is further evidence that Imam Ali (AS) was not affected by alcohol. If one questions Ali ibn Abu Talib (AS), then they are questioning the upbringing of the Holy Prophet (PBUH). Therefore in verse 5:90, Islam said stay away from the impurities such as alcohol whereby you will be able to be successful. The next verse (5:91) revealed, "Satan only wants to create hatred and animosity through intoxicants and gambling and to avert you from the remembrance of Allah and from prayer. So will you not desist?"

There are many cases where marriages and friendships are destroyed via alcoholism. That is why the biggest shame that has ever happened to the religion of Islam was that even though the Prophet (PBUH) reformed society in terms of alcohol, after his death alcohol was brought about again. Not only was it brought back, but it was brought back amongst the highest families of the Islamic state. The Abbasids with the caliph Harun al-Rashid, for instance, had their palaces in Baghdad full of alcohol. Nobody taught Harun about alcohol like Bahlool. Harun al-Rashid used to dislike the fact that people would tell him alcohol was haram, so he decided to go to Bahlool as he thought he would be wise enough to tell him that alcohol was fine. Bahlool used to act insane in order to protect the religion of the Holy Prophet and his Progeny. Harun asked Bahlool if there was anything wrong with eating grapes and Bahlool replied that there was not. Harun then asked about drinking water after eating grapes, Bahlool replied that it was acceptable. Harun then asked about eating grapes and drinking water under the sun. Again Bahlool replied that it was acceptable. So Harun said to him that alcohol was the same as it is a mixture of water and grape enjoyed under the sun, so it is equally permitted. Bahlool retaliated by saying that if dust was placed on Harun's head, would that be fine? Harun replied that it would. Then Bahlool said what if the dust was mixed with water. Again Harun replied that it would be fine. Then Bahlool said what about if he made it a brick and smashed it on Harun's head. Harun this time said that that would be an issue. Bahlool said likewise alcohol affects you physically and mentally. When components are mixed in the correct way, it can hurt you and devastate your mind. Unsurprisingly, this same Harun al-Rashid poisoned Imam Musa ibn Ja'far (AS).

Similarly, Walid ibn Yazid was an Umayyad caliph who used to have a swimming pool made up of alcohol. He wanted to submerge in the pool, and any liquid which he then took in would be alcohol. Even in the early days of Islam the relatives of the caliph used to drink. Umar ibn Khattab's son Ubaidallah was caught drinking one day and Umar wanted to punish him. Ubaidallah responded to his father that he would prefer a man who himself had never drank alcohol in his lifetime. Umar then replied that only Ali ibn Abu Talib had never drunk in his life. Uthman ibn Affan used to have a brother-in-law who was governor of Kufa by the name of Walid ibn Uqbah who was originally the man whom the Qur'an condemned in the time of the Holy Prophet (PBUH). In the Messenger of Allah's time, there was a verse that was revealed in 49:6, "O you who believe, when an evil man comes to you with news, verify the news because he may cause a group of people to fall into ignorance and they would be accused of something they have not done." This was revealed about Walid when he went to Bani Mustalaq. The Messenger of Allah had asked him to go to Bani Mustalaq and collect the taxes. Bani Mustalaq were not originally Muslims. Walid originally was not a Muslim either, and they did not like each other. They had all come out to welcome him when Walid went; he assumed they had come to attack him due to his hypocrisy. Walid went back to the Prophet and had told him they had all become disbelievers.

The Qur'an then immediately revealed this verse. Imam Ali (AS) used to say there are four things between what is right and what is wrong — between the eyes and ears. This should be instilled in society.

The Prophet excommunicated Walid from Medina; Uthman, however, had allowed his return during his caliphate and made him governor of Kufa. As governor, Walid used to lead the Prayer of Fajr and was so drunk he prayed it in four rukahs. In the fourth rukah he turned around and asked whether to continue. Imam Ali had punished Walid as Uthman didn't want to punish a cousin; Imam's greatest attribute was that he was not fearful of anyone's words in the face of Allah (SWT). There was once a family of al-Najashi who helped Imam Ali (AS) in the Battle of Siffeen and their son had a friend named al-Samaak who influenced him to go and drink in the holy month of Ramadan. The son and his friend caused chaos while drunk that night. When the news reached Amir al-Mu'mineen, the Imam asked that he should be punished even though he had been a family friend. The al-Najashi family wanted to avenge the Imam, and did so in the frontline of the Battle of Nahrawan, when the Imam had just acted upon the words of Allah.

Truly the accusation of Imam Ali ibn Abu Talib of drinking whilst praying is the most contradictory accusation because of two reasons: the Imam never came close to alcohol, and his brother was Ja'far ibn Abu Talib. Imam al-Baqir (AS) used to say that Allah loves Ja'far for five reasons: he never worshipped idols, he never lied, he never committed adultery, and he never drank alcohol. Abu Talib's children would never come near alcohol. They were raised in the purest of houses. Imam Ali had a son by the name of Uthman, the brother of Abu Fathlel Abbas. People questioned the Imam's choice of name, but Imam would say it was after Uthman ibn Marun, who was a companion of Imam and the Prophet during the days of Jahiliyah. He was one of the very few that didn't drink. The saddest part of Islamic history is that while the Holy Progeny looked after their religion by abstaining from alcohol, the same holy head that was kissed by the Prophet was in a bowl filled with alcohol in Yazid's palace. Imam Hussein (AS) was martyred and beheaded by the caliph Yazid's army, and the family of the Imam was brought to his palace to witness further atrocities to his holy head.

Lecture 15

Imam Hassan and the Treaty of Hudaybiya

The decision of Imam Hassan ibn Ali to enter a treaty with Mu'awiyah ibn Abu Sufyan is a decision which is widely misunderstood in the history of Islam. It requires a thorough analysis, as do any of the political constitutions which were stipulated by the Prophets or Imams, in order that we may understand the wisdom behind these agreements. In many Islamic circles, the biography of Imam Hassan is neglected but other personalities during his time are extensively studied. Therefore, it is important for us to affiliate ourselves and understand the basis of the treaty of Imam Hassan (AS), known in Arabic as "al-Sulh al-Hassan."

Unfortunately, in Islamic history, Imam Hassan (AS) is viewed as a weak character in both his personal conduct and his political affairs. In terms of Imam's personal conduct, both Muslims and non-Muslims historians alike view his personal conduct as that which does not befit a leader. In The Agha Khans, Will Frischaeur described Imam Hassan as the great divorcer. Likewise, Henri Lammens writes that the young Imam Hassan just married and divorced. In addition, Amir Ali in his book, The Spirit of Islam, mentions that Imam Hassan was fond of an easy and quiet life, again referring to the idea that all the Imam was interested in was marrying and divorcing. Regrettably this has always been a black mark amongst the life of Imam Hassan by historians.

This concept had begun from the time of Banu Abbas as they viewed him as someone who displayed a weak personal conduct, and al-Mansoor al-Dawaneeqi initiated this. Al-Mansoor al-Dawaneeqi, in the 144th year of Hijra, faced the major battle of his lifetime with Muhammad Nafs al-Zakkiya, who was a descendent of Imam Hassan (AS). When the Banu Abbas tried to come to power, they came with the slogan of "the family of The Prophet (PBUH)" to overthrow Banu Umayyah. However, when the Banu Abbas came to power, they ignored what they had said about the Ahlulbayt and maintained power according to the line of Abbas, the uncle of the Prophet (PBUH). Muhammad Nafs al-Zakkiya rose against al-Mansoor, while al-Mansoor himself wanted to deflect the idea of Imamat being with the sons of Ali ibn Abu Talib. Muhammad Nafs al-Zakkiya was from the line of Imam Hassan ibn Ali. Thus al-Mansoor spread the idea of Imam Hassan that remains in some circles today.

He said that although Ali was a rightful caliph, after him Hassan gave the Khalafa to Mu'awiyah as he was more interested in money and women. Al-Mansoor said that Hassan repeatedly married and divorced. Al-Mansoor persisted with this fabrication as he did not want anyone from Imam Hassan's line to receive the Khalafa from Banu Abbas. In the same way Imam Hassan supposedly gave his Khalafa to Mu'awiyah, al-Mansoor wanted his descendents to do the same. Later the books of hadith would write about Imam Hassan and how he was a person of weak personal conduct. Abu al-Hassan al-Mada'ini who lived until the 225th year of Hijra writes that Imam Hassan married seventy women in his lifetime. Even though Mizaan al-A'atadal says very clearly that Abu al-Hassan al-Mada'ini's claim of Imam Hassan marrying seventy women is untrue and this man should never be relied upon. Another of the famous scholars, Abu Talib al-Maki, wrote in his book, Quwwat al-Quloob, that Imam Hassan married three hundred women in his lifetime. However when one reads of Abu Talib al-Maki you find he says, "You should fear Allah as he is the most harmful to His Creation."

Abu Talib al-Maki narrates that Ali ibn Abu Talib was embarrassed of his son Hassan who used to marry and divorce repeatedly, to the extent that Imam Ali would say, "Do not give your daughters to my son Hassan." Then Abu Talib al-Maki narrates that the tribe of Hamadan came to Ali ibn Abu Talib and offered their daughters to Hassan and supposedly Ali said that their tribe would enter Paradise. These hadiths were in the books and in many of the books we have until today is tells of the weakness that Imam Hassan had, and that he just married and divorced. They say that his marriages and divorces took place in a fourteen year period, from when Ali ibn Abu Talib became caliph until Hassan ibn Ali's death. However this can be refuted. By the thirty-seventh year of Hijra Imam Hassan was married to three women. These three women were the only wives he had. If we say, for argument's sake, that in those fourteen years he married a fourth Islamically, then divorces the fourth one, he can then only marry three a year. Imam can only marry three a year because of the "iddah" periods when you divorce someone. Thus for fourteen years the maximum amount of wives he had would be forty-two and not seventy. In summary, on the first level, Imam Hassan was viewed as someone with a weak personal conduct.

On the second level, the Imam was seen as weak politically. Dr Taha Hussein in his book, al-Fitna al-Kubra, says that Imam Hassan disagreed with his father Imam Ali, and that he was Uthmani, not Alawi. Supposedly Dr. Hussein believes that the Imam followed the Khalafa, or leadership, of Uthman. He then narrates a weak tradition that one day Imam Ali saw Imam Hassan doing his wudhu' and when it came to the part of his feet he washed his feet and didn't rub them. Imam Ali then asked him as to why he didn't rub them, his son Hassan replied, "I am following the rightful Khalifa who washes his feet and you are the one who killed him." Therefore Dr. Hussein believed that Imam Hassan did not agree with his father, rather he inclined towards Uthman and the School of Uthman. This is why people like Dr. Hussein suggest that Imam Hassan was politically weak as he abdicated his Khalafa, or claim to caliphate. Imam Hassan made a treaty with Mu'awiyah and this meant that supposedly he gave up his leadership and did not continue to rule the Muslim state. On the other hand, the School of Ahlulbayt will not forget what The Prophet (PBUH) said of Imam Hassan (AS), "My son Hassan will bring peace between two quarrelling nations" and "Hassan and Hussein are your Imams whether they are standing or whether they are sitting."

The first hadith of the Holy Prophet (PBUH) is evidently of the peace treaty and the second hadith meant that Imam Hassan and Hussein are still your Imams whether they carry out a war or remain without a war. Unfortunately, some schools disregard these hadiths and disregard the idea that Imam Hassan is the rightful fifth caliph. These schools in Islamic thought believe that Imam Hassan and Mu'awiyah had a difference of opinion thus we cannot call them both rightly-guided. Furthermore, these schools take the Imam as someone who was not a political leader. This stems from their viewpoint that if someone rises with a sword rather than remain patient that that is someone who has carried out the greater jihad. When Imam Ali (AS) fought in many of the battles everybody said how he was so strong. But as soon as Ali ibn Abu Talib remained patient in the twenty-five years after his leadership was stolen, this gave the impression to everyone that Imam Ali was weak. On the contrary, the religion of Islam states that the major jihad is the jihad of the nafs, or self, and the minor jihad is the one with the sword. Thus, Imam Hassan (AS) carried out a peace treaty or "Sulh al-Hassan" so that he could conduct the major jihad. Every Imam of Ahlulbayt based their decisions on how The Prophet (PBUH) would act if he was present, hence Imam Hassan was once asked why he carried out a peace treaty with Mu'awiyah. He replied, "Because of Sulh al-Hudaybiya."

The Sulh, or Treaty of Hudaybiya, is the most famous treaty in the life of The Prophet (PBUH) and here Imam Hassan is saying that his treaty with Mu'awiyah is similar to the Prophet's treaty with the Quraysh. When you examine the treaty of Hudaybiya you will find that the wisdom of Imam Hassan is greater than what his followers believe it to be. Sulh al-Hudaybiya is mentioned in the Qur'an in 48:1, "Indeed, We have given you, [O Muhammad], your greatest victory." The misconception of this victory is that it was the day of the opening of Mecca, but the day of the opening of Mecca is mentioned in 110:1, "When there comes the help of Allah and the victory." Therefore, the opening of Hudaybiya is seen in Surah 48. The first aspect of Hudaybiya which clearly emerges is that The Prophet (PBUH) did not spread the religion with the sword as Allah (SWT) states in Surah 48 that the peace treaty is the "greatest victory." This meant that Badr, Khandaq, and Khaybar were not the greatest victories, even though they were carried out by the sword. Hudaybiya had in fact come from a dream of The Prophet (PBUH), as Allah communicates with the human through three different ways: an angel (Jibra'il), inspiration or via a dream known as "ru'ya." The Prophets before The Prophet (PBUH) who experienced a ru'ya from Allah are Prophet Ibrahim when he was asked to sacrifice his son Isma'il and Prophet Yusuf when he dreamt that the stars prostrated before him. Prophet Ya'qub then told Yusuf, "Do not tell your dream (ru'ya) to your brothers."

The Prophet saw himself dressed in his ihram. When the Prophet woke up he went to tell his companions, "I have seen a dream where we will be entering Mecca. Who will join me?" 1400 companions said that they will be joining him. When they had left Medina, Ali ibn Abu Talib was holding the banner, and Um Salama was the only wife of the Prophet who had come. The Prophet (PBUH) also took some animals as he declared that these would be sacrificed. The Prophet (PBUH) reminded his companions, "We are not going to Mecca to fight. Put your swords away. All you should have is the sheath of the sword."

On their way to Medina the Quraysh had heard of The Prophet (PBUH)'s journey towards Mecca, and they were scared as he had already defeated them in Badr and Uhud. They assumed that The Prophet (PBUH) had come in revenge after nineteen years of persecution and that this army he was leading will come and kill them. The Quraysh told Khalid ibn Walid to gather two hundred soldiers and kill him; the news of this reached the Prophet. The Prophet (PBUH) then told his companions to go the other direction towards Mecca through the "rocky road" so that they would avoid Khalid. The camel of The Prophet (PBUH) was a blessed camel, because when The Prophet (PBUH) wanted to build Masjid al-Nabawi he decided that wherever the camel would sit would be the place to start building the Masjid.

On the journey to Mecca, The Prophet (PBUH)'s camel decided to just sit there and stay stationary. So The Prophet (PBUH) told his followers that this must be a message from Allah (SWT) that they must stay there in the area between Medina and Mecca called "Hudaybiya." The Meccans had heard of this so they sent some envoys to find out its purpose. When the first envoy had come, The Prophet (PBUH) stated that they had come for umrah. The Quraysh did not believe this so they sent a second envoy. The Prophet (PBUH) said for for the second time they had come for umrah. The Meccans still didn't believe this and sent a Christian to ask the purpose of The Prophet (PBUH)'s journey, but The Prophet (PBUH) reminded them again, "The Quraysh have persecuted us for years. My religion is not a religion of revenge; I am coming towards Mecca with my companions peacefully and not to fight. Look at my companions. They are not recruited with swords."

For the third time, the Quraysh didn't believe The Prophet (PBUH) so they sent Urwa ibn Masood al-Thaqafi, the grandfather of Ali al-Akbar. Urwa asked the Meccans that if he goes to the Prophet and returns with the honest information will they listen to it sincerely or will they reject him like they did with the previous messengers. The Quraysh agreed to this, so Urwa went. Urwa went to Hudaybiya and greeted The Prophet (PBUH) by holding the beard of The Prophet (PBUH) to place it on his lap. Urwa's nephew al-Mughira told Urwa to take his hand away from The Prophet (PBUH), but the Prophet calmly told al-Mughira that this is how al-Thaqafi's greet each other and the Prophet was not against culture unless it went outside Islam. When Urwa asked the Prophet as to why they had come, The Prophet (PBUH) replied, "We have come to make peace with the Quraysh. I want my followers to see their families in Mecca for the first time [since they have left]."

Urwa went to the leaders of Quraysh and informed them that The Prophet (PBUH) had come peacefully. "Not only has Muhammad come to make peace with people who have killed many of his family and companions, there are also no soldiers like the soldiers of Muhammad. When he carries out wudhu', they jump to grab the water droplets that come off The Prophet (PBUH). If the saliva comes out of his mouth, they would go and hold it." The Quraysh were so stubborn that they rejected even a personality like Urwa. During the middle of the night, they sent seventy of their companions to go and attack the camp of The Prophet (PBUH). But when they had come, The Prophet (PBUH) had such a strong army that they held these soldiers. Some of the companions of the Prophet demanded that they should be killed. The Prophet (PBUH) decided that instead they should be freed. Some companions still persisted in saying that they should be killed, but then they realised that The Prophet (PBUH) had in fact come for a peace treaty.

The Prophet (PBUH) decided that in the same way they had sent envoys, he too would send out envoys; thus The Prophet (PBUH) wanted to send someone who had no blood of the Quraysh on his sword. The Prophet (PBUH) wanted to send out Umar ibn Khattab, but Umar said that he was afraid, so the Prophet sent out Uthman ibn Affan who had also not killed anyone in war and was from Banu Umayyah. Uthman had gone for nineteen days and had not returned. Many Muslims were wondering what they should do. Jabir ibn Abdullah al-Ansari narrated that the Prophet had a cup of water; some companions told the Prophet how nothing had happened even though he had promised victory. The Prophet (PBUH) placed his hand in the cup and water started to come out. Jabir narrated that 100, 000 could have quenched their thirst with the water. The Prophet had done this to assure them that he was certain and he took a bay'a from his companions, the "Bay'a of Ridhwan," or the Pledge Under the Tree. He asked them, "Do you all believe in my Prophethood? Do you believe that I say we will enter Mecca? I never did set a time when we will enter. If you believe in me, then pledge your allegiance." Uthman still had not returned and the rest of the companions pledged their allegiance. Allah (SWT) revealed that, "We were testing their beliefs so that we [would] know what is in their hearts."

Uthman then had come back and informed The Prophet (PBUH) that he cannot make peace with them as they are too strong. Umar agreed with Uthman on this matter. But The Prophet (PBUH) persisted in his idea of the peace treaty. That day Umar had gone to Abu Bakr and said, "Today I question the Prophethood of Muhammad. He said we are going to be victorious, but we have still not achieved victory." The Prophet (PBUH) waited patiently until the Quraysh sent Suheil ibn Amr. Suheil said that now they would make a treaty. The Prophet (PBUH) told Ali ibn Abu Talib to write down the treaty by starting with,"Bismillah al-Rahman al-Raheem..." Suheil said that this statement was not relevant to them as they didn't believe in Allah being Merciful and the most Beneficent. So, The Prophet (PBUH) asked what they would like to be written, Suheil answered, "Bismika Allahumma." This meant "In Your Name Allah," so Imam Ali wrote this. Then The Prophet (PBUH) said, "Muhammad The Prophet (PBUH)."Again Suheil said that this was something they didn't believe and if they had believed this then they wouldn't have fought them, so Suheil suggested they write, "Muhammad ibn Abdullah." Ali ibn Abu Talib looked at The Prophet (PBUH) and said, "Can I be excused from removing Muhammad The Prophet (PBUH)." The Prophet (PBUH) told Imam, "Do not worry, Ali. One day the same thing will happen to you." The Prophet (PBUH) had said this because in the Battle of Siffeen, Amr ibn Aas was watching Imam Ali when he was writing their treaty. Imam said, "This is a treaty between Amir al-Mu'mineen Ali ibn Abu Talib and Amr ibn Aas." Amr looked at Imam and answered, "If we had believed you were Amir al Mu'mineen (Commander of the Faithful) then we wouldn't have been fighting you." So Imam announced, "Subhanallah, a Sunnah like the Prophet's one". What happens with The Prophet (PBUH), happens with me."

The Prophet (PBUH) decided a treaty would be wiser than a battle because in war you do not see the hypocrisy of the opposition. However with a treaty, the terms are noted whereby you see to whom the true words belong to, if they are untrue they are exposed to society. The terms of the treaty included firstly that for ten years there would be no fighting between the Muslims and the Quraysh. Second, if a Quraysh comes towards Medina to become a Muslim we will give him back to the Quraysh. If a Muslim comes to the Quraysh, he does not have to be returned. Some companions questioned this term, but The Prophet (PBUH) reminded them that to be patient. Thirdly, if the Muslims of Medina want to engage in economic trade with the Quraysh, they will not be stopped. Fourthly, if the Muslims visit Mecca, they will not be harassed and can live there in peace. A few of the companions again questioned The Prophet (PBUH). As the treaty was being noted, a man named Abu Jandal, who was in chains, had come. He was the son of Suheil, the envoy of the Quraysh, noting down the treaty. Abu Jandal spoke to the Prophet, "Oh Prophet (PBUH), free me. I want to come and live with you in Medina. My father is an enemy of yours." The Prophet (PBUH) asked that he be freed, but Suheil said to the Prophet, "No, you cannot accept a Quraysh to live with you because in the terms we said he will have to be returned to the Quraysh."

The Prophet (PBUH) informed them they still have not signed the treaty. To which Abu Jandal exclaimed that it was still a verbal agreement. The Prophet (PBUH) told Abu Jandal to return to his father as this will pass over in a few months. Thus, the treaty had ended and the Muslims were able to enter Mecca in victory, and after a small period of time, The Prophet (PBUH)'s wisdom had emerged. The treaty meant that the Muslims would return to Mecca and the intention was that when they returned to their family and friends, there would eventually be more Muslims in Mecca without the need of a sword. Slowly more Meccans were becoming Muslims from the influence of those who visited them. Furthermore, The Prophet (PBUH) wanted to show the people of Mecca that Abu Sufyan and Abu Jahal were liars and against peace. This was seen when the Meccans did not honour the first term of the treaty; ten years of no fighting. Between the ninth and tenth year of Hijra, the Hudaybiya treaty was broken. Because of this Surah al-Taubah (Repentance) was revealed, Allah (SWT) wanted to tell the Prophet to dissociate himself from the Quraysh. The Banu Bakar was a tribe of the Quraysh. Banu Khuza'a were the tribe of the Muslims living there; in the middle of the night the Banu Bakar went and executed the Banu Khuza'a. The Prophet (PBUH) did not show the truth of the Quraysh through the sword, rather the hypocrisy of the Quraysh was revealed when they broke the treaty. Surah al-Taubah was sent to tell the Prophet that this meant no more treaties with the Quraysh should be made, and the Muslims must now defend themselves.

In the same way The Prophet (PBUH) exposed the Quraysh with Sulh al-Hudaybiya, Imam Hassan (AS) exposed Mu'awiyah with Sulh al-Hassan. People questioned Hassan's treaty with Mu'awiyah, but the Imam answered that he was doing what his grandfather had done in Hudaybiya. Imam Hassan knew his people really well; a hypocrite is harder to expose then a kafir. A kafir like Yazid, who used to drink alcohol openly and dance with young boys, can be exposed easily. Mu'awiyah was a hypocrite who used to pray and practice Islam in front of others, however he was discreet in committing haram. Imam conducted a treaty with him so that his hypocrisy would be exposed. Imam gave Mu'awiyah five terms and conditions in the treaty. The first was to protect the Sunnah of the Prophet (PBUH). The second was to stop cursing Imam Ali on the Friday minbar, and the third was to stop killing the followers of Imam Ali. The fourth term was that he (Mu'awiyah) should keep excluded what is 'in the treasury of Kufa, that is five million (dirhwns). So, handing over the authority does not include it (the sum of this money). Mu'awiyah should send al-Hassan one million dirham per year, he should prefer Banu Hashirn in giving and gifts to Banu Abd ash-Shams, and should divide one million (dirham) among the sons of those who were killed helping the Commander of the Faithful (Ali) in the Battle of the Camel and the Battle of Siffeen and should spend that from the taxes of Dar Abjard. The fifth term was that when Mu'awiyah died, the leadership would return to Imam Hassan or Imam Hussein (AS).

Imam Hassan chose not to fight because no one would ever have seen the truth of Mu'awiyah and the people would not follow the Imam. In regards to the five terms, firstly the protection of the Prophet's Sunnah, Mu'awiyah used to have Friday prayers on a Wednesday. Amir al-Mu'mineen has a hadith that states, "Give me one of Mu'awiyah's; I'll give you ten of mine." The followers of Mu'awiyah were so loyal to him that they were willing to pray Jum'uah prayers on a Wednesday. Further than this, the khutba, or speech of Jumu'ah, is meant to be done standing as the Prophet stood when he gave the khutba. However Mu'awiyah was the only caliph in history who did the khutba while sitting. Moreover, the protection of the Prophet's Sunnah was not carried out as he did not condemn adultery. He called his brother Ziyad, the son of Abu Sufyan, instead of Ziyad, the son of his father. This is because in Islam if someone has an adulterer as a parent, you name them "the son of his father."

The second condition of the treaty of Imam Hassan (AS) was the discontinuing of the cursing of his father Ali ibn Abu Talib on the minbar. However this was not carried out as the cursing of Ali ibn Abu Talib was carried out for ninety years until Umar ibn Abdelaziz stopped it. The caliphs after Mu'awiyah were as follows: Yazid then Mu'awiyah then Marwan then Abdel Malik ibn Marwan then Walid ibn Abdel Malik then Sulayman ibn Abdel Malik, and then it continued until Umar ibn Abdelaziz' Khalafa. Mu'awiyah used to encourage the cursing of Ali ibn Abu Talib to the extent that he ask Sa'ad ibn Abdel Waqas why he doesn't curse Ali ibn Abu Talib. The third condition was that Mu'awiyah had to protect the Shi'a of Imam Ali (AS). Mu'awiyah was the cause of the killing of Hijr ibn Adi al-Kindi. The Prophet (PBUH) used to say, "Hijr ibn Adi al-Kindi is the monk of the companions." Hijr used to pray one thousands rukaats per night and spoke out against Ziyad who used to lead Salat al-Jumu'ah whilst cursing Ali ibn Abu Talib. Ziyad could not take it when Hijr spoke out against him, so he wrote a letter to Mu'awiyah saying, "Hijr and his companions are blaspheming against Allah." This was a lie as all Hijr had done was speak out against the cursing of Ali. Mu'awiyah ordered an army against Hijr and for his companions to be executed. Before Hijr was executed, he was given a final wish, and so he said, "Kill my son, and then kill me. Now I die in peace knowing that my son died loving Ali and not Mu'awiyah."

Moreover, they executed Amr ibn Hamaq al Khuza'i, one of the great companions of The Prophet (PBUH). They even poisoned Imam Hassan ibn Ali (AS). They sent Samara ibn Jundub to Basra to kill eight thousand of the followers of the Ahlulbayt. Not only that, they sent Bisr ibn Arda'a to kill thirty thousand of the followers of the Ahlulbayt. Subsequently, the fourth condition was that the treasury of Kufa would be entitled to the blood families of Jamal, Nahrawan and Siffeen. He took this and started building numerous palaces in Sham. The final condition in which the Imam exposed Mu'awiyah was the area of Khalafa after him. Imam Hassan asked that he not appoint Yazid after him but rather appoint Imam Hassan, or Imam Hussein if he was absent. The second Mu'awiyah installed Yazid as caliph, Imam Hassan was the victorious one politically as this showed to all the Muslims how much of a hypocrite Mu'awiyah was. Mu'awiyah did not want to protect Islam but he wanted to protect Arab Nationalism and the Banu Umayyah. In his last days, Mu'awiyah was wondering how to make Yazid his successor, so he called Mugheera ibn Shu'ba for advice. Mugheera reminded him that Abdel Rahman, son of Abu Bakr, Abdullah ibn Umar and Hussein ibn Ali were still alive, and these men had greater rights over being caliph because Yazid was a drunkard and a womaniser. Mugheera asked that Mu'awiyah give Yazid two years whereby he would make him look religious to the people and then install him as his successor. Mu'awiyah then asked Ziyad for advice. Ziyad said that they should get a hadith from the Prophet which shows that something will happen and let Yazid be present at the incident. They looked at the hadith which states, "The army of Muslims that fight in Constantinople (Turkey) will be forgiven of everything by Allah."

So Ziyad told Mu'awiyah to show how Yazid was present at this battle, but was not fighting there, so Yazid could be the narrator. Mu'awiyah asked Yazid to go to Constantinople with the army led by Sufyan ibn Auf but not as a soldier. Yazid at the time was married to Um Kulthum and asked her to come with him; Marwan ibn Hakam allowed them to stay in the area of Farqaduni. When they went there had been a plague which had killed many of the soldiers. Mu'awiyah found out that Yazid had taken Um Kulthum with him and they had been drunk in Farqaduni, singing, "Let the army stay at Farqaduni, while I am in my house with my Um Kulthumi." Mu'awiyah became angry and sent him a message that he must reach the army as he needed to be in the hadith. So Yazid went to the battle and saw nearly everyone dead. They then were able to fabricate the hadith as Yazid being present there. Mugheera ibn Shu'ba sent thirty of the Kufan scholars to Mu'awiyah whereby they were prepared to give bay'a to Yazid. Mu'awiyah asked that they spread this news whereby Yazid has been forgiven of all his sins and could now lead the Muslim Ummah. Then Mu'awiyah asked the payments they received to write this hadith. They replied, "300,000 dirhams." The rumour was spread that Yazid was the successor of Mu'awiyah, which meant that Imam Hassan had exposed Mu'awiyah through pen and paper on a treaty, similar to how his grandfather exposed those in Hudaybiya.

In conclusion, one scholar brilliantly says, "Were it not for the treaty of Imam Hassan with Mu'awiyah there would be no follower of the Prophet living today. Imam Hassan could have allowed a war to happen where no one would be protecting the Sunnah of The Prophet (PBUH) and Ahlulbayt, or he waited to expose them to the Muslims, for a day when Hussein will avenge what has happened." Imam Hussein (AS) fought Yazid because Yazid differed from his father as Yazid was an open disbeliever whereas Mu'awiyah was an open hypocrite.

Lecture 16

The Rights of Neighbours in Islam

Neighbours are held at a high position in all communities, in the sense that a person looks for their neighbours when looking for protection and security. Islam values the neighbour in society to the extent that it has given them many rights. Therefore the discussion of neighbours in Islam is a discussion that is both ethical and jurisprudential, the former allowing us to understand the responsibilities we have towards our neighbour. Neighbour's rights are highlighted in jurisprudence as it allows us to understand the legal position of the neighbour. In our lifetime each human being will live with a neighbour. A neighbour can be someone you can choose or sometimes it is just luck. In some areas of the world, you do not choose who they live next to, whereas in other areas you do have the luxury to choose. A neighbour is an important component in society because neighbours can be a source of goodness and happiness, or destruction and bad relationships. In many countries you have a "neighbourhood watch," whereby each neighbour looks out for each other in this mini-community, for example, looing out for the elderly, children and the disabled.

Recently in the UK there was a television programme called "Neighbours from Hell" which focused on those who do not allow their neighbours to happily live their lives. Sometimes a neighbour can be a gift from Allah (SWT) and sometimes they are a trial. Every religion focuses on the neighbour as an important part of our development, for example, in the Book of Matthew, from 22:34 onwards, the famous line of Prophet Jesus states, "Love thy neighbour as thou lovest thyself." You have to love your neighbour in the same way you love yourself. Likewise we find the Holy Prophet (PBUH) in a hadith from the sixth Imam stating, "If your neighbour locks your door out of fear from stealing from them, this means you are not a mu'min or believer." Thus, this means as a neighbour you should be able to make everyone feel secure. It is fine if they lock their doors from outsiders, but if they lock their doors from you, this is not right. Amir al-Mu'mineen, in his final will states, "Fear Allah in relation to your neighbours. The Prophet (PBUH) recommended this so much that I thought they would have a share in our inheritance." This meant that The Prophet (PBUH) would always advise the Imam about neighbours, so Imam mentioned it as one of the ten things in his final will. Unfortunately, the topic of the neighbour is neglected, although many of our Prophets and Imams have discussed the neighbour. The position of the neighbour can be discussed here.

In the Arabic language, the word for neighbour is "jaar." In the Qur'an this word is mentioned in three different places, but where it is mentioned is not in the context of a neighbour but in the context of the root meaning of what a neighbour should be. The first place where "jaar" is mentioned is in 8:48, which says, "And when Satan made their deeds pleasing to them and said, 'No one can overcome you today, and indeed while I am your "jaar," or near.'" In the battle of Badr, Satan was disguised as a human and the Qur'an tells us the disbelievers were scared of the opposition because of how powerful they were. The disbelievers became frightened, so Satan reassured them by telling them that no one can overcome them as he is their "jaar." Here jaar doesn't mean neighbour, it means being "near" to them. Originally the word jaar meant someone who is near you; later on the word was used for neighbour. Another example of "jaar" is in 9:6, "And if any one of the polytheists seeks your protection (jaar), then grant him protection so that he may hear the words of Allah. Then deliver him to his place of safety. That is because they are a people who do not know."

When The Prophet (PBUH) found the disbelievers who broke the treaty of Hudaybiya, Allah ordered The Prophet (PBUH) to attack a group of them. But then there was another group of them that, Allah has said in this verse, if these polytheists ask you for protection, then grant them protection. In the first usage, the word "jaar" meant "being near" while the second usage means "being a form of sanctuary." The verse which was revealed about neighbours in Islam was 4:6, which divided our neighbours into two very different groups. "Worship Allah and associate nothing with Him, and to parents do good, and to relatives, orphans, the needy, the near neighbour, the neighbour farther away, the companion at your side, the traveller, and those whom your right hands possess. Indeed, Allah does not like those who are self-deluding and boastful." Here Allah (SWT) talks of the neighbour in context of shari'a, so why is the neighbour associated with shari'a? The reason is that shari'a doesn't deny that a non-Muslim may find it natural to look after your neighbour, but what shari'a does is it sets out the principles and rights of your neighbour. Islam said that there are two types of neighbours and they both have to be respected individually for what they are worth.

In verse 4:6, Allah says first to worship me, do not commit shirk towards me, respect your parents, the orphans, the poor, and then Allah says to respect your neighbours. In other words, after someone worships Allah, respects their parents, relatives, the poor, then comes your neighbours. Allah divided the neighbour into two types, the jaar that is "qurba" and the jaar that is "junub." There are three different opinions by the scholars of tafseer as to what these types mean. The first opinion is that jaar al-qurba is your relatives who are your neighbours while jaar al-junub are your strangers who are neighbours to you. But some of the scholars say that this opinion is weak as Allah has already mentioned your family and relatives in the beginning of the verse. The second opinion is that jaar al-qurba are those who live close to you and jaar al-junub are those who are distant. In Islam a close neighbour is considered to be those who live forty doors from you in every direction. At the time of The Prophet (PBUH), Ubaidallah ibn Bakra used to say,"My close neighbours are not my next door neighbours but they are forty doors to the left, forty to the right and forty to the front and forty behind." He used to make an effort to say Salamu Alaykum to everyone in his neighbourhood; his neighbours would always feel secure with him. He used to bring them money and food. Thus, with this opinion jaar al-qurba are close neighbours and jaar al-junub are those who are far. Then there is a third opinion which states that jaar al-qurba are your Muslim neighbours and jaar al-junub are your non-Muslim neighbours. Thus Islam gives rights to Muslim and non-Muslim neighbours over you.

The Prophet (PBUH) told his companions one day, "There are three types of neighbours; there is a neighbour with three rights over you, a neighbour with two rights over you and a neighbour with one right over you. The neighbour with three rights over you is Muslim, and who is your relative and your neighbour. The neighbour with two rights over you is your Muslim neighbour. Then there is someone in society who has one right over you, this is your non-Muslim neighbour. Whoever angers a non-Muslim has angered me." Just because someone's neighbour is non-Muslim, this does not mean we have a right to harm our neighbour. This is why Islam divided the neighbours' rights into a number of groups, four of them will be considered here.

1. not making noise

2. not going into their territory

3. when they are attacked you defend them

4. when they need financial assistance, you help them

When these four rights are examined, the religion of Islam will be seen in a beautiful light which has opened up the whole area of the neighbour. Firstly, the right of not making noise is important in regards to neighbours. For example, if a family has children and they are aware that their neighbour has work the following day, they should not make noise after a certain time in order for them to be able to sleep. A Muslim is one who does not just bring people from his prayer and sawm, but from his akhlaaq (manners) with others. The Prophet (PBUH) has said, "La'na, or curse, upon those who harm their neighbour."

One day someone came to the Holy Prophet (PBUH) and told him that there is this lady who fasts the whole day and she prays the whole night, however she hurts her neighbours. So what would be her position? The Prophet (PBUH) answered them by saying that she will be in Hell because she has not given the rights to her neighbour. In The Prophet (PBUH)'s life, his neighbour was his uncle Abu Lahab. In the beginning The Prophet (PBUH) did not mind having his uncle as his neighbour because Abu Lahab was very happy when his nephew was born; he even freed one of his slave girls. In Arabia, for someone to free a slave girl meant that they were very content. He would continue to respect The Prophet (PBUH) until the day it was announced that The Prophet (PBUH) was made a Prophet. Abu Lahab and his wife were described in a revelation of the Qur'an in Surah 111; it says that they will "be cast into a flaming fire, along with his wife, the carrier of firewood and thorny plants." His wife would leave the firewood and thorny plants outside the house of The Prophet (PBUH) so that they would step on it.

A narration also states that a young Fatima al-Zahra was walking one day when Abu Lahab and his wife used to throw these thorny plants on The Prophet (PBUH). Fatima would pick them up and her hand would bleed. Abu Lahab and his wife would carry out these acts and more. However The Prophet (PBUH) did not retaliate against his neighbours and remained patient. Similarly one day a man had come to The Prophet (PBUH) asking him what to do as his neighbours were making too much noise. The first time they came The Prophet (PBUH) said, "Be patient." This happened again the second and third time, until the fourth time The Prophet (PBUH) said something very unexpectedly. The Prophet (PBUH) told the person, "Pick up your belongings and throw them out in the streets." When the people would walk past, the man would tell them when they asked that his neighbour was harming him. Everyone then made la'na against his neighbour. When his neighbour had come to see this, he asked him to come back and promised to not cause havoc anymore.

Additionally, Luqman al-Hakim has said, "I have lifted the heaviest of metals and I have lifted the heaviest of iron, but I have never lifted something as heavy as a bad neighbour." Luqman meant that a bad neighbour can make someone live in fear and anxiety. Secondly, in Islam one of the rights of your neighbour is to not enter their territory. For example, some people may not know that if your neighbour's tree is nearby it is not permitted to take an apple from it. Allama al-Tabatabai narrates a story about how that which you take from your neighbour isn't yours can affect your child's concentration in prayer. One day there was a son who came to a Maulana who told him that he cannot concentrate in prayer. Maulana tried to give him advice with du'a and attempted to put him in the correct mode of prayer psychologically, however these efforts, as well as others, did not improve his concentration. Then he asked him a question, "Do you know anything of your mother when she was pregnant with you? Or when she was giving birth?" The student replied nothing was important that he remembered his mother telling him. When the student got home he asked his mother. She answered that was pregnant with him when one day she wanted to go out and get some food, however it was a cold day. She then saw her neighbours tree which was slanted in their garden. Her intention was to eat the fruit and to not make it ghasbi she would tell them after. But then she forgot to tell her neighbours so she fed him from ghasbi food. This she said was why he was not focusing in prayer. The Prophet (PBUH) has been narrated to have said, "Make sure you get permission from your neighbours when you build a building on your site." In the world today there is something called "planning permission" which means you cannot build something without letting the government know. The Prophet (PBUH) 1400 years ago discussed this. Your neighbour has their territory and you have yours. Moreover, even the scholars argue that it is not permissible to use the neighbour's water when it comes to performing ablution or wudhu'. Bishr al-Hafi, the famous companion of Imam al-Kadhim (AS), converted to Islam when he was asked by the Imam upon leaving his house (where music had been playing), "Is this house the house of a free man or a slave?" Bishr al-Hafi had a daughter who wanted to read a book but their light was not working, so she used the neighbour's lamppost, but Bishr said this was not their territory and she had to ask for permission.

The Prophet (PBUH) has a hadith that declares the following, "Do not look at your neighbours on the privacy of your Muslim brothers and sisters." However in society today they do not uphold the idea of not giving the neighbours their privacy, whereas the right of the neighbour mentioned by the Prophet says to not eavesdrop on them. In the Bible it mentions how Prophet Dawood looked over his territory into that of his neighbours, he saw the wife of his general wearing only a robe, and supposedly she took it off which led the Prophet to be infatuated. Apparently he then sent her husband to war so that he may be with her. This gives us proof that the Qur'an is not a copy of the Bible; the Prophet of God would never be mentioned as doing something like this in the Qur'an. The Prophet (PBUH) in another hadith states, "Whoever eavesdrops on his neighbours will be raised on the Day of Judgement with the hypocrites and will be exposed in this world." Thus, the second right of your neighbours is to not go into their territory without their permission or to eavesdrop on them.

The third right of your neighbour is to defend them when they are attacked, as your neighbour is like your brother. However, in Islam, if your neighbour has thieves entering their house, you should go in to defend them or phone the police for their help. But in the UK if you try and stop a thief from stealing inside someone else's house then you yourself will go to prison. Ubaidallah ibn Abbas, the cousin of Imam Hassan (AS), was given governorship by the Imam. Mu'awiyah sent Bisr ibn Art'aa, one of his commanders, to go and attack Ubaidallah. Bisr had killed thirty thousand Muslims when he was the general of Mu'awiyah. When Bisr went to attack Ubaidiallah, Ubaidallah ran away but left his children with his neighbour. That neighbour was holding Ubaidallah's children when Bisr had entered and asked that he give them to him. The neighbour persisted however and said, "I will never allow anyone to attack anything that belongs to my neighbour." Bisr said that he was only going to take the children, but now he wanted him too, the neighbour then said that if he wanted the children then he should take him instead. Bisr then executed that neighbour. The stand was of great principle, which showed the physical protection of his neighbour. Imam Zain al-Abideen (AS) says, "If your neighbour is being attacked you either help through physical or verbal means."

The fourth right is when your neighbour needs financial assistance so you help them. The Prophet (PBUH) would always mention how if you bring lots of food back home, hide them as your neighbours may not be able to afford this. Now we live an environment were everyone in your area has the same wealth, but at the time of the Prophet they would have neighbours from different classes. Sayyed Mahdi Bahr al-Uloom was one of the great scholars of the Ahlulbayt who even had conversed on one occasion with the twelfth Imam. One day Sayyed Mahdi became angry with his student Sayyed Jawad al-Amuli who was a mujtahid. Sayyed Jawad narrates that he was once sitting at home; he was about to eat when the door knocked and it was Sayyed Mahdi's slave who said, "Sayyed Mahdi refuses to eat tonight unless you come and eat with him." Sayyed Jawad thought this must have been an emergency and as soon as he entered he saw Sayyed Mahdi who looked at him and shouted, "Do you have respect for Allah (SWT)? Do you believe in Allah (SWT)? How can you allow your neighbour to move into your neighbourhood without you going to ask about what he needs? You have a new neighbour and for seven days you have not even gone to say Assalamu Alaykum to him. Don't you know he went to the green grocer, but he didn't have any money on him and he asked the grocer if he can have some time to pay him? The grocer refused to give him the food and he went home to his children empty-handed. How can you call yourself a scholar of the Ahlulbayt when you are sitting at home not helping your neighbour? If you were a Muslim and you believed that your neighbour had no right over you, your Islam would have finished." Sayyed Jawad looked puzzled and answered, "Maulana, what shall I do?" "Take this food and give it to your neighbour. Sit with him, eat with him. Take this money and put it under his rug because this is the right of your neighbour over you in Islam." Sayyed Mahdi Bahr al-Uloom showed here the importance of helping your neighbour financially even if they do not ask for help.

Our fourth Imam, in Risalat al-Huqooq, has written, "The right of your neighbour is that you guard them when they are present and you honour them when they are absent. You do not look for their imperfections and their faults. If you find that they have faults, put a veil between you and their faults. If they invite you for dinner, go. If they are sick, visit them. If they die, go to their funeral. If they need help financially, give them a loan. " The idea in Islam is that the neighbour was the spectrum of society, if you neglect their rights then you have neglected the rights of the whole of society. Islam did not stop there, not only do we have neighbours in this world but we have neighbours in the next world. There are also neighbours in the world of Barzakh, or the grave.

Once Prophet Musa (AS) knocked on someone's door and asked if he could have dinner with them that day. He welcomed him inside, although he did not know that this was Prophet Musa, and he said his house was open to strangers. When the Prophet was sitting with this man he noticed that he kept on leaving the room and coming back again and again. Prophet Musa asked him where he was going and the man replied he was going to his ill mother. Prophet Musa decided to go speak to her but found that she was whispering too low, so he asked her son what she was saying. The man answered, "O my son, may Allah bless you for you welcomed a stranger into our house to feed them. I wish that Allah (SWT) allows you to meet one of his messengers one day." Prophet Musa looked at him, smiled and said, "I am Prophet Musa. Before I knocked on your door today I asked Allah to give me a neighbour in Paradise. Allah directed me to your house, saying, "Because of his respect of his mother in old age, he will be your neighbour in Paradise."

Furthermore, Muslims are always asked to be buried next to someone who was a pious person. This is because your neighbour in the grave can stop the punishment coming to you if they were a great believer. Abu Bakr and Umar wanted to both be buried next to The Prophet (PBUH); this means that the buried is not just dead; this means that you have a neighbour in the next world too. Maulana Yazdi narrates an incident whereby the importance of your neighbour in Barzakh is highlighted. He says his friend had died but he wasn't very religious, he prayed and fasted but had a few points that were not great. He saw his friend in the dream and saw him calm. Yazdi asked him why he was so relaxed. His friend replied, "On the first day when I died the punishment was severe, then while we were in our graves the lady who was buried next to me was visited by Imam Hussein (AS). When Imam came, he sent his salutations and called out to stop the punishment of this lady, which made all the graves around her have their punishments seized." Yazdi then asked his friend, "Who is this lady?" "The wife of Ustath Haddad." When Maulana Yazdi woke up he immediately went looking for Ustath Haddad, who told him his wife was buried on the same day as his friend. Maulana then asked Ustath if his wife had ever visited the shrine of Imam Hussein (AS), but Ustath replied no. He then asked if his wife had any relationship with the Imam. Ustath replied no again. Maulana then told him the dream and Ustath then recalled why Imam had visited her. "My wife would always recite Ziyarat Ashura. I am sure this is why Imam visited her." Thus your neighbour in the Hereafter can be your sanctuary just like your neighbour in this world.

The famous caliph of the Buyid dynasty, when he wanted to die, asked that he be buried next to Imam Ali (AS) and said that he wanted to be his neighbour. Likewise, many people want to be buried in Wadi al-Salam because they want to be in the vicinity of the Prophet and the Ahlulbayt. The caliph asked to have the following saying on his tombstone, "And their dog is outstretched, with his forelegs at the entrance." This is verse 18:18 in the Qur'an, where it talks of the dog of Ashaab al-Kahaf. The caliph wanted to be like the dog of Ashaab al-Kahaf for Imam Ali (AS) just to reside near him. When Imam Hussein was going to die, he said he wanted two people to be buried near him, his son Ali al-Akbar and his six-month-old son Abullah.

Lecture 17

The Battle of Badr

The holy month of Ramadan is a month of spirituality and reform as well as peace and prosperity. Furthermore, this month honours the great personalities and events in Islamic history. For example, the martyrdom of Amir al-Mu'mineen, the birth of the grandson of the prophet Imam Hassan (AS) and the death of Khadijah, the Mother of Believers. When we look at these personalities we seek to take lessons from them and apply them to our own lives. Some of the greatest events in Ramadan include the Night of Power and the Battle of Badr, the first battle in Islam. The Battle of Badr is unfortunately neglected in many Islamic circles as its importance and position in history is underestimated.

Like any battle, an examination of the Battle of Badr involves its background, its purpose, the events which occurred, the reason why the Prophet defended Islam, and the aftermath of the battle. In this way we can apply these lessons to our lives today. Badr was remembered years after it had happened to remind the Muslims of the greatness of it. Many companions who took part in the battle would call themselves a "Badri," which allowed them to be recognised as fighters in the battle. Likewise, many pointed towards personalities who took part in the battle. The caliph Umar ibn Khattab would base his economic policy on those who fought in Badr, those who came later, and those who converted to Islam before and after the battle. Imam Zain al-Abideen (AS), in his famous sermon in Syria in front of Yazid's empire, came forward and said, "I am the son of he who fought in Badr and Hunayn. I am the son of he who was a Mekki and Medani, a Badri and Uhudi." This meant that he was highlighting his grandfather Ali ibn Abu Talib who was amongst those who fought in Badr. The caliph Umar ibn Abdelaziz stopped the cursing of Ali ibn Abu Talib when he discovered the position Ali had in the Battle of Badr. Therefore, there is a need to study this battle which occurred on the seventeenth of Ramadan in second year of Hijra.

Firstly, in order to study the battle, the background must be looked at. The Prophet was forty years old when he became a Prophet and he was in Mecca for the first thirteen years and Medina for the latter ten years. In the first thirteen years he and his companions experienced a lot of oppression from the pagan circles of the Arabs. Likewise, in Christianity and Judaism, as they were monotheistic religions, they faced periods of oppression from the ruling classes. In terms of the oppression faced by the Muslims, you had companions like Bilal who was tortured simply because he was a black slave who joined Islam. Ammar ibn Yasir's parents, Sumayya and Yasir, were executed because of their belief in Islam. Many others were tortured severely. The Prophet himself would go down in prostration in prayer and Abu Jahal would throw the intestine of an animal towards him. Even in the middle of his Prophethood, many of his companions had to leave Arabia and go to Africa in order that to receive sanctuary from the Christian priest, Najashi. In the thirteen years of living in Mecca, this oppression was never once retaliated, nor did Allah send a revelation to retaliate. Eventually the Prophet went to Medina on the Night of Migration because, at the end of the thirteen years, the Meccans sought to kill him. The Prophet managed to leave Mecca and go to Medina. At fifty-three years of age the Prophet had not fought a single battle. Even when The Prophet (PBUH) reached Medina, the Meccans still sought to attack him, and still The Prophet (PBUH) did not retaliate.

When he had reached Medina, the Arabs were angered for three reasons as to how he was able to leave Mecca safely and how he went to Medina. The first reason was that they were unhappy that a fellow Arab tribe was willing to welcome him to Medina. The two tribes of Medina were the Aws and Khazraj who had fought each other in the past but had managed to reunite with the Prophet's migration and come towards the religion of Islam. The second reason the Arabs were unhappy was that the economic stranglehold they had over Mecca had diminished. The third reason the Arabs were angry was that Prophet Muhammad (PBUH) had managed to convert many of their sons and daughters to Islam. Many of the great aristocrats of Mecca had families who came to Islam. For example, Utba ibn Rabi'a had a son named Hanthala, and who was the brother of Hind, who had gone to Medina with The Prophet (PBUH). Some Arabs did not rest, for people like Abu Jahal said, "I will not rest until I kill Muhammad, even if I have to chase Muhammad to Medina."

Abu Jahal used to stay on the outskirts of Medina, and would attack the caravans of the immigrants along with their villages and crops. Yet many of the Muslims would ask the Prophet if they could retaliate. The response of The Prophet (PBUH) was to remain patient. The Prophet had known that the Meccans were trying to attack Medina. Until, at the beginning of Jamad al-Awwal, the Prophet had heard that Abu Sufyan had mobilised the caravan to Syria. At the time the Arabs had two directions: in the summer they would travel to Syria and in the winter they would go to Yemen to collect an amount of expenditure. The Prophet had heard that Abu Sufyan had brought weapons from Syria in preparation of his army attacking Medina. So the Prophet told Talha, or in another narration it says Adi ibn Hatim, "I want you to go and find out what Abu Sufyan has brought from Syria."

The Prophet did this to confirm the allegations, and when Talha returned he said the caravan was headed by Abu Sufyan, surrounded by forty guards. The caravan was made up of fifty thousand dirhams and a thousand camels; Abu Sufyan had brought artillery to come back to Mecca. When the Prophet heard this, he told his companions that it was their role to go and stop this caravan, because in the same way that Abu Sufyan attacked their caravans, they must do the same before they recruit their army. Abu Sufyan heard of the possibility of an ambush, so he asked his servant Damdam to go quickly towards Mecca, and before he reached there he must pierce the nose of the camel and cut its ears. He also asked Zamzam to tear his shirt in the hope that when he entered Mecca and claimed the Muslims had done this that they would believe it. Zamzam entered Mecca saying, "O people of Mecca, I have come with news from the caravan of Abu Sufyan. The caravan of Abu Sufyan has been attacked by Muhammad and his companions. My shirt is torn and my camel has been attacked. Surely you cannot accept this." This meant that they had lost money so when they heard that the caravans were attacked, Abu Jahal stood up and said this shall not be accepted, he will take a thousand soldiers and seven hundred horses and camels to attack them.

Meanwhile, The Prophet (PBUH) was in Medina and told his companions that they had to go to the caravan of Abu Sufyan. Eighty of the immigrants and two hundred and thirty-three of those from Medina came with him. This meant that 313 people came with the Prophet. They went to the southwest village of Medina, which was named Badr, and when they reached there, the Prophet asked Ali ibn Abu Talib to find out if Abu Sufyan had come past. When Ali came to the wells of Badr, he found three of the Arabs talking amongst themselves, "Get ready, the army is coming and we need to fight." He took two of them, who were from the tribes of Bani Hajjaj and Bani Aas. They then told the Prophet how the army from Mecca was coming as you have ambushed their caravan. The Prophet told them he hadn't ambushed Abu Sufyan's caravan. He realised that this was a rumour used to aggravate the Arabs to come and fight the Muslims. The Prophet was in a predicament because all he had was 313 people with him, with the Meccan soldiers numbering at least a thousand. The Prophet then looked at the soldiers and asked if they were willing to defend their land. Abu Bakr and Umar came forward and said that the Arabs are of a great glory that has never been defeated, thus was this a good idea. Then Miqdad al-Aswad stood up and said, "O Prophet of God, you are the one who made us submit to God and we gave our hearts to God through you. We went through years of torture without once holding our swords against them, as you told us to remain patient. O Prophet, we will not be like the children of Israel who said to Musa, 'Go you and your Lord; we will stay behind at home.' We will say, 'We will be with you and your Lord.'"

The Prophet (PBUH) saw the passion his companion Miqdad had, who was of the Muhajiroon, or the immigrants. So he then turned to ask the people of Medina, because their first pledge to Muhammad was that they would defend him, but this did not include a war. So he asked their leader Sa'ad ibn Manaf if his soldiers were prepared to be alongside him, to which Sa'ad answered, "Oh Prophet (PBUH), if it means we have to drown in the sea alongside you, we will be there." At this moment the verse was revealed which gave the philosophy of why the Prophet Muhammad had to defend himself, "To those against whom war is made, permission is given (to fight) because they have been oppressed, and verily, Allah is most powerful for their aid; (They are) those who have been expelled from their homes in defiance of right, because they say, 'our Lord is Allah.' For had it not been for God's repelling some people through the might of others, there would surely have been pulled down monasteries, churches, synagogues, and mosques in which the name of Allah is commemorated in abundant measure. Allah will certainly aid those who aid his (cause) for verily Allah is full of Strength, Exalted in Might" (Surah 22, verses 39 and 40).

If the religion of Islam was only about mosques, why did Allah (SWT), through this verse, want the Prophet to defend the other holy places too? The reason Prophet Muhammad (PBUH) rose in Badr was so that he could defend any institution which believed in the monotheism of One God. Thus the rise of Badr was to prevent the oppression of the Muslims, Christians and Jews. Allah demanded that the Prophet rise against the Meccans, as not doing anything meant that the institutions of the religions of the One God would be no more.

The Prophet (PBUH) wanted to camp in Badr on the area of soft ground. Habbab, a companion, came towards him and first took permission to ask a question before he said, "O Prophet of God, is the place where you have decided to camp revealed to you by God or was it your own decision?" The Prophet answered, "No, this was my decision." Habbab then asked, "May I give you advice about where to camp as I am an expert in the desert?" The Prophet responded that he may advise him as The Prophet (PBUH) was never a dictator and encouraged dialogue. "Don't rest your soldiers on the soft area; rest them on firm areas where they are closer to the wells of Badr. If you rest them on high ground the water will be accessible, for you are near the wells of Badr."

The Prophet thanked Hubbab and took on this advice to camp close to the wells. At the same time, Prophet Muhammad (PBUH) was victorious due to the help of Allah (SWT) because the Qur'an says that Allah helped them when they were few in number. But also because Allah helped them sleep easily in the night – Allah had sent down an abundance of rain to make the ground softer. The rain was also sent by Allah so that they may purify themselves at night. Surah 8, verse 11, states the following, "[Remember] when He overwhelmed you with drowsiness [giving] security from Him and sent down upon you from the sky rain by which to purify you and remove from you the evil [suggestions] of Satan and to make steadfast your hearts and plant firmly thereby your feet."

When the opposition had come, they were in an arrogant mood. Abu Jahal claimed, "We do not need our main soldiers to fight. Let our slaves fight and they will destroy the army of Muhammad." Not all of the Arab leaders were present at Badr. Abu Lahab was too lazy to come so he sent his slave al-Aas ibn Hashim as he had promised him four thousand dirhams. Of course Ibn Hashim did not return. Umayyah ibn Khalaf was the man who tortured Bilal, his slave, until the day Bilal said he would not follow his Arab aristocracy rather he followed Islam, whereby black and white are equal before God. Umayyah ibn Khalaf then tortured him on the sand hills of Arabia by placing hot rocks on his body until eventually Bilal was released. Umayyah did not want to come to Badr as he was afraid he would one day be defeated by the Muslims. A day before the battle, someone came to Umayyah and said, "Here is some kohl, you may be seen as a woman as you are not coming with us to war. You tortured many of Muhammad's soldiers when they had done nothing. Now when we want to attack them, you're sitting behind him." This made Umayyah change his mind and come to battle. When they had come to battle, Allah (SWT) shows how he helped the Arabs in a further instance, in Surah 3, verse 13, "Already there has been for you a sign in the two armies which met – one fighting in the cause of Allah and another of disbelievers. They saw them [to be] twice their [own] number by [their] eyesight. But Allah supports with His victory whom He wills. Indeed, in that is a lesson for those of vision." And in Surah 8, verse 44, "And remember when ye met, He showed them to you as few in your eyes, and He made you appear as contemptible in their eyes: that Allah might accomplish a matter already enacted. For to Allah do all questions go back (for decision)." Allah here is saying how he made the Muslims look larger in number so that they may be victorious, while the Arabs looked few in the eyes of the Muslims.

Before the battle, Utba ibn Rabi'a, the father of Hind, heard how Abu Sufyan's caravan had reached Mecca. So he told the Meccans how they were fighting Muhammad if it had been a false rumour. He was secretly scared to face his son Hanthala in battle, who was on the side of The Prophet (PBUH). But Abu Jahal called Utba a coward who just didn't want to face his son. However, because of Arab pride, Utba replied that he will still fight in Badr even if it meant he had to face his son. At the start of the battle, the Arabs would be in a combat which involved an introduction with three soldiers opposite three other soldiers. So Utba came forward, "I am Utba, son of Rabi'a. On my left is my son Waleed and on my right is my brother Shayba. O Soldiers of Muhammad, show us your greatest soldiers." Hamza, the uncle of the Prophet stood against them and said,

"I am Hamza, son of Abdul Muttalib. On my left is Ali, son of Abu Talib, and on my right is Ubayda." Hamza managed to kill Shayba and Ali killed Utba as well as Waleed. They were warriors who were of quality and not quantity. Ali ibn Abu Talib later on in the Battle of Siffeen would say to Mu'awiyah, "O Mu'awiyah, come and fight me one on one! Do you not remember what I did to your maternal grandparent and uncle at Badr?"

On the day of Badr, Ali ibn Abu Talib was as fierce as a lion. When Sa'ad ibn Waqas was asked about Badr, Sa'ad answered, "The day of Badr belonged to Ali ibn Abu Talib because in the beginning of the battle Ali had said these lines, 'I am like someone who is possessed. It is for a day like this that my mother gave birth to me." Imam al-Shafi'ee narrates that a person of the tribe of Kunani came to Mu'awiyah and asked him how Ali ibn Abu Talib was in Badr, Mu'awiyah, who had observed the battle, said, "Ali ibn Abu Talib, in Badr, was like a lion roaring through the soldiers. Nobody could get in his way." Imam Ali (AS), on that day, was only twenty-four years of age, yet he was a youth who valiantly defended his cousin and his Prophet while he was the flag bearer. The Badr army could not believe how an army of 313 was defeating an army of a thousand. Two of the Meccan's great leaders were killed, the first being Abu Jahal who tortured the Prophet and killed many monotheists for years. Abu Jahal died in an embarrassing manner which showed off his arrogance. When Abdullah ibn Masood was at the beginning of the battle, he came to The Prophet (PBUH) and said because he was so short he did not know what to do. So The Prophet (PBUH) said if any of the leaders who have ambushed their caravans and executed the Muslims are about to die, that he go and ensure that they are dead. Abdullah ran to Abu Jahal who was lying on the ground close to dying, Abu Jahal looked at him and declared, "I do not want you to kill me; I cannot take one of the shortest men being the death of me." This shows the extent of Abu Jahal's arrogance, which has been narrated in a hadith by the Prophet, "Abu Jahal is more arrogant than Pharaoh, because when Pharaoh was drowning in the Red Sea, he had said he believed in a God. However Abu Jahal, in his last moments, was more concerned about the height of his killer."

The second Arab leader who was killed was Umayyah ibn Khalaf, the man who tortured Bilal. He attempted to run away when he saw Abdel Rahman ibn Auf who had converted to Islam, so Umayyah reminded him of their friendship. Abdel Rahman was turning to take him to a safe place when Bilal saw this; Bilal eventually avenged Umayyah and killed him. Eventually after a while the remainder of the Meccans ran away, and this gave the Muslims their victory. The Muslims had lost fourteen soldiers in Badr, while the opposition had lost seventy – thirty-five of whom were killed by Ali ibn Abu Talib. Fifty Arab prisoners were caught, and the Prophet asked his soldiers their advice as to what to do with these soldiers. Some companions asked that they be killed while Abu Bakr asked that they be ransomed. So the Prophet agreed with Abu Bakr, however he said that the prisoners should not be held in ropes. Then the Prophet said they should be fed, clothed, live amongst them and be treated equally. The ransom is that if they teach ten children how to read and write then they can be freed. The Prophet wanted to build a state of education; this gives further proof that The Prophet (PBUH) did not spread the religion by the sword.

The Prophet (PBUH) then said that from the opposition there were soldiers who were compelled to fight and some were good human beings, for example, his own uncle Abbas. Abbas was caught by Abu Yaseer. During the night The Prophet (PBUH) could not stand to hear the groans of his uncle so he demanded that he be released in addition to those who were compelled to fight them. Furthermore, The Prophet (PBUH) collected many of the spoils of war; some of his companions were not fighting sincerely as they only fought to collect the spoils. One of his companions, Sa'ad ibn Waqas looked at The Prophet (PBUH) and said, "Are you going to give me the same as one of these water carriers and gardeners when I am from the tribe of Bani Zuhra?" The Prophet (PBUH) replied, "Haven't we removed these inequalities? All of you should have come sincerely to this battle, not to receive spoils, but rather to remove oppression from Arabia." Some of The Prophet (PBUH)'s soliders were bickering about the spoils of war instead of rejoicing over the victory against oppression. The Prophet (PBUH) then asked Abdullah ibn Ka'ab to come forward so that he may give out the spoils of war. Ali ibn Abu Talib told the Prophet, "If we have removed oppression, this is enough for me. I do not need any spoils of war." One of the great Arab ministers which The Prophet (PBUH) had seen not fighting in the battle had been caught as a prisoner so The Prophet (PBUH) asked that he be released. The Prophet (PBUH) told his companions that this man must be freed as he didn't have the intention to fight them and he had never bothered them in Mecca.

The Qur'an said to the Prophet, in Surah 8, verse 9, "[Remember] when you asked help of your Lord, and He answered you, 'Indeed, I will reinforce you with a thousand angels, following one another.'" Surah 3:124, however, says Allah assisted him with three thousand angels and not a thousand – "[Remember] when you said to the believers, 'Is it not sufficient for you that your Lord should reinforce you with three thousand angels sent down?'" God assisted Prophet Muhammad with a thousand angels and in the latter verse it said Allah would send you another three thousand if he wishes to. This meant that Allah had no limit to his blessing when his servants aimed to protect his message. The angels did not fight alongside the Prophet but they were there to give certainty to the minority, that in any land the minority can lead the majority if the majority represents injustice. The angels came to give certainty to the hearts of the believers.

Zaynab, one of the stepdaughters of The Prophet (PBUH), had a husband named Abil Aas ibn Rabi' who was in the opposition and was caught. She came to the Prophet and said, "O Prophet of God, my husband has been caught. Will you not release him? I am willing to give away the necklace my mother Khadijah gave me for my inheritance." The Prophet (PBUH) took the necklace and told the companions of how Zaynab wanted her husband freed and that she was willing to ransom the necklace to the treasury of the Islamic state. The companions agreed to this and her husband was freed. This is proof for the event of Fadak, because Ibn Abil Hadeed, in "Sharh Nahj al-Balagha," says he was having a discussion with his teacher Abu Ja'far al-Alawi, who told him of Zaynab after Badr. Ibn Abil Hadeed asked his teacher, "Where did she get this necklace from?" His teacher replied, "From her father and mother Khadijah as inheritance." Hence, Ibn Abil Hadeed answered, "If Zaynab was able to inherit from her parents, then how can Fatima al-Zahra not inherit Fadak from her parents?"

In conclusion, the Battle of Badr was seen as the greatest victory in Islam where 313 soldiers were united with each other. Thus the main message is that Muslims must remain united, and that Muslims must defend monotheistic religions as the Prophet did in Badr. Lastly, one should note the importance of the number 313. In the same way that the first battle of Islam was won with 313 soldiers, when the Messiah returns with Prophet Jesus, they will be victorious with an army of 313.

Lecture 18

The Case of the Pleading Woman

The verse in question, Chapter 58, verse 1, is seen as one of the most pivotal social verses in the Qur'an. This verse is used by many academics when discussing the reforms of the right of the wife in Islam. Pre-Islamic Arabia gave no rights to the female; psychologically, it was seen as a male chauvinistic society. It did not acknowledge the presence of the female in terms of the legal boundaries that should exist in a community of all the creations of God. On the contrary, the female was seen as a lower creation than the male. The majority of pre-Islamic females did not have any rights; psychologically, families were willing to reach a level where they would feel sad or angry at having baby daughters. Reading Surah 16 of the Qur'an, the verses come forward to say that their faces blacken with sadness when the news arrives of a female being born to them. In 16:58, it says, "And when one of them is informed of [the birth of] a female, his face becomes dark, and he suppresses grief."

Many people ask why there was so much dismay when the news of a baby girl being born reached the family; there are normally four reasons that are given. Firstly, they were ready to kill the female infant out of fear of poverty. They believed that the female required a certain amount of financial investment and that later on she would not be of any use to them. Therefore, in the Age of Ignorance, they would decide to bury the female infants alive. Ch. 17, verse 31, states, "And do not kill your children for fear of poverty. We provide for them and for you. Indeed, their killing is ever a great sin." This verse reminds the human being to never kill their baby out of fear of poverty as Allah will provide for them, and it is a greater sin to kill them. On the second level, economically the female was of no use to them in the markets of Arabia. So they concluded it was better to end her life rather than give her any position in the economics of Arabia. On the third level, the female would be of no use when it came to tribal wars. Although the irony is that, in the battle of Uhud, The Prophet (PBUH) was defended by a female. On the fourth level, the female was useless because she had to be married off to another family and the in-laws could be people they despised. They did not want the shame of their daughters going to in-laws they despised. Many of the great companions of The Prophet (PBUH) had parents whose lives changed upon the revelation of the verse in Surah 81, which says, "And when the girl [who was] buried alive is asked, for what sin she was killed?"

This verse is talking about how on the Day of Judgement the female will ask why she was buried alive and what sin she had committed. The companion Ammar ibn Yassir had parents who were affected when this verse was revealed. His mother Sumayya had lost two sisters before she was born. Even the second caliph himself mentions that in the Age of Ignorance he buried alive his baby female too. Women were not given any rights, particularly in the case of marriage. When The Prophet (PBUH) came with Islam, he sought to provide great exemplars of females who had come before. For example, the Qur'an named a whole chapter after Maryam. Then there is the discussion in the Qur'an of the lady named Aasiyah, who was married to Pharaoh yet died as a martyr in the cause of God. The Qur'an mentions females to give a source of guidance to the new converted females in Arabian society. The Prophet (PBUH) recognised the process of reforming the rights of females within Islam. This examination will be based on the following questions: What does verse 58:1 mean and what does the title of the chapter mean? What other marriages existed in Arabia which The Prophet (PBUH) sought to reform? What are the rights of the wife in Islam and why are they not being protected in communities today? What type of wife does one have when he honours her rights as Islam has requested?

The verse quoted in the intro comes from an interesting chapter in the Qur'an named "Surah al-Mujadilah," or "The Pleading Woman." Sometimes chapters in the Qur'an are named after Prophets, such as Yusuf, Muhammad, or Ibrahim. Some are named after great human beings such as

Luqman. Some are named after tribes, for example, Surah Bani Israel. But Chapter 58 is entitled "The Pleading Woman," which was revealed about a story on the rights of the wife. There was a lady named Khawla bint Tha'laba who was married to Aus ibn Samit. They had children together and were married for a long time. Aus was returning home one day when he told his wife he wanted her to satisfy his needs at that moment. Khawla replied it had been a difficult day and she needed an opportunity to cater to the house then she would cater to him. Aus stormed out of the house and said to her that she was to him "like the back of his mother," which in Arabia meant that he could no longer have conjugal relations with her. In other words, in the same way that he doesn't have conjugal relations with his mother, this applies to her too. When he had left, Khawla was in dismay. When he had returned, he told her it was a rash decision and he wanted to return to married relations with her. So, this lady went to The Prophet (PBUH) to ask him if Aus could return to her. At the same time, The Prophet (PBUH) received a revelation, Chapter 58, verses 1 and 2, "Certainly has Allah heard the speech of the one who pleads with you, [O Muhammad], concerning her husband and directs her complaint to Allah. And Allah hears your dialogue; indeed, Allah is Hearing and Seeing. Those who pronounce thihar among you [to separate] from their wives – they are not [consequently] their mothers. Their mothers are none but those who gave birth to them. And indeed, they are saying an objectionable statement and a falsehood. But indeed, Allah is Pardoning and Forgiving."

Allah (SWT), through this revelation, wanted The Prophet (PBUH) to know that there is no more conception of "Zihar" because someone cannot just simply state that there would be no more relations between the pair. When a man takes a lady from her household, he tells her household that he will take care of her. She is not a material to be let go in this way. The same lady, Khawla...When she was living in the time of Umar al-Khattab, she was once walking in the street when she saw Umar. She said to him, "Umar, now you are Khalifa of the Islamic state, do you remember when I used to call you Umri (my life). When you deal with the people, deal with them with justice." The person sanding next to Umar ibn Khattab looked at him, stunned. He said to him how can a lady speak to the caliph like this. Umar then spoke, "How can I reply to a lady that Allah (SWT) answered her supplication with a chapter in the Qur'an?"

Allah (SWT) not only said He heard the cry of the pleading woman, but also named the chapter after her. Thus, Islam wanted to show Arabia the great rights of women and that the belief of the first woman being born from the rib of the first man is false. Women are created from the same clay as man. Nor do Muslims believe that the female is the cause of sin. The same way people are heard when they are crying, Khawla was heard too in Chapter 58. This can provide solace for ladies who are going through harsh marriages or the many around the world who are going through domestic abuse. These women who think they have no way out…they can have faith through Surah 58, "Allah heard the speech of the one who pleads with you, [O Muhammad], concerning her husband and directs her complaint to Allah."

The story in Chapter 58 also highlights that the decisions we make about our relationships may be taken too quickly. Maybe sometimes we do not try to be more understanding or patience…because a School of Islam should not allow divorce to be that quick. A school of jurisprudence should now allow you to simply message your wife, "Divorce, divorce, divorce," and that means it has finished between the two. Allama al-Hilli, the great scholar was once involved in a debate on this issue, about not coming to a rash conclusion based on Chapter 58. The sultan of the time, in an argument with his wife, said, "Divorce, divorce, divorce," but a few days later he missed her. When he had wanted to revoke the divorce, they told the sultan that all the Schools in Islam did not allow it except for "Rawafidh," or "The Rejecters," meaning the School of Ahlulbayt.

Allama al-Hilli was called in. He took off his shoes, and everyone bowed down to the sultan, except Allama, who just said "Assalamu 'alaykum." The sultan said to Allama, "How dare you enter my palace, keep your shoes and not bow down to me?" Allama answered, "In the School of Rawafidh, we do not bow down to anyone except Allah (SWT). The reason why I brought my slippers was that once The Prophet (PBUH) left his slippers outside to find the Hanafi's had stolen them." The sultan asked the advisor as to whether this had been true or not, but the advisor told him that there were no Hanafi's at the time of The Prophet (PBUH). So the sultan said, "There were no Hanafi's in the time of The Prophet (PBUH)." Allama al-Hilli apologised, "I'm sorry. It was definitely the Maliki's." The advisor then explained to the sultan that the Maliki's had came a hundred and fifty years after The Prophet (PBUH). So Allama al-Hilli corrected himself, saying, "Sorry, I meant the Shafi'ees."

After this, the sultan told him they were not there at the time of The Prophet (PBUH). Allama corrected himself again. "The Hanbali's stole the slippers of The Prophet (PBUH)." The sultan again explained that they were not there during the time of The Prophet (PBUH). Allama informed the sultan, "If all those schools didn't exist in the time of The Prophet (PBUH), then can you tell me which School existed during the Prophet? The School of Ahlulbayt are not the "Rejecters," rather our school protected the Message of The Prophet (PBUH) from day one." Allama al-Hilli was able to revoke the divorce of the sultan, and this showed that the School of Ahlulbayt protected the rights of the wife.

When The Prophet (PBUH) initiated Islam, there were certain marriages which were abolished while others needed reform and other marriages continued. The marriages which continued from pre-Islamic Arabia was the mut'a marriage, or temporary marriage. Temporary marriage existed before Islam and continued in Islam, except that Islam provided strict conditions upon it. The type of marriage which needed reform was the marriage of the ex-wife of an adopted son. The Prophet (PBUH)'s adopted son Zaid was married to Zaynab, the cousin of The Prophet (PBUH). They ended up divorcing each other. The Prophet (PBUH) then married Zaynab with the intention of allowing this in Islam because in pre-Islamic Arabia this would not happen. The type of marriages which needed abolishing and changing was the marriage of swapping wives, "zawaj al-badal," which occurred in pre-Islamic Arabia. This concept may happen in some circles today, which suggests that there is more than one Age of Ignorance. The Prophet (PBUH) abolished this as this mentality is not accepted in Islam whatsoever. A second type of marriage which was abolished was when the husband would want a child from another family so he would ask his wife to be with another man for nine months. A third type of marriage which was abolished was "sheghar," when two men swap their sisters around for marriage. A fourth type of marriage was when someone's father was married to two wives. One was their natural mother, and if their father died, they placed a cloth on the second wife and she became their inheritance. This society of pre-Islamic Arabia gave no rights to the wife; The Prophet (PBUH) thus built the concept of marriage on the understanding of mercy and reciprocal love. As 30:21 says, "And of His signs is that He created for you from yourselves mates that you may find tranquillity in them; and He placed between you affection and mercy. Indeed in that are signs for a people who give thought."

The rights of the wife in Islam are numerous. The first right is that she can choose her potential partner. The media may attack the religion with their assumptions of "forced marriages," however this is not the case in Islam. Both sides have a choice as to who they marry. Parts of illiterate Arabian states do have forced marriages, but this is their culture and this has nothing to do with the religion. Some families look for attributes that are not supported by Islam, such as prestige and wealth, rather than looking for morals or spirituality. When the Prophet allowed his daughter to marry Amir al-Mu'mineen, he looked at the attributes of piety and morals. Many came to propose to Fatima such as Abdel Rahman ibn Auf, who said that Fatima didn't accept this. Note that the Prophet had no say. Likewise, Abu Bakr and Umar ibn Khattab said that Fatima did not accept their proposal. When Fatima was told about Ali ibn Abu Talib, she gave a silent approval. The female in Islam is allowed to decide for herself, and is allowed to engage in talking with the potential partner.

The second right of the female is the dowry in Islam. Greek society paid the dowry which was what the lady was worth. They looked at the female and decided what she was worth. The female was not honoured in terms of the dowry. The Arabs used to have a different type of dowry. The Arab father-in-law would look at the person coming to propose to his daughter. He would wait to see which was the offer of the highest dowry because the dowry in pre-Islamic society would go to the father. Hence, the Qur'an revealed 4:4, which says, "And give the women [upon marriage] their [bridal] gifts graciously. But if they give up willingly to you anything of it, then take it in satisfaction and ease."

Thus the dowry was asked to be given graciously and not with the idea that you are buying a wife. This dowry is a right of the economic dependence of the wife. There was a man who couldn't pay the dowry to his wife. He said to The Prophet (PBUH) that he knew it was her right but he couldn't afford it. The Prophet (PBUH) asked if he could teach the Qur'an and his wife accepted this. This is the simplicity of the dowry; it does not have to be sums of money which have been made obligatory in dowries today. The origin of the dowry is completely different to the dowry today, to the extent that in Los Angeles, a dowry was reported to reach one million dollars. The Prophet (PBUH) himself has said, "The worst of the wives is the one that asks for a high dowry."

The Prophet (PBUH) never put a limit on the dowry. Umar ibn Khattab once tried to put a limit to the dowry, but a lady reminded him that The Prophet (PBUH) himself didn't put a limit. Whereas communities today have dowries which are the highest but provides the futile of relationships.

Haroon al-Rashid's wife was Zabeeda, and he gave her a dowry of one million dinar, and he also gave her a dress that is narrated to originally have been from Abda bint Abdullah ibn Yazid ibn Mu'awiyah. Abda was married to Hisham ibn Abdel Malik. When Banu Abbas achieved victory over Banu Umayyah, they took all their belongings. So the Abbasids took the dress of Abda which required a hundred people to carry. This dress was the dowry for Zabeeda, but what did this extravagance bring them?

The third right of the female is physical satisfaction. In the same way the woman has to look beautiful for her husband, he also has to take care of his physical appearance. At the same time, the physical desires of the female have to be met. It is said that nine tenths of the desires are given to the female and nine tenths of the modesty is given to the female. But this is nine tenths of female modesty in public and nine tenths of desires with her husband. A'isha, the wife of the Prophet, was once speaking to The Prophet (PBUH) in one narration and asking him if he remembered Uthman ibn Meth'oon. There is a narration that says Imam Ali (AS) named his son after Uthman ibn Meth'oon because he never drank alcohol in the Age of Ignorance. A'isha said that Uthman's wife was the most beautiful wife in Arabia, but now her hair was dishevelled and she was not looking after herself anymore. But Uthman's wife replied that her husband fasted in the day and prayed in the night with no inclination to satisfy her desires as his wife. When The Prophet (PBUH) heard this, he went to Uthman and told him that this was not taqwa. Worship and one's wife should be compromised as the wife's right is to be satisfied.

The fourth right is the right of dialogue with the wife. The Prophet (PBUH) says, "The person who engages in dialogue with his wife is greater than being in my mosque in Medina for one whole night." It is important to engage in discussions with the wife, such as discussions affecting the future of the Ummah. Dialogue is one that interests both of them as a couple in order to seek to build intimacy. There were some characters in history that needed dialogue to maintain their relationships. Zuhair ibn al-Qayn…had it not been for his wife he would not have fought alongside Imam Hussein (AS). Originally he was an Uthmani who had come from hajj. When the message form the third Imam came to Zuhair, his wife wanted to know what it was about so she told him to talk to her. When she found out, she told Zuhair to go to the son of Fatima and be alongside him. This moment of dialogue between the husband and wife, allowed him to go to the battle and fight for the Imam and his Lord.

A further right is that akhlaaq, or morals, are maintained with the wife. There are many who return home to take out their anger and rudeness on their wife. In 4:19, Allah says, "And live with them in kindness." Sa'ad ibn Maath was the head of the Ansar in Medina. When he was being buried, his congregations was one of the biggest. People came to The Prophet (PBUH) and said, "Look at Sa'ad and the way he has lived his life. I'm sure Allah is honouring him." But The Prophet (PBUH) said that he may be punished in the grave because he would show the worst of akhlaaq to his wife and family. The public Sa'ad was building Islam, the private Sa'ad was a different character. In Islam you have to show your wife the best of akhlaaq because you have taken this responsibility, therefore you have to honour and respect this responsibility.

In history when a husband honours his wife's rights, and when a husband completes these rights, the wife will never forget her husband when he passes away. Nai'la al-Farafisa was the wife of Uthman ibn Affan, and she was married to him for seven years. Originally she was a Christian from Kufa. When Uthman got killed in Medina…when he was being struck, they chopped her finger. She sent the finger to Mu'awiyah in a latter saying, "My husband was being killed in Medina and you were sitting down. Now you tell Ali ibn Abu Talib that he is the cause. Ali ibn Abu Talib had sent Hassan and Hussein to protect him." Mu'awiyah loved Nai'la's beauty. He would constantly write letters to propose to her. Out of her frustration one day, she wrote back. In the letter she said, "What is it that you like about me?" Mu'awiyah said, "I like your white teeth. They are like pearls." So Nai'la took out one of her teeth and sent it back to him and wrote, "Do you think after Uthman ibn Affan, with the way he treated me, that I will come to you?" Even if you have certain differences with certain personalities the values still remain the same.

As a second example is Rabab, the wife of Imam Hussein (AS). The Imam honoured each of her rights. When Imam died on Ashura, all the other ladies on return to Medina had a ceiling to cover their homes. Rabab, however, said, "I do not want a roof because I cannot protect myself from the same rays of sunlight that burnt Imam Hussein's body on the tenth of Muharram." For a year after Karbala Rabab allowed the rays of sunlight to come upon her whilst she was in that house. Khadijah, the "Tahera" of the people of Mecca, sacrificed everything for Islam which led to The Prophet (PBUH)'s hadith, "This religion would not have been built were it not for the wealth of Khadijah and the sword of Amir al-Mu'mineen."

Three years of economic sanctions were placed upon her and The Prophet (PBUH). She had so much wealth yet she died without affording a kafan in her grave. A narration from Asmaa bint Umays says that she saw Khadijah crying before she passed away. When Asmaa said to her, "You are the four women of Paradise, alongside Aasiyah, Maryam, and Fatima, your daughter. Why are you crying?" Khadijah replied, "I am not crying from fear of death. I cry for my daughter Fatima. A lady always needs her mother to confide in before she gets married. Whereas my daughter will have no mother to confide with when she will get married."

When The Prophet (PBUH) came to cover Khadijah with her shroud, it wasn't big enough to cover all of her body. The narrations says that he supplicated to Allah, Khadijah has given everything in the way of Islam. She was the wealthiest of women, yet now she does not have a shroud to cover her fully. Ya Allah, I am your servant Muhammad and I ask you to help me." The narration says that Jibra'il came with five shrouds. He told him the first shroud was for Khadijah and the second was for him. Jibra'il continued to say that the last three were for his daughter Fatima, her husband Ali and their son Hassan. The Prophet (PBUH) then asked him where the shroud for Imam Hussein was. Jibra'il replied tyour Ummah will end up killing him. Fifty years after the Prophet died, Hussein lay on the ground, beheaded without a shroud.

Lecture 19

The Similarities Between Prophet Jesus (AS) and Imam Ali (AS)

The relationship between Jesus, son of Mary, and Ali, son of Abu Talib, is one of the most fascinating relationships in the religion of Islam. This relationship, studied in-depth, is beneficial to us as both personalities act as exemplars to millions around the world today and throughout Islamic history. The biographies of both of them may give you an understanding of how they have acted as beacons of lights and as role models. Many of the productions and pieces of literature created today are portraying their lives. Both these personalities have acted as forces of attraction and repulsion to groups of people in societies. This in-depth examination will look at the similarities and differences that arise, and will conclude by deciding whether they are more similar or more different.

Prophet Jesus (AS) is a both a contemporary and historical figure – contemporary in that his biography is looked at today, which can be seen in the films, Passion of the Christ and the Da Vinci Code. Jesus, the son of Mary, is seen as one of the arch-Prophets in Islam, alongside Prophets Nuh, Musa, Ibrahim and Muhammad (PBUH). Jesus was the Prophet that came with the message known as the Evangel, or in Arabic the "Injeel." When we look at the life of Prophet Jesus we see many parables mentioned in the Qur'an. These stories that are narrated by Muslims may show how important this figure is in Islam. Recently a book was published called, "Jesus through Shi'ite Narrations," which includes narrations mentioned by the Ahlulbayt. As an example, one of the narrations includes when Jesus asked Allah (SWT), "Ya Allah, who is the most thankful servant of yours?" Allah (SWT) replied, "O Prophet of God, at the end of your road, he will be the most thankful of my Blessings." Prophet Jesus went to the end of his road and found a lady seated on the ground. When the Prophet came near her, he found that she was blind; she had no hands and no feet. He wondered how this woman could be the most thankful when she had lost so much, so he asked her, "Are you thankful for what Allah has given you?" The old woman answered him, "Of course, how can I not thank the Lord who did not give me the feet which walks to what is forbidden or the hands which touch what is forbidden? He also gave me no eyes so I cannot see what is forbidden."

On another occasion within our narrations about Prophet Jesus (AS) there is a beautiful example of jealousy. The Prophet used to walk on water and when he would travel from city to city, he would take a companion who was short and firmly built. When Prophet Jesus was able to walk on water, his companion could not, so he would hold on to him to walk across. It is narrated that on one occasion this companion started thinking how he was able to walk on water equally like the Prophet, however he was not a Prophet himself. But as soon as he had finished this thought, he fell in the water; Jesus picked him up and asked him why this had happened. The companion replied, "A moment of jealousy entered me. I thought you were a Prophet who was able to walk across water and therefore so could I, but I am not a Prophet. So I thought I should reach Prophethood as well. So Allah made me lose this blessing I had." Jesus then told him, "Always ask forgiveness when you are jealous because it can affect you. The moment you lost your sincerity you drowned in the water."

Many of the narrations of Prophet Jesus (AS) come from Amir al-Mu'mineen. Whenever he began any narration about Prophet Jesus he would say, "Shall I tell you about my brother Jesus?" On one occasion the Imam was asked, "Which six was born not from a womb?" The Imam answered this, "The six not born from a womb are Prophet Adam and Eve, then the snake in the story of Prophet Musa, then the camel in the story of Prophet Salih. Then the sheep in the story of Prophet Ibrahim, then the birds in the story of Prophet Jesus." Prophet Jesus had the miraculous ability to create birds from clay. In another question to Ali ibn Abu Talib, he was asked, "Which five Prophets have special names?" Imam said, "The Prophets Joshua, Jonah, Khithr, Jesus and Muhammad. Joshua's original name was Thil Kif', Jonah's original name was Yunus, Khithr's original name was Hayqal, and Jesus' original name was al-Massih, or the Messiah. Lastly, Prophet Muhammad's original name was Ahmad."

Likewise, in another narration, Imam Ali told his companions about Prophet Jesus. "Jesus used to use a stone as his pillow and the moon as his lamp. He used to eat rough food; he never had a wife to try him or a son to grieve him or wealth to amaze him. He used to never mount a horse as he would walk on foot and he would always use his two hands." Jesus "us[ing] his two hands" means that he never had a servant in his life. Furthermore, Imam narrates that Prophet Jesus would say, "The dinar is the illness of the religion. The ulama (or scholars) are the doctors of the religion. So whenever you are ill, always go to the scholars unless they have been affected by the dinar, then leave them."

Today there are those who are more interested in wealth rather than the people, so here it is saying go towards people who are sincere and humble. Therefore, you find in many situations that Ali ibn Abu Talib would narrate parables of the life of Prophet Jesus. This is why The Prophet (PBUH) compared Imam Ali with Prophet Jesus, "O Ali, your position is the same as Prophet Jesus in the sense that there are a group of people who loved you so much that they gave you a position you do not have. Then there are a group of people who hated you so much that they were willing to curse you on the pulpit. The third group of people know you truly. They are your Shi'a." This meant that Prophet Jesus was like Ali also in that there were three groups of people that:

1. either made him so high as to be God
2. loathed him so much that they insulted him and his mother
3. were his true followers and disciples

These three groups of people will be examined in this analysis in regards to Prophet Jesus (AS) and Imam Ali (AS). With Prophet Jesus the first group of people were those who made him God and worshipped him as God, or named him "the son of God." This group of people exist today and name the trinity as "the Father, the Son and the Holy Spirit." While there are those who are from different sects, the idea is the same in that Jesus can raise the dead to make them alive, walk on water, heal the blind, cure the leper. Therefore they concluded that Jesus is God, and they also say that the father came down on earth in flesh as the son so that he may cure mankind from sin. They believe that mankind was born in sin because Prophet Adam (AS) sinned when he ate the forbidden apple, so his descendents are thus sinners until God sacrificed his son so that mankind can be forgiven of their sins. This is rejected in Islam because if everyone was born a sinner then why would they be accountable for something they did not do. Also, if we say that we were all born sinners, then what was Prophet Adam born as? This means that Adam must have born pure because he later sinned, therefore in the same way mankind are born pure, as only later on do they commit sins. In summary, the idea that Prophet Jesus was sacrificed for man's sins is a complete fallacy in Islam. The idea that Jesus is the son of God is also refuted because that would make Adam or Prophet Dawood his son. All of mankind are God's children as God is our Sustainer, Nourisher and Protector. When al-Ma'moon brought our eighth Imam in front of a Christian priest, the priest asked him what Imam's opinion was of Prophet Jesus and Muhammad. Imam Ridha replied, "Jesus is a Prophet of God, and we respect him highly. Muhammad is the highest of the Prophets of God and we respect him higher than any other Prophet. This is because Muhammad fasted and prayed more than any of them." The Christian priest was angered and said, "How can someone pray more than the Lord Jesus? He prayed throughout his life." The Imam replied, "If he is your Lord then tell me who was he praying to?"

Likewise when Jesus was crucified Christians believe that he said, "O my Lord, why hast thou forsaken me?" If Jesus was so willing to die for mankind's sins then why was he complaining to God? Also, if the belief is that God came down in flesh then who was he speaking to? If God has separated, which means that which is separated is limited and defined, that which is defined cannot be worshipped. The Lord is omnipotent, omniscient and everywhere whilst being closer to me than my jugular vein. In the incident of Mubahila, when the Christians of Najran asked Prophet Muhammad (PBUH) about his opinion of Jesus, the Prophet replied that Jesus is a prophet of God. When The Prophet (PBUH) then asked these Christians how they viewed Jesus, they answered that Jesus is the son of God. The Qur'an replied, "Indeed, the example of Jesus to Allah is like that of Adam. He created Him from dust; then He said to him, 'Be,' and he was." Likewise, Prophet Adam had no parents, which gives him more of a reason (and likeness) to be the son of God, however in Islam, Adam and Jesus are both Prophets with no fathers. This was the first group of people who elevated the position of Jesus to God.

The second group of people hated Jesus so much that they insulted him and slandered his mother. If someone believes that Allah's will can break the law of cause and effect, then they can believe that Mary was a virgin and that fire can be cold for Ibrahim. The children of Israel, however, did not understand Allah (SWT), and that if Allah wants something, He can say, "Be, and it is." The children of Israel slandered Mary so much that they called her an "illicit" woman and a woman of adultery. Even though they heard from Prophet Zakariya that Mary would fast in the day and worship in the night, they still insulted her. The Bible says that the children of Israel killed the Prophets and insulted the Virgin Mary. Similarly the children of Israel insulted Jesus, saying, "You are the king of the Jews?" It was the Jews who went to the Romans and informed them that Jesus believed he was the king, while overtaking the Roman Kingdom. They wished to crucify him, but the same Lord that made his virgin mother give birth to him is the same Lord that saved him from crucifixion. Surah 4, verse 157, says, "And [for] their saying, 'Indeed, we have killed the Messiah Jesus, the son of Mary, the messenger of Allah.' And they did not kill him, nor did they crucify him; but [another] was made to resemble him. And indeed, those who differ over it are in doubt about it. They have no knowledge of it except the following of assumption. And they did not kill him for certain." Islam believes that they did not kill him, nor did they crucify Jesus, rather they made him appear to look like one of them. The Romans went to collect Jesus, but Allah made the person who insulted Jesus resemble him.

The third group who have a relationship with Jesus are those who understand the true Jesus. There are a number of them in the Qur'an, the first being "Ashaab al-Ukhdud," who are mentioned in Surah 85. They were the Christians who were executed by the Jewish Empire. There was a holocaust at that time wherein the Jews would burn the Christians who believed that Jesus was a Prophet of God. Secondly, "Ashaab al-Kahaf" were the Christians who understood the position of Jesus and that he was a Prophet of God. Thirdly, in Surah Yaseen, Chapter 36, verse 14, it says, "We sent to them two, but they denied them, so We strengthened them with a third, and they said, 'Indeed, we are messengers to you.'" These two disciples were John and Jonah; Jesus had sent them to the land of Antioch, whereby the people rejected them, so Jesus then sent Simon. Eventually some of the people came towards their message. These disciples did not worship Jesus and used to say that he was the Prophet of God.

Likewise there were three groups with Imam Ali (AS), just like Prophet Jesus (AS). The first group were those who loved him so much that they called him God; they originally began in the time of Imam Ali and were headed by Abdullah ibn Wahab al-Sabai'. Some people confuse this character with a Yemeni Jew, and a concocted myth in the world of hadith. One only has to examine the background of his proponents such as Sayf ibn Umar in the world of hadith sciences. Some people believe that the Shi'a originated from Abdullah ibn Saba' and Yemeni Jews. They also say that Abdullah ibn Sabai' was someone who created friction between Imam Ali and A'isha as well as between Abu Dharr and Talha. But in reality there was no one named Abdullah ibn Sabai'. These traditions were created to fill in the gaps so that people would not ask questions about certain personalities. The School of Ahlulbayt completely disregard this myth of Abdullah ibn Saba' as the fact is that there was hatred towards Ali ibn Abu Talib. But Abdullah ibn Wahab al-Sabai' was the leader of the Khawarij. He came to Ali ibn Abu Talib one day and said, "We love you and worship you because you are God." Ali ibn Abu Talib said to him, "Repent to what you have just said." Abdullah ibn Wahab al-Sabai' persisted until Ali ibn Abu Talib ordered him to be burnt alive because anyone claiming that Ali is God has to be burnt alive in an Islamic state.

One day Amir al-Mu'mineen was on a camel when he saw people in Ramadan eating. Straightaway the Imam thought that they were either ill or travelling. When the Imam asked them why they were eating, they answered, "You are who you are. We worship you, O son of Abu Talib, and after this there is no need for any obligatory actions." Amir al-Mu'mineen put his cheek amongst the dust from the floor and spoke, "Allah (SWT) made me from this dust and he will return me to this dust. I am a servant of Allah and nothing more." A further group of people who worshipped Ali ibn Abu Talib were the Nusayri's. Muhammad ibn Nusayr was a person who worshipped Ali and was an extremist. In the time of the Abbasid Empire, after the Ghaybah, Nusayr would say he was one of the doors to Imam Mahdi. Musa ibn Furat was a secretary of the Banu Abbasids, and they allowed Muhammad ibn Nusayr to rise with his Nusayri followers.

A fourth group of people ignorantly worship Ali ibn Abu Talib whilst believing they should not pray as Ali died in prostration. This Imam was prostrating to Allah (SWT), so how can we, his followers, not do the same? Imam was praying to the Lord that nourished him and he used to always thank Allah for his blessings. When Mu'awiyah ibn Abu Sufyan used to not pray, they would call him a kafir, but when Ali ibn Abu Talib doesn't pray they call him Allah. The famous lines of poetry states, "I wonder about those who call Ali God, how great a God we have if Ali is his slave." This means that if you want to know great the Creator is, you look at the creation. Similarly, the group known as "al-Khaddabiya" used to say that Imam Ja'far al-Sadiq (AS) was God. When the sixth Imam found out about this group, the Imam would say, "May Allah curse these people. They are polytheists and infidels. I am a servant of Allah; I also will be raised on the Day of Judgement. We, the Ahlulbayt, are superior but we are still the servants of Allah. Whoever loves this group is our enemy and whoever hates them is our friend."

In another narration the sixth Imam was told that there were those who believe in "tafweedh," who say that Allah created the Ahlulbayt, and the Ahlulbayt then feed people to cause them to die. Imam said, "This has nothing to do with us. These people are cursed and polytheists. Allah is behind every action." Moreover, in the time of the ninth Imam there were a group of people that believed Imam Jawad (AS) was God. Hashim ibn Abi Hashim used to believe the ninth Imam was God. Likewise, with the tenth Imam, people such as Ali al-Qumi would believe he was God. The eleventh Imam was also believed to be God by people such as Ali al-Hasaka who would worship Imam Hassan al-Askari whilst believing there was no need to practice Islam. The followers of the Ahlulbayt always get attacked with misconceptions such as worshipping the Ahlulbayt, and the cause of this is through people like Ali al-Qumi and Ali al-Hasaka. There is also a misconception that the Shi'a believe that the Prophethood should have gone to Imam Ali (AS), and sometimes it is not their fault that they think like this. It is some extremists who may have caused this. Imam Ali used to say, "Our enemies are not those who disbelieve. Our enemy is our own ignorance."

The sixth Imam also says, according to the fiqh of Ahlulbayt, that "a person who believes that any of the Imams are God, those people are prohibited from being given an Islamic burial, a kafan, and a washing, or ghusul. You are not allowed to be in their jenaza/funeral, you cannot recommend them for marriage, you are allowed to inherit them but they cannot inherit you, and they die as infidels." Therefore, there were groups who made Ali ibn Abu Talib God. Then there was a group who hated Ali ibn Abu Talib, and would insult him from the minbar, starting from Mu'awiyah, and his son Yazid did the same. After this his family would continue this tradition; Marwan ibn al-Hakam, Abdel Malik ibn Marwan, Waleed ibn Yazid, Sulayman ibn Abdel Malik…they would insult Ali ibn Abu Talib, even though he was the son-in-law of The Prophet (PBUH) and the man who held the message of Islam. Abdullah ibn al-Kaw is someone who has been narrated by Imam al Bukhari…Abdullah ibn al-Kaw used to curse Ali ibn Abu Talib with his tasbeeh after Salat al-Fajr. Meanwhile, Imam Ali would finish his prayer and give his money to Abdullah from "al-bayt al-maal." Imam would treat people nicely even if they insulted him as he didn't fear the people, he feared Allah (SWT). Hatred towards Imam Ali (AS) came from Arab nationalism; he had killed their fathers at Badr and Uhud. For example, Mu'awiyah did not forget that Ali had killed his grandfather and uncles. The hatred was of such an extent, that when the people of Syria heard that Imam was dying, they questioned whether he even prayed to be hit whilst prostrating.

Lastly, there is a group who love Ali ibn Abu Talib as he should be loved rightfully. This group love the friends of Amir al-Mu'mineen and they hate his enemies. Night and day they pray to Allah (SWT) to withdraw his Mercy from the enemies of Ali. People like Abu Dharr al-Ghaffari, Ammar ibn Yasir, Malik, Salman, Miqdad, Jabir, and Hijr sacrificed their lives for Ali ibn Abu Talib. Abu Dharr al-Ghaffari died praising Ali ibn Abu Talib. The enemies of Islam made him die alone in a desert out of his love for Ali ibn Abu Talib. Until today, Ali ibn Abu Talib's followers are those who love him, honour him and take him as the true successor of The Prophet (PBUH).

Lecture 20

Imam Ali (AS) and his Concentration in Prayer

Imam Ali (AS) had many great attributes, and amongst the greatest of them was his concentration in prayer, or prayers. This attribute has been revered by many scholars and historians. As we know every act of worship requires an optimum amount of concentration because behind these acts there is an aim and benefit for the human being. Concentration requires the presence of the heart in an action and not only the presence of the tongue. Every act of worship needs optimum concentration in order to taste the true flavour of that worship, such as the hajj pilgrimage. If the hajj is simply a movement of "Labayk Allahuma Labayk," without engaging with the words, then the real meaning behind hajj is misunderstood. True concentration is when an attentiveness to the act allows you to taste the real fruit of that act. Likewise with fasting, if you do not concentrate when you fast then you will not taste the flavour of that fast. Concentrating in fasting is the awareness that your senses are liable to sin so you do not go towards it. Prayer is no different; a person can only taste the real flavour of prayer when they concentrate.

Many Muslims come forward today and admit that they cannot achieve high concentration in their prayers, thus prayer has become a chore. Many du'as consist of asking Allah (SWT) to raise us in our prayer. Surah 23, verses 1 and 2, says, "Certainly will the believers have succeeded. They who are during their prayer humbly submissive." This verse is from Surah al-Mu'minoon or "the Believers," and this is what we aim for. There are other chapters in the Qur'an entitled "al-Munafiqoon" and "al-Kafiroon" (the Hypocrites and the Disbelievers), which we do not aim to be. The first attribute that Allah (SWT) gives in the Chapter of the Believers is of those who "during their prayer [are] humbly submissive." Allah does not just mention the attribute of praying, rather he mentions those who are concentrating and are submissive. The du'a recited after Asr prayers states, "O Allah, I seek refuge from you from a prayer that doesn't raise me." This supplication focuses on a prayer which raises our position towards Allah. The Prophet (PBUH) used to always state, "Prayer is the Mi'raj of the Mu'min."

On the Night of Mi'raj the Holy Prophet (PBUH) went to the highest of the heavens and above. So when The Prophet (PBUH) said prayer is the same mi'raj, he meant that we are raised to the same station he sought to reach in our prayers. If we want to know how to reach these levels, we have to submit to it completely, so the scholars of spirituality divide the performers of prayer into four groups. They say that the first group are those who are negligent towards their prayer and make many mistakes in it. The second are those who Satan whispers in their ears throughout prayer so they do not concentrate. The third are those who strive to a level where they are able to overcome Satan for most of their prayer. The highest level is the fourth group who Satan does not come near at all. They see Allah before their prayer, during their prayer and after their prayer. The scholars said that the first group are punishable, the second are accountable, the third are striving and thus are not punished. The fourth group are Godly human beings on earth.

Therefore, in this examination of how Imam Ali (AS) achieved the highest concentration in his prayer, the title of this analysis refers to the techniques we can learn which Imam used to achieve concentration. If you begin these techniques, hopefully you can see improvements in your own prayer. The analysis involves the following questions: How important is our attitude when concentrating in prayer? How important is it that we know the benefits of prayer? How important are the timings of prayer and do they effect our concentration? What is the appetiser before prayer that the Ahlulbayt focused on, their Shi'a are lazy on, and Imam Ali was struck in? How should we stand in prayer and how does this affect our prayer? How important is it to recognise someone is responding to your words in prayer?

The first step of concentration in prayer concerns the person's attitude in approaching prayer. Psychologists have said that if a human being wants to complete a task 70% of completion depends on attitude and 30% depens on intellect. For example, if a genius approaches an examination with 70% intellect and 30% attitude they may do not as well as they perceived. The same applies to prayer, because the first step is to reflect on your attitude before you approach it. The mosque's "mihrab" is usually opposite us when we pray. The word mihrab comes from the word "harb," which means "war." This indicates that you entering a war with Satan. Thus, the attitude when approaching prayer means that you are ready for the battle with Satan. If your mind has wavered then you have been defeated by Satan. Amir al-Mu'mineen used to say, "There are three types of worshippers; there is one who worships God who fears of going to Hell, this is the worship of a slave. The one who worships God to attain heaven, this is the worshipper of a business man. Then there is the one who worships you so submissively that even if there is no heaven and hell, they recognise they are free through worship." The Qur'an then came and said there are two types of people who approach the prayer and never achieve concentration. The first of them is mentioned in Surah 4, verse 43: "O you who have believed, do not approach prayer while you are intoxicated."

The first group of people who cannot achieve concentration in prayer are those who are intoxicated. This could mean alcohol. Imam al-Nasaei used to state that Abdel-Rahman ibn Auf once led prayer in a state of intoxication so this verse was revealed about him. The second group who do not concentrate are those who are lazy. This is stated in 4:142 of the Qur'an: "Indeed, the hypocrites [think to] deceive Allah , but He is deceiving them. And when they stand for prayer, they stand lazily, showing [themselves to] the people and not remembering Allah except a little."

There are many who delay their prayer when they get home because they find themselves tired and lazy. Amir al-Mu'mineen, when he was struck in his prayer, said, "I have won, by the Lord of the Ka'aba." Imam said this because he became victorious against Satan in the "mihrab" of the mosque. Imam had two enemies at his last moments; Satan and his killer, Ibn Muljam. The Imam had the most perfect attitude when he approached prayer. He knew he was not distracted by Ibn Muljam as the people knew the only time he would not be distracted would be in prayer.

The second area of achieving concentration in prayer is the belief and understanding of the benefits of prayer. Psychologically, if you believe in the benefits of prayer then you can concentrate in prayer. When a non-Muslim asks you as a Muslim what are the benefits of prayer, the response is not that it is obligatory. The response is that it builds humility in an otherwise arrogant creation. Since a human being would not bow down to anyone, Allah wanted to remind the human that one day he had come from clay and one day he will return to clay. So, it is good that we prostrate to remind ourselves where we have come from in humiliation. Amir al-Mu'mineen used to say, "Mankind you came from a drop of semen and you leave as a piece of dust. You don't know when you came and you don't when you'll leave. So why do you walk around like you know everything?" There will be a day when no human can control the angel of death who will take your soul away. Amir al-Mu'mineen goes further and says in Nahj al-Balagha, "Look at the peacock. It is the most insecure animal. It stretches its feathers to look at them because it is insecure about its skinny legs." Anyone who is arrogant must be hiding something as they are insecure just like the peacock.

Likewise, prayer was introduced to bring humility to the human being. Our fourth Imam says, "If you knew how much reward you were receiving whilst you are in prostration, you would never lift your head from prostration." The Arabs could not understand the concept of prayer as they were so arrogant that they would say, "O Muhammad, how can our backsides be higher than our heads?" Thus the first benefit of prayer is that it makes us humble human beings. Secondly, another benefit of prayer is that it teaches us the discipline of time because punctuality is one of the greatest of attributes. Without punctuality the human is not successful in this life. 4:103 states, "And when you have completed the prayer, remember Allah standing, sitting, or [lying] on your sides. But when you become secure, re-establish [regular] prayer. Indeed, prayer has been decreed upon the believers a decree of specified times."

Prayers have been set at specific times for the believers. If one delays praying their prayer, they will not concentrate properly. Allah (SWT) wanted to test us to see if we have that much love for praying on time, then He will provide us with the light that allows us to remove Satan in order to concentrate. If we have an appointment with another creation of whom our life is in their hands, then we endeavour to reach their appointment. If I am willing to turn up on time for the creation, then how can we not be on time for the Creator? Our rizq, life, blessings and health is in fact within the hands of the Creator.

Sometimes other Schools in Islam assume that the School of Ahlulbayt do not pray properly as they do not separate their prayer, but instead combine their prayer. However, there is not a single Qur'anic verse which states prayer should be prayed via five periods of the day. The Qur'an mentions three periods in the day. 17:78 says, "Establish prayer at the decline of the sun [from its meridian] until the darkness of the night and [also] the Qur'an of dawn. Indeed, the recitation of dawn is ever witnessed." The verse focuses on three periods; likewise The Prophet (PBUH) used to pray combined prayer and at times used to also pray separated prayer. The School of Ahlulbayt believe that, like The Prophet (PBUH), there is no harm combining or separating. But given the fact that our school took the easy option, we should not abuse it and pray our three prayers late.

In addition, the prayer has an appetiser, just like in every act there is an appetiser. The Ahlulbayt gave us an appetiser that we do not use enough. Amir al-Mu'mineen himself died during this appetiser and not during Salat al-Fajr. One day a man came to the eleventh Imam and said to him, "I am one of your Shi'a." The Imam then told him, "A real Shi'a is one who prays fifty-one rukaats a day." Each prayer is prayed after Salat al-Nawafel, or the "Sunnah prayers." These are appetiser prayers to prepare you for the five prayer. Before Fajr two rukaats are prayed, before Dhuhr eight rukaats are prayed and before Asr eight rukaats. After Maghrib is four rukaats and after Isha one rukaat. Generally we pray seventeen rukaats of the five prayers, but if you add the Nawafel mentioned above and the Namaz-e Shab/Salat al-Layl, you get fifty-one rukaats. Thus if we pray seventeen rukaats, we cannot say we are Shi'a. We must say we are trying to be Shi'a because we are not doing the Nawafel. Sayyed Khomeini has a lovely line in his book, "O Brothers, have you heard the Hadith Qudsi from Allah which states, 'My servant seek nearness to me through the Nawafel until he attains my love for him. I become the eyes by which he sees and the ears by which he hears and the mouth by which he speaks. When he calls upon me, I answer him. When he asks me, I give him.'"

Allah (SWT) found the Nawafel so beloved to Him...because if a person prays the Nawafel before the prayer, then watch the difference in their prayer. Just like a main meal is enjoyed after appetisers, the main prayer is enjoyed through the Nawafel. The Prophet was also told by Allah, "And from the night time pray a few extra rukaats, as spiritual boosts for you, so I will raise you to the maqam mahmood." Maqam mahmood is the highest level The Prophet (PBUH) could reach; he would reach it through the Nawafel before the obligatory prayers. Imam Ali (AS) was struck in the Nawafel of Fajr which is what made him victorious. Abdel Rahman ibn Muljam reached the Imam as Salat al-Juma'a had not commenced. Everyone was praying the Nawafel so Ibn Muljam reached Imam quickly. It is as if Imam Ali's concentration comes from the Nawafel that he would pray before the obligatory set of prayers.

Our fourth Imam, in Risalat al-Huqooq, has a stunning line which says, "The right of prayer on you: You magnify Allah through your stillness and the bowing of your head." These are two key areas for concentration; those who move a lot will not focus on what they are saying and who they are standing before. Imam says Allah is magnified through our stillness; the creation surely can be still for five minutes for the Creator. Imam says to also magnify Allah through the bowing of the head, as if to stand in humiliation out of the aura of Allah that surrounds him. The Prophet (PBUH) used to say, "Pray every prayer as if it is your last prayer."

The final technique for concentration is the most important which is the belief that Allah is responding to your words in prayer. If you believe that Allah will respond to you then this allows you to speak in a way of passion and commitment. There are some who speak the words of prayer as if no one is listening to their words. Imam Ali gave us so many supplications to read while we are in prostration that must be said with passion and the belief that Allah will respond. For example, "Ya Lateef, irham abduka al-thaeef" must be said with passion and humiliation. This is translated as "O Glorious One, have Mercy on Your weak servant." Another example is "Ya Wali al-Aafiya, asaluka al-aafiya, aafiyat al-deen, wal-dunya wa alakhira." This is translated as "O Master of our health and goodness, we ask you for more health and goodness. The health and goodness of our religion of this world and the Hereafter." Imam used to also recite the following du'a knowing Allah would respond, "Ilahi, kifani izzan lian akuna laka abda, wa kifani fakhran an takuna li rabba. Ilahi, anta kama ahib, fajalni kama tuhib." This is translated as "O my Lord, it's enough of an honour that you are my lord, and its enough of an honour for me to be your servant. You are as I like, so make me as you like."

Many historians believe that Imam's greatest moments came in his prayer. Firstly, when it was asked of him, "O Ali, do you prefer to be in a mosque praying to Allah or do you prefer to be in heaven?" Imam answered, "I prefer to be in a mosque praying to Allah. In a mosque praying to Allah, Allah is pleased with me, whereas in heaven I am pleased with myself. " Secondly, when they narrate that an arrow from battle was stuck in his ankle, they asked the Prophet as to when they could take it out. The Prophet answered, "In Imam's prayer, as he does not listen to anyone else but His Lord when he is praying."

Thirdly, Imam gave his ring away in rukoo' and became Allah's "Wali" on earth. 5:55 states, "Verily, your Wali (Protector or Helper) is Allah, His Messenger, and the believers, those who perform al-salat (iqamat al-Salat), and give zakat, and they bow down (submit themselves with obedience to Allah in prayer)." When the poor man came in the mosque of Masjid al-Nabawi, Imam answered the poor man by handing him his ring in prayer. Some may find it difficult to understand how Imam answered him in his prayer while he was concentrating, however the Imam was in mi'raj which raised him towards Allah. Allah answers the du'a of any poor man, so the poor and the Mi'raj of the Believer connected in one moment. A poor man in the mosque of The Prophet (PBUH) asked God for some wealth, another servant of Allah was in the state of mi'raj in his prayer. Thus Allah answered the supplication of the poor through the servant, so Allah used the "waseela" of Ali ibn Abu Talib in his rukoo' to answer the poor. As soon as the Imam gave his ring, he was at one in servitude to Allah and servitude to his people. The verse states, "waliyukum" which means "your Wali" is one who gives charity whilst in prayer. This gives proof that Amir al-Mu'mineen is the Wali of Allah.

The fourth greatest moment of Imam and prayer was on Wednesday, the 19th of Ramadan, when he was struck by Ibn Muljam. The narrations state that he was either in the house of Um Kulthum or Sayyeda Zaynab. Sayyeda Zaynab narrates that on a night like this her father Amir al-Mu'mineen broke his iftar at her house, when she had prepared yoghurt and bread. Her father looked towards her and said, "When have you ever known me to have a meal this grand? Do you not know that anyone who has such a grand meal will have a prolonged Day of Judgement?" So Sayyeda Zaynab took some of the meal away. She narrates that her father pointed at his stomach and he said that he wanted to return to his Lord with a light stomach. She did not know what he meant, and throughout the night, the Imam would recite supplications, including his Munajat. The Imam would then walk towards the door and come back repeatedly; he would also look outside and say, "This is the night that The Prophet (PBUH) promised me. This is the night I ask Allah to congratulate me when He meets me." At that moment Sayyeda narrates that he asked for some water so that he may perform his wudhu'. The Imam explained to his daughter that he was scared because he saw The Prophet (PBUH) saying in a dream, "Come back to us." As he was leaving, the door got stuck, so he called to himself, "O man, do not be afraid of death. In this life you are either laughing or crying."

When the Imam left the house, the ducks began to make noises when they saw him as if they knew these were the final moments of Imam. When the Imam entered the mosque, he saw a man sleeping on his stomach and told him not to sleep this way as it was the sleep of Satan. This man was Abdel Rahman ibn Muljam. Imam walked towards his prayer and prayed the Nawafel of Fajr, then he entered his rukoo' and his sujood (prostration). Ibn Muljam came behind him and struck the Imam on his head, the same head that The Prophet (PBUH) would touch, and the head that Allah (SWT) allowed to be born in the Ka'aba. The Imam called out, "I have been victorious, by the Lord of the Ka'aba."

Lecture 21

Examining the Final Will of Imam Ali (AS)

The final will or "wasiya" of Amir al-Mu'mineen just before he passed away is one of the greatest documents in Islamic history and literature. It requires a thorough analysis for it is a document full of advice and wisdom. The aim here is to apply these principles in our lives, and therefore his wasiya must be studied by all Muslims. The will itself occupies a prominent position in Islamic thought and a prominent position around the world. Many governments encourage citizens to write a will as this will safeguard the future of that citizen and their relatives.

The word for will in Arabic is "wasiya," and Islam encourages wasiya to be written for a number of reasons. The first reason is legal, as Islam aims to cover five areas within a society – property, honour, intellect, life and religion. Every human has a certain amount of property or assets, and Islam teaches you how to look after these assets, while recognising that when we pass away the assets will have to be transferred. This encourages someone to write a wasiya, someone to execute the wasiya and someone who oversees the execution of the wasiya. Legally, the wasiya is found to be important as there are many non-Islamic states, therefore the wasiya must be stressed upon. If the wasiya is not written, a person's assets would be distributed according to the laws of the country that he or she lives in. In Islam two thirds of the assets are determined from what the Qur'an and Sunnah says, and one third is determined upon the person's discretion.

The second reason writing a will is so important in Islam is due to social reasons. This is because there is a great likelihood that families will not speak to each other when there hasn't been a will left behind. This causes misunderstanding as to the shares of the inheritance. Many times there may be a verbal will but not a written will. The third reason for the writing of a will is that it is spiritually important, as many of us die without performing acts of worship. For example, there are those who did not perform hajj, or those who have missed prayers. Thus if they state in their wills that they could not go to hajj, then they can allow someone else to perform it for them spiritually. In the Qur'an, Allah (SWT) makes it clear that the writing of a will is an obligatory act, thus it says in 2:180, "Prescribed for you when death approaches [any] one of you if he leaves wealth [is that he should make] a bequest for the parents and near relatives according to what is acceptable – a duty upon the righteous." The verse starts with "kutiba 'alaykum," or prescribed for you, and whenever Allah (SWT) mentions this in the Qur'an, this means that He has made it obligatory on you. For example, 2:183 says, "O you who have believed, decreed upon you is fasting as it was decreed upon those before you that you may become righteous." Allah (SWT) is saying that fasting has become obligatory on you. In 2:180, it says it "has been prescribed for you when death approaches one of you…" This doesn't mean that we know when we die. The verse is ensuring the will should be written before you pass away. Then the verse says, "if he leaves wealth." This can be relevant to any property, and "bequeath" means to leave to someone else.

Likewise in the world of hadith, the position of the will is made clear. Imam Ali (AS) has said, "Whoever dies without writing a wasiya, he will die as if he lived in the times of ignorance." And the hadith of The Prophet (PBUH) proceeds to say, "Whoever dies a death without knowing the Imam of his time will die as if he lived in the times of ignorance." Both these hadiths interlink as we will be asked about our will and our Imam on the Day of Judgement. As the Qur'an says in 17:71, "One day We shall call together all human beings with their (respective) Imams. Those who are given their record in their right hand will read it (with pleasure), and they will not be dealt with unjustly in the least." This means that man will be raised with their Imam; likewise Allah says that the People of Ignorance had no Imam, so those who do not know their Imam will be like those who were ignorant. Similarly, the People of Ignorance did not believe there was a Day of Judgement thus they had no understanding of the assets that they had and that the transferred assets will be questioned. In another hadith Imam Ali says, "Whoever dies and does not write his will, it means he lacks reasoning and humanity." Here the Imam is saying that it is not rational to think that you will die with your family left to deal with your affairs. Then the Imam says it shows a lack of humanity because this can lead to misinterpretations between family and relatives.

Imam also says, "There are two types of wills – al-wasiya al-ahdiya and al-wasiya al-tamleekiya." Al-wasiya al-ahdiya includes two subtypes – Allah's rights over us and fellow human beings rights over us. Allah's right over us includes acts of worship, for example going to hajj once in your lifetime. So al-wasiya al-ahdiya is when a person writes down what obligatory acts he has missed in order for this to be transferred to their family/relatives. Once a lady came to the Prophet telling him how her father passed away and did not perform hajj, would this mean they should perform it for him? The Prophet (PBUH) replied, "If your father had a loan, which he owed the people, the loan will have to be paid back. Allah's loan is greater, so hajj will have to be performed equally."

The second subtype of al-wasiya al-ahdiya is making up the people's rights on you. This includes situations where you owe someone money. This relates to an incident that happened with our sixth Imam. Just before Imam al-Sadiq (AS) passed away, his slave girl Saleema narrates that he called his companions, gave them seventy dinar and said, "Go and take it to my cousin Hassan." Both the companions and Saleema reminded the Imam how Hassan was someone who fought him. But the Imam persisted in saying that he owed him the seventy dinar. "Thus I do not want to be one of those who breaks the covenant with a relative," he said. Also, before Muslim ibn Aqeel was killed by Umar ibn Sa'ad, Muslim said, "There are three things I leave in my wasiya." Umar ibn Sa'ad wanted to stop him but Ibn Ziyad said he could finish what he was saying. So Muslim ibn Aqeel continued, "The first thing in my wasiya is that I owe someone some money (wasiya ahdiya), the second is that I would like an Islamic burial, and thirdly, tell Imam Hussein (AS) not to come here." Umar ibn Sa'ad declared that none will be given, but Ibn Ziyad said that the first one may be fulfilled as he respected his debt to someone else. However the other two will never be accomplished for him. Therefore the first wasiya is ahdiya, Allah's rights on us and the people's rights on us.

The second type of will is wasiya al-tamleekiya, and which is in areas that are mustahab, meaning areas that are recommended and not obligatory. For example, writing that you want your house to become an orphanage. This isn't obligatory but is recommended. Another area of a wasiya is offering advice to your family before you pass away. This can be anything such as reminding your family to stay attached to the religion. Before Amir al-Mu'mineen passed away he gave this last type of wasiya, which every Muslim is recommended to read and even memorise. As the famous saying goes, "The words of the leader are the leaders of words." Imam Ali's wasiya includes words that are useful to us today in contemporary society as he writes it so eloquently.

Imam Ali (AS) began the wasiya by saying, "This is the will of al-Abd lillah Amir al-Mu'mineen Ali ibn Abu Talib." Imam believed that the greatest achievement he attained in his life was that he became Abd-Ullah which means "the servant of Allah (SWT)." In Islam this is the highest position you can attain. This can be seen with what Allah (SWT) said to The Prophet (PBUH) on the Isra and Mi'raj. Allah said, "Glory be to the Lord who ascended his servant to the heavens." This meant that Allah gave his Prophet the greatest attribute which was being called "Abd" or "servant" of Allah, which led him to the heavens. It is like Allah is saying that The Prophet (PBUH)'s servitude was so perfect that his name is "Abdullah." This is why in our prayer we state, "I witness that Muhammad is his slave and his Messenger (Rasool)."

The first thing The Prophet (PBUH) achieved was to be called "abd," in the same way that Imam Ali (AS) opened his will with "Abdullah." Imam then informed his son Imam Hassan (AS), "O Hassan, on the lands of Najaf you will see a grave which has already been dug for me, it was dug by Prophet Nuh. On the grave, you will see the statement, 'This is the grave dug by Prophet Nuh for Abd al-Salih (the Pious Servant) Ali ibn Abu Talib.'" Many hadiths by Imam Ali stress that his honour is to be the servant of Allah. Or even the du'a that Imam Ali would recite, "O my Lord, it is enough of an honour that I am your servant, and it is enough of an honour that you are my Lord. You are as I like, so make me as you like." Further than this, in Imam Ali's whispered munajat, he says, "My Master, O my Master, you are the Master and I am the servant. Who is there for the servant except for the Master?" Imam Ali finds, through his servitude, that he is weak and humble before him, yet he finds his happiness through serving Allah (SWT). Imam additionally shows this when he says, "Ya Allah, I do not worship you as a servant out of fear of Hell because that is the servant of a slave nor do I worship you because I want heaven because that is the worship of a businessman. I worship you because of thanksgiving towards You. This is the worship of a free man." So when Imam began his wasiya, he wanted to show that the highest position one should reach is being the servant of Allah (SWT).

Then Imam continues by saying, "O my sons Hassan and Hussein, I advise you to be conscious of Allah and steadfast in your religion. Do not yearn for this world and do not be seduced by it. Do not resent anything you have missed in it." Imam states in another saying, "The world deceives someone other than me. I have divorced you three times." Imam here is not saying that he is not willing to live in this world; however he is saying that he only wants the pleasures from this world that will please Allah (SWT). The power of the world included the Khalafa, or the power of him being caliph. After The Prophet (PBUH), the right of Imam being caliph was taken from him, and during this Abu Sufyan came towards Imam. He said, "Ali, I have thousands of soldiers ready to fight those who took your leadership." But Imam replied, "Abu Sufyan, you are the one who fought The Prophet (PBUH), how can I trust you? I know you can give me the world, but I don't want this Khalafa. I want a Khalafa which Allah gave me on the day of Ghadeer." This meant that the world was in Imam's hands yet his philosophy is that one "should not yearn for this world nor be seduced by it. Do not resent anything you have missed."

When Umar ibn Khattab left a "shura" of six, he asked them to pick a leader amongst them. Eventually they had chosen Ali ibn Abu Talib, but they asked Imam if he would follow the Sunnah of The Prophet (PBUH) and Abu Bakr and Umar. Imam said that he would only follow the Sunnah of The Prophet (PBUH) which came from Allah (SWT), but had the Imam aimed for this world he would have taken this Khalafa. When they found the Imam to only believe in the Sunnah of The Prophet (PBUH), they rejected him for the Khalafa.

Subsequently, in the wasiya, the Imam says, "Fear Allah in relation to the orphans and attend to their nutrition. Do not forget to remember their interests in the middle of yours." After the Battle of Nahrawan, Imam Ali (AS) was walking back like an innocent human being; no one would know he was caliph when he walked. He saw a lady carrying water who boiled and stirred it, when he came close to her she told him, "I am unhappy with the world. May God curse Ali ibn Abu Talib. Ali takes my husband and brothers to war while my children are orphans and Ali comes back alive." Imam then asked her if he could help her. She then asked him to carry the bread and dough for her everyday. So Imam would then do this every morning in the heat. Imam did not care that she had abused him, he still feared Allah by caring for her orphans. One day her daughter saw the Imam and told her mother who this was. She ran towards the Imam and she cried towards the feet of the Imam, "O Ali ibn Abu Talib, forgive me. I did not know your behaviour was like this." The Imam went to the floor and answered, "I ask you to ask Allah to forgive me, just in case I have hurt you in any way."

Following this, the Imam says in the wasiya, "Fear Allah in relation to your prayers, they are the pillar of Islam and the best of deeds." The true followers of the Commander of Faithful are those who do not neglect their prayer or create excuses to pray late. Ali ibn Abu Talib's three great moments in his life came in prayer. The first was when the arrow was stuck in his ankle. When the companions asked The Prophet (PBUH) as to how they could cure this, the Prophet asked that they release while Imam was in prayer. So the companions took the arrow while the Imam was praying. When he had finished, he asked where the drops of blood had come from. The second greatest moment of Imam was when he was in ruku' and he was inspired by Allah to give his holy ring to the poor. When Allah then revealed verse 5:55, "Your guardian can be only Allah; and His messenger and those who believe, who establish worship and pay the poor rate, and bow down (in prayer)." The third great moment of Imam was when he was struck in his prayer by Ibn Muljam. Because his prayer was his pillar of the religion, when he had finished his prayer after being struck, he said, "I have been victorious by the Lord of the Ka'aba." Then the Imam told his sons that Ibn Muljam must be protected and given something to drink as he may be thirsty. Imam advises in his wasiya, "Fear Allah in relation to His House. Do not abandon it for this will abandon your dignity." The Imam had such a relation with the Ka'aba as he was the only person to be born within it, and the Ka'aba attested to him.

The Imam concluded his wasiya by saying, "Maintain communication and exchange opinions amongst yourselves. Beware of disunity and enmity." Unfortunately, many communities of the Shi'a today are not united. When the Imam finished the Battle of Jamal, in front of him was Talha, Zubair, Marwan ibn al-Hakam, Sa'eed ibn Aas and Abdullah ibn Zubair. Imam tried the hardest to unite with Talha and Zubair. He said to Talha, "O Abu Muhammad, me and you grew up with each other. How are we fighting each other?" Imam said this to ensure unity. Marwan ibn al-Hakam, Sa'eed ibn Aas and Abdullah ibn Zubair were the cause of the battle, nevertheless the Imam let them go when he had caught them. Even in the battle of Siffeen, he tried to foster unity. Mu'awiyah did not let water be given to the Imam and asked Amr ibn Aas whether they should give Imam water. Amr ibn Aas then admitted that the Imam himself would give them water if he was in their position. The Imam asked his companions to go get the water, which meant Mu'awiyah's army had no water. When the Imam heard of the opposition being thirsty, he asked his companions, to which they replied, "No, as they did not give us water earlier." However, Imam told them that the opposition can have the water. Imam even stopped enmity in a war. Imam said, "I cannot bear to see the horses of Mu'awiyah's army thirsty, let alone the soldiers." Everything the Imam said in his wasiya...he acted in the same way.

On the night of the twenty-first of Ramadan, the Imam read out his wasiya to those around him, which included Sayyeda Zaynab, Imam Hassan, Imam Hussein, Abu Fathlel Abbas, Muhammad ibn Hanafiya, Um Kulthum and others. Imam Ali (AS) read the following, "In the Name of Allah, the Beneficent, the Merciful. This is the will of Abdullah Amir al-Mu'mineen Ali ibn Abu Talib. I witness that there is no Allah but Allah and I witness that Muhammad is His servant and Messenger. My advice, O Hassan and Hussein, is to be conscious of Allah and steadfast of your religion. Do not yearn for this world nor should you be seduced by it. Do not resent anything you have missed in it. Proclaim the truth and work for the next world. Oppose the oppressor and support the oppressed. O my children, my relatives and my followers, my Shi'a who hear this message, I advise you to be conscious of Allah, to strengthen your ties and remove your differences, for The Prophet (PBUH) says, 'Reconciliation of your differences is greater than all fasting and prayer.' Fear Allah in relation to your prayers as it is the pillar of your religion and the greatest of your deeds. Fear Allah in relation to your fasting, for it protects you from Hellfire. Fear Allah in relation to your zakat for it cools Allah's Divine Anger. Fear Allah in relation to your neighbours for The Prophet (PBUH) recommended this so much that I thought they would share from the inheritance. Fear Allah in relation to the orphans, attend to their nutrition and do not forget their needs in the middle of yours. Fear Allah in the poor and needy, allow them to join you. Fear Allah in relation to the woman and the slave girls for The Prophet (PBUH) stressed on this. Fear Allah in relation to His House, and as long as you live do not abandon it, for if you abandon it, you abandon your dignity. Fear Allah in relation to your relatives, attend to them, and go visit them, for Allah will lighten your punishment on the Day of Judgement. Remain attached to the Qur'an; nobody should surpass you in being intent on it, or more sincere in implementing it. Persist in jihad with your money, your souls, and your tongue. O Children of Abdul Muttalab! Do not shed the blood of Muslims under the banner: The Imam has been assassinated! Only the assassin should be condemned to death. If I die of this stab of his, kill him with one similar stroke. Do not mutilate him! I have heard the Prophet, peace be upon him, say: 'Mutilate not even a rabid dog.'"

Lecture 22

Imam Ali (AS), the Voice of Human Justice

One of the greatest attributes of Amir al-Mu'mineen was his justice, an attribute which was manifested throughout his life, particularly in his four-and-a-half years as caliph. Although some scholars view the four-and-a-half years as being the most turbulent years in Islam, other scholars view it as the greatest four-and-a-half years in terms of any successor of The Prophet (PBUH). The Imam performed justice as proved by Muslims and non-Muslim analysts, who say that he established the most just government of Islamic history. This government can be taken today as an example of justice within its administration, governors and society as a whole.

Non-Muslims come forward and praise the justice of Imam throughout his Khalafa. George Jordac wrote a book entitled, "The Voice of Human Justice," which until today is seen as one of the greatest analyses of the Imam. Jordac was not from an Islamic background – he was a Lebanese Christian. When Jordac was asked about why he had written about Imam considering Imam was a Muslim, Jordac said, "Ali ibn Abu Talib is not just for the Muslim world, but he is for all of humanity." Jordac used to keep the sign above his door, "There is no youth but Ali and there is no sword but Thul Fiqar." Jordac explains how he was brought up on the principle that although Ali doesn't share the same religion as him, he was a man of justice. Jordac brings the character of Imam as a universal example, a status we should endeavour to encourage.

When all other leaders in history are examined, we do not look at their religion but rather their humanitarian principles are examined. For example, Gandhi is not viewed as a Hindu; rather he is examined on his stand for justice as he sought to remove injustice from his society. Or a character like Martin Luther King is not examined on the basis of being a Christian, rather he is looked upon by his stand against oppression, and he as well sought to bring justice to his society. When Che Guevara is analysed, you do not focus on his background, but rather what he stood for. Likewise, when Ali ibn Abu Talib is analysed, Muslims define him as a Muslim rather than a human being who had general humanitarian principles that are universal. Justice, knowledge, generosity and eloquence are universal principles which means they are not restricted to a certain religion. In 1997, Kofi Annan made a survey which he sent to all the countries, including Islamic ones, asking them what is the most just document that has ever been written by a human being. The result was Imam Ali's letter to Malik al-Ashtar. The Imam was revered by the United Nations. Imam was not just a Muslim leader but was a humanitarian who should be in the same books as the likes of Gandhi and Martin Luther King. Yet unfortunately there are many who do not know of the Imam. This brings us to our role here, which is not examining the justice of a Muslim caliph, rather it is to examine the justice of the greatest human being who implemented it after The Prophet (PBUH).

The examination of Ali ibn Abu Talib's justice answers three questions. Who instilled this justice in Ali ibn Abu Talib? Did Ali ibn Abu Talib administer justice only as a caliph? How did Imam Ali (AS) administer justice in the Islamic state in his four-and-a-half years as caliph? Firstly, a great personality in history always would have a great teacher who instilled those great qualities within them. Imam Ali (AS) was taught by The Prophet (PBUH) as he was born in the cradle of the Prophet, wherever the Prophet would go, Imam would follow. When The Prophet (PBUH) became the Prophet of God, the main philosophy behind his Prophethood was that he was the manifestation of Allah (SWT) on earth. One of Allah's attributes is that He is "The Just." Therefore the Prophet manifested this justice on earth. In the School of Ahlulbayt, the second "Usool al-Deen" after tawheed is 'adala, which is the belief that Allah is The Most Just. In other words, Allah's Justice is instilled in his Messenger, and this was a covenant instilled in the line of Prophet Ibrahim (AS). Surah 2:124 says, "And (remember) when his Lord tried Abraham with

(His) commands, and he fulfilled them, He said: 'Lo! I have appointed thee a leader for mankind.' (Abraham) said: 'And of my offspring (will there be leaders)?' He said: 'My covenant includeth not the unjust.'" Ibrahim asked Allah about his line following him, and Allah replied that none would be unjust.

When The Prophet (PBUH) came to Arabia, Imam would watch how he would instill justice. The Prophet instilled economic justice, such as women's rights to inherit and the right to have their dowry, which was not there before. Politically, The Prophet (PBUH) introduced justice through forming the "Constitution of Medina." This was a constitution between the Muslims with the Christians and the Jews. In this constitution, the Prophet established justice in that every Jew had a right to worship in their synagogue; every Christian had a right to worship in their church and the Muslims to worship in their mosques. If a Jew harms a Muslim, then he must be punished; if the Muslim harms the Jew, then they are to be punished. Imam would see how the Prophet would give the rights to the Jew, Muslim and Christian. The Prophet (PBUH) made it clear to the Imam that justice is achieved through sacrifice and honouring the trust of people who gave you the leadership. On the night of Hijra when The Prophet (PBUH) told the Imam to sleep in his bed, he also told him, "There is a trust of the people of Mecca…when you wake up after sleeping in the bed, ensure you give the people their trust back before coming."

When Imam stayed behind in Mecca, Hanthala ibn Abu Sufyan went to Umayr ibn Wael and made a deal with him. Hanthala asked Umayr if he could get some money out of Imam Ali (AS). He would give him his mother's necklace. He explained to him how Imam was remaining, and everyone believes in Muhammad's trust, so Imam would return everything. Umayr was asked to go tell the Imam that the Prophet owed them a hundred mithqal of gold and that he wanted it. When Umayr told the Imam this, the Imam was skeptical, so Umayr swore by the Ka'aba while touching it. The Imam then asked of his witnesses, to which Umayr replied his witnesses were Abu Jahal, Akrama, Uqba and Abu Sufyan. Imam then went to ask the witnesses individually who all gave different timings as to when The Prophet (PBUH) had taken the loan. Imam concluded that the Prophet doesn't owe them any money, and Umayr admitted that it had been a bribe from Hanthala. Thus, no one would mistrust the Prophet.

The Prophet (PBUH) ensured trust was available in the Islamic state with Muslims and non-Muslims alike. They would trust the Prophet so much that both parties would entrust their belongings to him. When The Prophet (PBUH) established social justice, after the Battle of Khaybar, Bilal was taking the women of the Jews past the dead bodies of their husbands. When Bilal reached The Prophet (PBUH), the Prophet asked him why he did that. The Prophet (PBUH) explained to Bilal that this was social injustice and may have oppressed them; although they were there enemies they must be respected. The Holy Prophet (PBUH) considered every aspect of justice and this was replicated and manifested by Imam Ali (AS).

The Imam was the fourth caliph, so throughout the twenty-five years between The Prophet (PBUH)'s passing away and his Khalafa he did not remain quiet about this injustice. The Prophet (PBUH) passed away in the eleventh year of Hijra and Imam became caliph in the thirty-sixth year of Hijra. Imam would speak out with reasoning, as Plato states, "A wise man has something to say whereas a fool has to say something." Imam Ali was a wise man when one day, when Umar ibn Khattab had been caliph, a lady came to Umar and said, "O Khalifa, I have committed adultery, punish me." Umar ibn Khattab asked his companions to bring the punishment so he may punish her, but Imam said, "Wait, you must ask her why she committed adultery." So when she was asked why she committed adultery, she answered, "I was living in an area of famine, I had nothing to eat. There was only one man who had some food and I was thirsty. I went to him, so I asked him if could have something to eat. The reply from him was that he would give me something after I satisfied his desires. I rejected this and left, but on the third day my eyes had sunken in their sockets. So I was compelled to commit adultery with him to allow me to survive." The Imam then told Umar to not punish her because in verse 5:3 it says, "But whoever is compelled by hunger, not inclining willfully to sin, then surely Allah is Forgiving, Merciful." Although the Imam was not the caliph at this time, he spoke out against injustice. It is also narrated that Umar ibn Khattab used to say,"If it wasn't for Ali ibn Abu Talib, I would have perished."

Further incidents include when Imam saw Marwan ibn al-Hakam giving Uthman ibn Affan bad advice, or when he saw Walid ibn Uqba drunk in Salat al-Fajr when he was governor of Kufa. Imam did not remain silent; rather he spoke out against these situations. Ali ibn Abu Talib advised Uthman to not walk with Marwan as he would make him commit injustices. Imam also asked Uthman to remove Walid as governor. Moreover, Imam Ali would tell his sons Hassan and Hussein to go and stand by the door of Uthman to give him water so that this would be just towards him. However, when the Imam became caliph, the companions of Uthman turned against him and accused him of killing Uthman. The Muslims carried out injustice against Amir al-Mu'mineen with this accusation, even though the Imam had helped Uthman. For four-and-a-half years of being caliph, the Imam was involved in three civil wars – Jamal, Siffeen and Nahrawan. Someone came to the Imam and said, "In the days of Abu Bakr, Umar and Uthman there were no wars, whereas you have had three wars." The Imam looked at him and said, "In their time they dealt with people like me, whereas in my time I deal with people like you." The Imam meant that the type of people in his Islamic state were those causing disunity, but the Imam's aim was to remove and eradicate injustice. This can be seen in his hadith when he was caliph, "If you give me the seven regions of the world and everything under the sky to disobey Allah and unjustly take away the husk of barley from an ant, I shall not do so. In my eyes this entire world is inferior to a leaf that may be pressed in the mouth of a locust." This shows that the Imam's main aim was to be just to the extent of not even removing a grain from an ant.

The Imam instilled justice in six different ways. The first way was justice with his family because the Imam practiced in his own home what he preached on the pulpit. Ali ibn Abu Talib saw the Prophet say once, "I do not just instill justice in the people; if my daughter Fatima were to steal, I would cut her hands." Fatima al-Zahra (AS) would never steal, yet this statement was given to show the people that this justice would be implemented to his family also.

Likewise, Ali ibn Abu Talib instilled justice with his family first; his brother Aqeel would come and visit the Imam. Imam said when Aqeel once came on his visits, "My son Hassan, go and get a cloak to cover your uncle, it might be a bit cold." They went to the roof of the house and they both had eaten. Aqeel asked the Imam, "Is this all the food? The 'bayt al-maal' is in your hands and you give me this dry food?" The Imam replied, "This is a blessing from Allah (SWT)." Then Aqeel admitted, "I'm in debt. I need 100,000 dirhams. Get this from the bayt al-maal." The Imam said, "As soon as the share of bayt al-maal comes to me, I will give it to you. But I cannot give you [a share that is not mine]." Aqeel insisted, "How can you not give bayt al-maal to your family when you are caliph?" The

Imam then took him to the market stalls, and asked him if they should go and break their boxes to get the money. Imam said, "This money belongs to the poor people of Kufa who go everyday to earn their living." Aqeel refused this, saying, "No, how can we take their money?" The Imam then informed him, "You are afraid of taking their money, but not scared of taking the bayt al-maal of all of the Muslims? Aqeel, I have another idea. Let's go to Heera town, we take our swords, find an individual, and take his money." Aqeel replied, "But we would have been stealing from that individual." The Imam asked him again as to why he had said this. "You have a problem stealing from one man, but not stealing from the whole nation?" Then Aqeel apologised and invited him for food. The day the Imam went he asked how Aqeel had made this if he had needed money. The Imam reminded him that the same heat coming from the iron rod near them will burn him on Judgement Day if he steals from bayt al-maal.

The Imam established justice even with his sister Fakhita. She was living in Mecca when the Imam was in Medina. Fakhita's husband was with the Quryash who were attacking The Prophet (PBUH). The Prophet had told Imam to stop injustice if he saw it in Mecca. Imam Ali (AS) saw his own sister protecting the kuffar of the Quraysh. The Imam entered his sister's house while his face had been covered. When Fakhita saw him she said, "Leave my house; do you not know who my brother is?" The Imam caught the Qurayshi people, and he revealed who he was to her. Thus the Imam removed injustice even if it was being committed by his own family member.

Additionally, the Imam removed injustices with his companions. Talha and Zubayr were Imam's companions; Zubayr was his first cousin but Talha was not as close as Imam had killed Talha's father and brothers at Badr. Zubayr had even defended Imam at Saqeefa and wanted to take his sword out. Talha and Zubayr did not say a word against the Imam when he was not caliph, but as soon as the Imam became caliph, they turned against him. When Imam became caliph, he changed some policies of Uthman, including giving everyone three dinars even if they were converts or originally Muslim. Talha and Zubayr came to Imam and said, "We need to see you." When they entered, the Imam blew out a candle that was on and lit another. Talha asked Imam why he had done this, to which Imam answered, "The first candle was bought from the money of the Muslims; you have come to me for personal affairs, so I must light the candle I bought with my own money." Talha and Zubayr would say to Imam, "We fought for this religion from the start with the Prophet. Why is our bayt al-maal equal to everyone else?" Imam reminded them, "If it is about this concept, then it was me who was with the Prophet from day one. If it's about who fought, I fought the most defending the Prophet and his religion. I take the same as you, even if I am the caliph."

Talha and Zubayr then asked if they could be governors of Basra and Kufa. But the Imam said he could not trust them. They then went to Mecca and assembled all the troops against Imam. They took with them thousands of soldiers, but the Imam did not fear justice. At the start of the battle the Imam reminded them of their friendship and brotherhood. The Imam only fought back after the third arrow of the opposition was released. Talha and Zubayr despised the Imam because of his justice; hence, thirteen thousand soldiers on Talha and Zubayr's side and five thousand on Imam's side died in the Battle of Jamal. The Imam would always spend the wealth of the Islamic state knowing he would be accountable for it.

The third group the Imam displayed justice to were his governors of Egypt, Kufa, Medina and Basra. He placed Uthman ibn Hunayf in Basra. One day Imam had heard of Uthman's dinner, which led to Letter 45 in Nahj al-Balagha. The Imam wrote to him, "Ibn Hunayf! I have received information that a person of Basra invited you to a dinner and you immediately accepted the invitation...the invitation of a person who invites big officers and rich people and from whose doors poor persons and hungry paupers are turned away rudely. Now look to your Imam. In this world he has satisfied himself with two old torn and coarse garments and two pieces of bread (one in the morning and one in the evening). I know that to adopt such a hard way of life is beyond you but at least try to be pious. I swear by Allah that from this world I have neither amassed gold nor have I gathered wealth and possessions nor have I changed these coarse and old garments of mine with even an ordinary raiment from your treasury. Verily, under the sky we had only Fadak as our personal property but we were deprived of it; it tempted them, and they took it by force, and we had to bear the wrench patiently and cheerfully. The best judge is the Lord Almighty."

Imam respect Ibn Hunayf, however he reminded him of his activities even if he was a governor. The Imam even goes on to say, "Shall I be satisfied simply because people call me 'Amir al-Mu'mineen' (the Leader of the Faithful Muslims)? Shall I not sympathise with the faithful Muslims in their calamities? Shall I not be their partner in their adversities? Shall I not be their fellow-sufferer? Shall I not set an example for them to patiently, courageously and virtuously bear privation?" The Imam wanted to taste what the fellow believers are going through to be equal to them.

The Imam's other governor of Medina, Sahal ibn Hunaif, wrote a letter to Sahal telling him how many people have left him and are going to Mu'awiyah. The Imam told him not to worry as they have forsaken the truth and have gone towards injustice. Again, the Imam sends a letter to Malik al-Ashtar, the same letter Kofi Annan had rewarded in 1997. The one line from that letter is on a plaque in the United Nations, "Know O Malik, that the Egyptians are of two categories; they are either your brothers in faith or your equals in humanity. Forgive them as you would want Allah to forgive you. Be merciful to them in the same way you would want Allah to be Merciful on you." In Egypt there were Muslims and Coptic Christians, hence the Imam wanted to allow justice for all.

The fourth area the Imam protected with his justice were the weak people. He would administer justice with the black people and with the women of the community. Similar to how the Prophet protected these two groups of people, the Imam did as well. Once a black youth came to Imam Ali (AS) and asked him to cut his fingers. The Imam asked why. The man told the Imam that he had stolen. The Imam informed him, "But there are nineteen conditions. This includes that you know the law, you are sane, and being in need." The Imam went through all the conditions and found that he had to administer the punishment. When they cut his fingers, this youth started walking in the markets; some of the Khawarij asked what evil man had done this to him. The man answered, "Do you know who cut my fingers? It was Imam al-Muttaqeen and Sayid al-Wasiyeen (Master of Successors). I am honoured the Imam cut my fingers. I would never allow anyone to administer justice on me but Ali ibn Abu Talib because he is just in everything he does." When Imam Hassan (AS) heard this, he took this youth to his father, and told him what had happened. Imam Ali brought his fingers and held them where they had been, and the hadith says that the man's fingers became attached miraculously.

In another hadith the oppressed women had nobody to go to except Imam. One day there was a lady called Sawda from the tribe of Hamadan; she had gone to Mu'awiyah to make a complaint. Mu'awiyah had heard about her from the Battle of Siffeen, when she used to write poetry for the soldiers to be motivated to fight for Ali. Sawda complained to Mu'awiyah against his governor Bisr who had been oppressing them. Mu'awiyah remarked, "I hope he oppresses you more. I do not care." Sawda turned to say, "May Allah have Mercy on that man who was buried whilst justice was buried with him. Look at the difference between you and Ali ibn Abu Talib. One day I had a complaint and he treated a woman justly. I informed him of his unjust governor and the Imam raised his hand to pray, "Ya Allah, forgive me if I have appointed an unjust governor. You know I do not wish to spread injustice." The Imam then began to cry. "You, Mu'awiyah, mock me whereas Ali opened his door for me." Mu'awiyah apologised and removed Bisr from the governorship. Therefore, the fourth group that Imam ensured justice for were the weaker people in society.

The fifth group of people the Imam carried out justice with were the non-Muslims in the Islamic state. He knew that they may be unjustly treated by the Muslims. One day Imam Ali was walking and saw a blind Christian begging on the ground. Imam turned to his companions to say, "Why is this man begging? What was he doing before this?" The companions answered saying that he used to work but now he was no use to them so he was left behind. Ali ibn Abu Talib sat down next to him and announced that he would not move until someone would help this man as they had only used him when he was strong and had eyesight. Eventually one of the companions came and decided to help the blind man. Imam's vision of justice and humanity was not narrow; it encompassed Muslim and non-Muslim alike.

Likewise, in the famous incident of when the Christian took him to court, the judge called him, "Abu Hassan," so the Imam asked that he be called instead, "Ali ibn Abu Talib." The Imam found it unfair that he would be called by his title whereas the Christian would be called by his name. When the judge found the Imam to have no witnesses he awarded the case to the Christian. The Christian looked at Imam and said, "This is a day where I have seen Allah's justice on earth. Look at me, I have taken the Khalifa to court. I am a Christian and you are a Muslim. A decision has gone against you and he says, 'The decision is yours. Keep what you have.'" This man then converted to Islam, and died alongside the Imam's army on the battlefield.

In every area, Ali ibn Abu Talib would establish justice; in the Battle of Nahrawan a beautiful incident emerges. The Imam was fighting one on one with the Khawarij. One of the soldiers came towards him, and the swords got stuck. Imam lifted his sword to find two swords in his reach. The soldier said, "I heard you never reject anyone if they ask you for anything. Give me my sword back." The Imam gave him his sword, but instead of continuing the man said he wanted to be one of his followers. The Imam answered, "Do not say you want to be one of my followers. Say you want to follow the justice of Allah wherever it goes."

In conclusion, there is a story that says that Mu'awiyah caught Adi ibn Hatim one day. Adi's father Hatim al-Taei was known for his generosity in Arabia. Mu'awiyah looked at him and said, "Adi, where are your sons Tarafa, Turaif and Taref?" Adi answered, "They died under the banner of Amir al-Mu'mineen, Ali ibn Abu Talib at Siffeen." Mu'awiyah concluded, "So Ali has done injustice to you? He takes your sons to war whereas Hassan and Hussein are still alive." Adi then said, "It's not him that has done injustice to me. I am unjust to him because I am alive. By God Ali ibn Abu Talib was the most far-sighted and strongest of men; he talked with righteousness and decided with clarity. He was an ocean of knowledge and wisdom. He loved the simple life and wore short clothes. He was a man who did not like the pomp of the world, but rather wanted the solitude of the night. He would scrutinize himself and have pity about the past. When he was with us, he was one of us. When we would ask him for something, he would give it to us. He would always say to us to come visit him; he would come sit next to us. He would like the honest and kind. He used to love the poor. Although he was humble, we were inspired when we sat with him. It's as if I see him now, his teeth like a string of pearls. The strong did not fear his injustice and the weak did not lose hope of his justice. I remember seeing him one dark night in his place of worship, he was crying like a person bitten by a snake, bereaving someone. That was Ali ibn Abu Talib. I miss Ali like a mother whose baby is beheaded in her lap. Does the world allow you to forget Ali ibn Abu Talib?"

Every one of Ali's lines was about administering justice. Some of the justice we saw, some were only revealed after he had passed away. When Hassan and Hussein buried their father, they were returning home and saw a man crying. When Imam Hassan (AS) approached this man, he found this man crying over a man who had come every night to feed him but hadn't come for the past three nights. Imam Hussein (AS) then realised who it had been and informed the man that it had been their father who had just passed away.

Lecture 23

Is the Qur'an the Word of God?: Arabic Linguistics

The analysis of the Qur'an being the word of God includes four stages, the first being predictions and prophecies. Then it involves scientific principles, historical accuracies and the final is the unique linguistic genre or the unique literary form of the Arabic of the Holy Qur'an. Every Prophet of God that came to his people with a miracle...this miracle would be better than the particular speciality that was prominent at the time. For example, Prophet Moses came with a miracle that was considered magical amongst the dominant magicians in the Egyptian province. The people's magic was only one which deceived the human eye, such as the sticks which deceived the people into thinking they were snakes when, depending on the heat, the sticks moved towards mercury. Whereas, when Prophet Moses (AS) came with the miracle, the stick literally turned into a snake, therefore his miracle was superior to the speciality of that era. This miracle would be a sign for a people of his time.

Likewise, Prophet Jesus (AS) had come with his miracle at a time in which medicine and healing was important. At this time, physicians were at their highest level. Allah (SWT) thus gave him a miracle which allowed him to cure the leper, the blind, and even raised the dead to make them alive. The Qur'an was revealed at a time when Arabia was flourishing in poetry, so it would prove to be miraculous as it showed a superior form of the Arabic language. It must be noted that the Qur'an is the only book that sets a challenge to mankind in its verses, so as to make the people contemplate its words originating from an essence of something much higher than any being.

Allah (SWT) sets forward two challenges in the Qur'an, the first being in Chapter 11, verse 13, "Or they say, 'He (Prophet Muhammad,(PBUH) forged it (the Holy Qur'an).' Say: 'Bring then ten forged surahs (chapters) like unto it, and call whomsoever you can, other than Allah (to your help), if you speak the truth!'" Nobody answered this challenge. Then Allah (SWT) revealed in Chapter 10, verse 38, "Or do they say, 'He forged it?' Say: 'Bring then a surah like unto it, and call (to your aid) anyone you can besides Allah, if it be ye speak the truth!'" These challenges by the Qur'an are so bold that not any other Holy Book has made them. The Qur'an was requesting challenges if they are truthful. But what was so unique about Arabic linguistics that made the people come towards Islam? What is so unique about the literary genre of the Qur'an? What is so unique about the literary content of the Qur'an? Why is it important that a Lord speaks not only in Arabic but with a legal system tied within it? What is the rational deduction through the Arabic language? Were there any Muslims or non-Muslims who have challenged the Qur'an and why did they fail from the time of the Messenger until 1999?

The first aspect as to why the Arabic of the Qur'an is miraculous is that the Qur'an has its own unique genre; it is able to explain a particular concept through the usage of rhetorical and cohesive features. A rhetorical feature is the art of using metaphors or assonance or rhetorical questions in a sentence to persuade someone about a concept. Assonance is the use of the same vowels being repeated but with different meanings. For example, in a metaphor in Chapter 7, verse 176, Allah talks of scholars who change what they say depending on who they are speaking to, and so Allah wanted to show that this scholar cannot rest, "And if We had pleased We would certainly have exalted him thereby; but he clung to the earth and followed his low desire, so his parable is as the parable of the dog; if you attack him, he lolls out his tongue, and if you leave him alone, he lolls out his tongue. This is the parable of the people who reject Our communications. Therefore, relate the narrative that they may reflect." The metaphor used describes the scholar without principals as being similar to a dog that keeps sticking its tongue out even if you bring something towards it or leave it. The dog only sticks its tongue out due to heat in its body; the scholar has so much heat in his body that he cannot rest in this world. A further rhetorical feature, assonance, is used in the Qur'an in Chapter 12, verse 84, "O my grief for Yusuf!," which translated in Arabic is "Ya asafaa ala Yusuf!" This sounds a lot better in Arabic as both words sound similar but have different meanings – one means "grief" and the other is "Yusuf" his name. But Allah brings both words together to make the language simpler to understand. A rhetorical question is also beautifully used in the Qur'an in Chapter 55, verse 60, "Is the reward for good [anything] but good?" Here, the Qur'an isn't asking for a response to the question, but for people to contemplate and comprehend a concept better.

The cohesive features in the Qur'an are ones which connect more than one concept in a sentence grammatically or lexically, for example, "lam, wa, and fa" are cohesive features. When the letter "waw" is used, it is not just used for its literal meaning of "and," but also for reasons such as incident, swearing by something, tafseer/explanation and so on. Chapter 5, verse 55, "Verily, your Wali (Protector or Helper) is Allah, His Messenger, and the believers, those who perform al-salat, and give zakat, and they bow down (submit themselves with obedience to Allah in prayer)." The "waw" in this verse is used as a cohesive feature, or for the incident purpose, which is that of when Imam Ali (AS) in prayer gave away his ring.

"Wa at-teeni, wa az-zaytoon" This verse uses the letter "waw" here to swear by Allah's creation. The Qur'an mixed the rhetorical and cohesive features in a manner that the Arabs had not seen before, and it further made these two features inseparable in every sentence. The Arabs, however, used cohesive features many times, and when it had come to rhetorical features, they used them on rare occasions. The Christian poet Louis Cheikho used to say that Arab poetry used to come up with many cohesive features while having very few rhetorical features. He then said that the only book which uses cohesive and rhetorical features in a way in which they are inseparable is the Qur'an. This is the first miracle of the Qur'an in relation to the Arabic.

The second miracle within the Arabic of the Qur'an is its unique literary form. All Arabic literature in pre-Islam is divided into prose and poetry, then prose is split into "straightforward speech," or "mursal," and "rhyming prose," or "saj'." Poetry in the Arabic language has sixteen patterns called al-bihar (which translates as waves in the sea). Poetry is classed as one of sixteen bihar, dependent on the number of syllables. For example, the bihar of "Kaamil" has a particular number of syllables. Thus any Arabic literature falls into mursal, saj' or a bihar. With the exception that is the Holy Qur'an, the Qur'an is not mursal/straightforward speech as there are numerous verses that are not straightforward and can rhyme. But at the same time, the Qur'an isn't just poetry, and isn't one of the bihar as the syllables are not always the same. For example, Surah Kawthar has syllables of 3, 3, and 4 in every verse. If the verses were all the same number of syllables, then it would be one of the bihar. The Qur'an, furthermore, isn't a form of saj' or rhyming prose as the Qur'an has its own saja'. Saj' alone has no fusion of poetic literature and prose, whereas the Qur'an mixes poetry and prose, i.e., one verse can consist of poetry and prose. For example, when Zulaykha found out that all the women were talking behind her back about her stalking Prophet Yusuf (AS), she replies to them in Chapter 12, from verse 31 onwards, using poetic literature then prose. This is not saj'. In verse 32, the beginning is in poetic literature, and then she speaks of herself in prose. Holy Qur'anic saj' is a fusion of poetic literature and prose.

Moreover, saj' has a concentrated number of rhetorical features (metaphors, assonance and rhetorical questions) whereas the Qur'an has an unlimited amount of rhetorical features. In addition, saj' always ends in rhyme, but the Qur'an doesn't always end in rhyme, thus a further reason for the Qur'an not to be saj'. For example, Surah Fil, or the Chapter of the Elephant – each line ends with a rhyme except for the last, which does not rhyme. Hence, it is not saj'. Hence, those who claimed the Qur'an was a mursal. This was proved to be wrong. Or those who came forward saying the Qur'an is bihar – this was denied too. Those presenting it as saj' were also denied as it blends poetic literature and prose.

The third argument on the miraculous nature of the Qur'an is the integration of a legal system being built. That is why, if anyone, after the challenge of the Qur'an, suggests a sentence of Arabic to contend with it will have to bring one coinciding with a legal system. When Allah (SWT) sent the Qur'an, it didn't just present the eloquence of the Arabic but also had certain fiqh behind which word is used where. For instance, with the words "ba'al" and "zawj," they both mean husband and are both used in the Qur'an. When Allah (SWT) uses the word "ba'al," it has connotations which are different from the word "zawj" in divorce. "Ba'al" refers to a husband that has a right of divorce over his wife; "zawj" refers to a wife who has a guardian who may have the authority in a matter of divorce.

When Allah (SWT) uses a word in Arabic, there is a word used for its legal connotations and another word for another connotation. Therefore, the Arabic in the Qur'an has its own unique linguistic genre coupled with its own jurisprudence system, which then brings us upon the rational deduction of the Arabic.

The Qur'an was written by an Arab as a non-Arab would not have that much knowledge of rhetorical features. Some argue that the Prophet may have written the Qur'an, however the language of hadith by the Prophet Muhammad (PBUH) is completely different from the language of the Qur'an. The Prophet is also an "ummi." He was not illiterate, but he was never formally taught how to read or write at a particular institution. He wasn't taught by a human but by Allah (SWT).

Some may also argue that the Qur'an had been written by any Arab. We reply that the best Arab poet at the time was Walid ibn Mugheera who mastered saj', mursal and the sixteen bihar. One day Walid heard the Qur'an being recited by the Prophet and was astonished how the Qur'an did not display the properties of the linguistic categories. Abu Jahal found Walid in a sense of confusion and Walid said to him, "Muhammad has something which is not in this world, it is out of this world. I'm mesmerised by this language, and it can't be Muhammad, as he had never been taught this." However, Abu Jahal advised him, "Walid, you would not be referred to as the greatest poet in Arabia if you admit Muhammad's words are superior." Walid here is put in a position where he was caught between being arrogant and humble; unfortunately he chose the former path. The Qur'an responded in Chapter 74, verses 18-25, "For he thought and he plotted; And woe to him! How he plotted! Yea, woe to him; how he plotted! Then he looked round; then he frowned and he scowled; then he turned back and was haughty; then said he: 'This is nothing but magic, derived from of old; this is noting but the word of a mortal.'" The Qur'an wanted to show, that if someone states that it is the words of a magician, they are indirectly stating it is superior to them. But Walid was so arrogant that even though he knew the Qur'an broke all the laws in Arabian literature, he still referred to it as the word of a mortal.

We find that until today the challenge of the Qur'an still stands, where a single chapter hasn't been brought forward. This Holy Book doesn't fall into Arabian literature; it is a mixture of rhetorical and cohesive features which are inseparable. There have been challenges from the time of the Prophet. Musailamah the Liar, for instance, used to state that he was a prophet himself just like Muhammad, but he was rejected as the Arabs would say to him that he had not come forward with a book like Muhammad. Musailamah responded with the idea that he could match the words of the Qur'an, and in response to the Chapter of the Elephant, he stated the following:

> "O, the elephant!
> What an elephant!
> And what makes you think of the elephant?
> It has a ropey tail and a long trunk.
> What of the trifles of our Lord's creation."

But the Arabs mocked this attempt as anyone could have simply put those words together describing an elephant. Truthfully, it was a poor attempt which any one could have come up with. After this, the renowned Iranian man of literature, Ibn al-Muqaffa', came forward with his challenge. He came up with, "In the name of the Compassionate, the Merciful Light." But this was not much different from the usual, "In the Name of Allah, the most Beneficent, the Most Merciful." A further challenge came from one of the greatest poets in history, Abu l'Ala al-Ma'ari, who was a blind poet in Syria. His attempt was the following: "I swear by the horse and the yellowish camel which lopes along al-Ruhayl." He defended this by saying he used "waw" thus a cohesive feature, rhetorical feature being a metaphor and a concept. But there is no concept in the statement. But when the Qur'an talks about, for example, the fly which steals something from you and you won't be able to catch it, it is providing a scientific principle in that the fly has an enzyme which breaks down the food outside its body. But with al-Ma'ari's statement about a horse and camel, no concept is being put forward except random Arabic words. The difference between the creation and the Creator is that the Creator not only masters the language but is able to place scientific principles within it. The creation can use a language without any principles being entailed.

The Baha'i Bab also imitated the Qur'an, however that failed. Yahya ibn Hakam al-Ghazal was a character that lived in the Andalus [Spain] who produced an attempt to imitate Chapter 112 in the Qur'an. On the way to doing so, he was overcome by fear and said he should not question the words of Allah (SWT). Recently, in 1999, there was a Christian group, who came forward with "al-Furqan" in an attempt to style it as the new Qur'an, however, this Furqan that they made contained words that either fell into the category of mursal, saj', or bihar, and failed to have a mix of cohesive and rhetorical features. Hence Allah (SWT), by creating this unique literature, wanted the Muslims to protect the Qur'an. No human can produce the same scripture, not even the prophets.hAllah (SWT) wanted us to be confident with this Book, and to remind those who question it with Chapter 10:38 – to bring a surah like it.

Unfortunately, there were characters in history that disrespected the Qur'an after the death of the Prophet of Allah, for instance, Mu'awiya ibn Sufyan. In the Battle of Siffeen, he stuck the Qur'an on the end of a spear in front of the Muslims. Muslims respect the Qur'an so much that it is never placed on the floor. How can one place it on the end of a spear? A second insult to the Qur'an is changing the meaning of the verses and who they were revealed about. For example, Surah 2, verse 207 says, "And there is the type of man who gives his life to earn the pleasure of Allah. And Allah is full of kindness to (His) devotees." This was revealed the night when Imam Ali (AS) slept in the bed of Prophet Muhammad (PBUH) on the night of Hijra, thus the sacrifice of his soul for the pleasure of Allah (SWT). When the Prophet had asked Ali ibn Abu Talib to do so, Imam replied, "If you are at peace then my soul is for your soul and my body is for your body." After saying this, Imam prostrated and repeated al-Hamdulillah three times. When the Prophet reached the mosque of Qiba before entering Medina, some people asked to enter Medina, however Prophet Muhammad (PBUH) said he would not enter until Ali ibn Abu Talib was by his side. When Imam reached Qiba, he was wounded so the Messenger ofhAllah (SWT) used his saliva to heal the wounds of Imam, in respect to Imam's sacrificial night. This verses' tafseer was unfortunately changed by Mu'awiya. Instead of it being about Ali, they changed its tafseer to being about Abdul Rahman ibn Muljam. Samara ibn Jundub was paid four hundred thousand dinars to change that hadith, and because Abdul Rahman had stricken Imam Ali with a sword, he had given his life tohAllah (SWT).

The third disrespect to the Holy Qur'an is that the people praised in it were oppressed and martyred; all our Imams were either poisoned or martyred. Let's not forget the tragedy of Karbala, where Imam Husain (AS) and his family were killed, leaving the women and children walking in chains to Sham. Imam Zain al-Abideen (AS) narrates that when he had entered Sham a man came to abuse him, Sayyeda Zaynab (SA), Sukayna, Ruqaya and Um Kulthum. The Imam asked the man if he had read the verse in Chapter 8:41 which states, "Know that whatever property you may gain, one fifth belongs to God, the Messenger, the kindred, the orphans, the needy and those who need money while on a journey. (This is the law) if you believe in God and what We revealed to Our Servant on the Day of Distinction when the armies confronted each other. God has power over all things." The Imam then stated, "Have you not read Surah 42:23? 'No reward do I ask of you for this except the love of those near of kin. And if any one earns any good, We shall give him an increase of good in respect thereof. For Allah is Oft-Forgiving, Most Ready to appreciate.' What of Chapter 33:33? 'Allah only desires to keep away the uncleanness from you, O People of the House! and to purify you a (thorough) purifying.' Do you know who these verses refer to?" The man replied no. The Imam then pointed at the women and the children and said, "These verses refer to us, the Ahlulbayt." The man then cried and asked for forgiveness.

The Prophet (PBUH), in a famous line states, "O people, I leave among you two weighty things that are important and must be followed. You will not go astray if you hold them tight. One is the book of Allah and the other is my progeny, my Ahlulbayt – for Allah, the Merciful, has informed me that these two shall never separate from each other until they reach me in heaven at the Pool of al-Kawthar." Only a few years after the Prophet had died, the people neglected this hadith. Arabic grammar was put into a profound systematic structure by Imam Ali (AS). Imam had taught Abu al-Aswad al-Du'ali how to structure the Arabic language. After the Prophet (PBUH) had died, those who were meant to protect the Qur'an, the Arabic language and the religion were completely oppressed.

Lecture 24

Is the Qur'an the Word of God?: Predictions & Prophecies

Chapter 30 of the Holy Qur'an occupies a prominent position within Islamic thought; it is entitled Surah al-Rum, which is translated as "the Romans," and is a chapter that requires in-depth examination. This is because it is a chapter that affects everyone, in which many lessons may be learnt and many examples may be derived. It is a chapter with a historical basis and a contemporary significance.

Many scholars have the opinion that the twenty-third night of Ramadan is "the night of power." When the Imams of Ahlulbayt were asked about which of the nights of Ramadan is the "night of power," they would give general as well as specific responses. Sometimes if someone was to ask the Imams, they would say that the night of power Ramadan is the night of nineteenth, twenty-first or twenty-third. On some occasions, they would specifically say the twenty-first or the twenty-third. On one occasion, someone came to Our Holy Prophet (PBUH) and said, "O Prophet of God, I cannot keep skipping one night and coming back for another when I have many camels and livestock. Can you inform me what night I should focus on?" The Holy Prophet (PBUH) replied, "The twenty-third night is the night of power." People usually ask why Allah (SWT) doesn't just let us know of the "night of power," but Allah (SWT) wants us to receive as many bounties as possible by us making every night as important as the other.

Amongst the actions which are to be performed on such a night is the recitation of three specific chapters of the Qur'an, as well as other actions which consist of supplications, asking for forgiveness and asking for repentance. The three chapters are are as follows: Surah al-Ankabut, Surah al-Dukhan and lastly, Surah al-Rum, the chapter we seek to examine. When examining these three chapters, Imam Al-Sadiq (AS) used to state, "I swear by God that whoever recites these three chapters will definitely enter paradise." The Imam here is making a statement that whoever lives by the principles of these chapters will be one who will receive paradise. This is why I would like to dissect one of these chapters, Surah al-Rum, which is underestimated and understudied. Unfortunately many Muslims recite the chapter without being aware of its importance, particularly in contemporary discussions. It is a chapter that is of the utmost importance when discussing whether or not the Qur'an is the word of God. Why does the chapter begin with "Alif, Lam, Mim?" What is the significance of these unconnected letters? How could you use this chapter to prove that the Qur'an is the word of God? What is the history of Islamic-Roman relations and how important is the Roman Empire when we discuss the Imam of Our Time?

The chapter begins with "Alif, Lam, Mim." Some chapters in the Qur'an begin with unconnected letters; they can either start with one letter, for example, "Qaf," two letters, such as "Ta Ha" three letters such as with al-Rum, "Alif, Lam, Mim" or even Surah Maryam which starts with five letters, "Kaf, Ha, Ya, Ayn, Saad" There are various opinions in Islamic thought as to what the intention of Allah (SWT) was in beginning some chapters with unconnected letters. One opinion by Allama Tabataba'i is that Allah (SWT) challenged the Arabs of the Quraysh to see if they could determine the hidden message behind these letters if they did not believe it was the word of God. Furthermore, Allah (SWT) was trying to say to the Arabs to use these letters to produce a chapter like the Qur'an. A second opinion states that when the Holy Prophet (PBUH) recited verses of the Holy Qur'an, the Arabs reached a stage of envy that led them to clap and jeer whenever he would recite a verse. It was as if they wanted to put their hands over their ears. Thus Surah 41, verse 26, states, "And the disbelievers said, 'Do not listen to this Qur'an and engulf it in noise. Perhaps you may be victorious this way.'" Thus Allah (SWT) wanted the Prophet to recite something unique that would grasp the Arab's attention by the recitation of these random letters which would be new to them.

In this way, the Arabs stopped the clapping and jeering. A third opinion states that these letters refer to the Qur'an, as in Surah al-Baqara you find a verse that says, "This is the Book [the Qur'an], whereof there is no doubt, a guidance to those who are pious." The letters are immediately followed by the statement about the Holy Qur'an, thus they refer to it. A fourth opinion suggests that these letters refer to the Holy Prophet (PBUH), such as "Ya Seen, I swear by the Holy Qur'an full of wisdom, most surely you are one of the Messengers."Most surely 'you' are the Messenger" refers to the Prophet, straight after the letters " Ya and Seen" and Yaseen is one of the names of the Prophet. A fifth opinion is that Allah (SWT) is abbreviating one of His attributes in the letters, such as "Aleem" the All-Knowledgeable; therefore Allah (SWT) abbreviates this in "Alif, Lam, Mim." These are the opinions regarding the letters, however the ultimate opinion belongs to Allah (SWT).

The verse continues in Surah al-Rum, verse 2, "The Romans have been defeated." This verse is the verse used to prove the Qur'an is the word of God, and it is the responsibility of Muslims worldwide to prove this argument justifiably. There are four ways to prove that the Qur'an is the word of God, and they are the Qur'an's predictions and prophecies, unique linguistic genre, scientific miracles, and lastly, the Qur'an's historical accuracies in contrast to other books which consist of mistakes. The first way will be conducted on the predictions and prophecies – if you want to prove that a book is the word of God it is logical to start with predictions of events before they actually occur. For example, if one looks at the Book of Isaiah or John in the Bible, there are prophecies in which Prophets tell you, "I will tell you about an event prior to it happening." This prophecy cannot be a calculated guess, nor can it be given by someone who manipulates an event. Surah al-Rum, the Chapter of the Romans, states "The Romans have been defeated in the lowest part of the earth, but they after their defeat shall be victorious within a few years."

In the year 613, the Romans had been completely annihilated by the Persians. The emperor Heraculus was the head of the Roman Empire, known as the "Byzantines," which were destroyed by the Persians under Kisra. The Persians were able to take the land of Antioch, the land of Syria, the land of Jerusalem, the land of Egypt, and the land of Armenia from the Romans. The Romans at the time were Christians and the Persians were fire-worshippers, thus those that believed in God were defeated by those that didn't. The Romans were defeated in such an embarrassing manner that they reached a stage whereby they had to melt their gold and silver in their churches in order to make money and support their army. However, the Qur'an stated that the Romans will be victorious after this defeat. In response to this verse, the polytheists of the Quraysh mocked the Qur'an. These polytheists didn't believe in the words of the Qur'an and were taking a stand similar to the Persians in that they didn't believe in God and they would be victorious against the Prophet like the Persians' defeated the Roman Christians.

When Heraculus regained his bravery he was able to retrieve Armenia, Nainawa and Jerusalem. When he had captured Jerusalem, he received the two things the Christians wanted the most, which was the church of the Holy Sepulchre and the Holy Cross. This allowed them to regain their pride. When the Qur'an had revealed this verse, the Romans had been destroyed, and the Qur'an had predicted this nine years prior to their victory ("within a few years" as the Holy Qur'an states). When the Holy Qur'an says, "in the lowest part of the earth," this was due to the Romans being defeated near the Dead Sea, which is 399 metres below sea level. This depicts the Qur'an's stature in scientific principles.

Likewise with Islam, the people of Quraysh attempted to defeat it from the start, with examples such as Abu Lahab, Abu Jahal, Waleed, 'Utba and Abu Sufyan. Thus Allah (SWT) wanted to reveal this chapter to say that you may have been defeated in the beginning, but persevere as the Romans were victorious later on. Islam shall be triumphant over the Quraysh as well. Ten years after this verse, Prophet Muhammed (PBUH) defeated the Quraysh at the Battle of Badr. This involved 950 soldiers against a mere 313. But the Muslims consisted of warriors such as Imam Ali (AS), al-Miqdad, Hamza ibn Abdul Muttalib, and Ubaid ibn Hareth. These people had witnessed the revelation of the verse in Surah al-Rum, and asked the Prophet (PBUH) what it had meant. To which the Prophet replied, "Wait and see. This is a prediction from Allah (SWT), and if Allah (SWT) wants to prove his words are true, He will make predictions, as some humans will not believe unless a prediction comes true." There are other predictions in the Qur'an similar to Surah al-Rum, such as Surah 111, "Perish the hands of the father of flame. His wealth and his children will not benefit him. He will enter a Fire full of flames."

As predicted by the Qur'an, Abu Lahab's money and children did not benefit him in the end. The Qur'an predicted these events years before

Abu Lahab's death, which occurred after Badr, and the Qur'an predicted this way before Badr. Abu Lahab did not go to the Battle of Badr as he hired someone to fight for him and he would pay him when this person would come back alive. One of the soldiers of the Battle of Badr had come back to Mecca. The soldier let Abu Lahab know that he saw the Muslims being victorious and unseen forces fighting alongside them. Someone seated next to Abu Lahab who was the servant of Abbas, the uncle of The Prophet (PBUH), replied, "Those were not unseen forces. They were angels." To which Abu Lahab replied, "So you believe in what Muhammad believes in?," whilst picking up a bar and hitting and torturing him. Abbas, or some narrations say his daughter-in law, stood up with another pole and started hitting Abu Lahab while he was striking the man. This brought about an injury to Abu Lahab's body which developed an infection, to the extent that no one would come near Abu Lahab – not even his sons 'Utba and 'Utaiba. The Qur'an states in Surah Lahab, "Destroyed were the hands of Abu Lahab. His wealth avails him not, neither what he had earned. Soon will he roast in a flaming fire along with his wife, that carrier of slanderous tales, and upon her neck shall be a rope of palm-fibre." When Abu Lahab heard this verse, he didn't believe it as he did not understand how his wealth and his family would depart him. Furthermore, Abu Lahab believed that he would never reach the hellfire that the Prophet (PBUH) spoke of. This was thus the second prophecy that the Qur'an made.

The third prophecy is about Waleed ibn al-Mugheera, who was a man that mocked The Prophet (PBUH) and Allah (SWT). The Qur'an predicted that Waleed would die in an embarrassing manner. Accordingly, Waleed died from a splinter in his foot. Waleed had too much pride to kneel down and take it out as he believed people should not see him come down to what he believed was a lower class region. In Chapter 74, the Qur'an revealed in verses 16- 17, "By no means! Surely he is inimical to Our messages. I will make a distressing punishment overtake him." Waleed's sons converted to Islam and left him, his wealth diminished and he died in a disgraceful manner just as the Qur'an prophesized.

A fourth prophecy involves verse 25:85 in the Qur'an, "Verily, He Who has given you, (O Muhammad), the Qur'an (ordered you to act on its laws and to preach it to others) will surely bring you back to the Ma'ad." Ma'ad means place of origin, and for the Prophet (PBUH), this is Mecca. When the Holy Prophet left Mecca he believed his return was precarious and unlikely. This was because of certain characters that were there such as

Abu Jahal, Abu Lahab, Abu Sufyan, Waleed, and 'Utba. However, these characters all died except for Abu Sufyan. Some companions did not think they would ever go back to Mecca to see their families and homes again. However this prophecy made by the Qur'an proved otherwise. When The Prophet (PBUH) finally entered Mecca, some companions offered to kill Abu Sufyan, however the Holy Prophet replied that he should be forgiven in the hope that he will come to the path of Islam.

The fifth prophecy is in 48:27, "Allah indeed showed His Messenger the true vision, one fully in accord with reality. If Allah so wills, you shall certainly enter the Inviolable Mosque in full security. You will shave your heads and cut your hair short, and do so without any fear. He knew what you did not know, and He granted you a victory near at hand, even before (the fulfilment of the vision)." When the people heard this verse, they didn't believe that they would return to Masjid al-Haram and shave their heads in hajj, as they had already performed two umrahs. Allah (SWT) wanted to promise the Muslims that they would return to their homelands as hajj pilgrims. During the Hudaibiyah treaty one of the companions looked at the Prophet (PBUH) in disbelief and remarked, "Today I question your prophethood, O Muhammad." The narrations state that the Prophet and his companions did perform a pilgrimage to Mecca, which was the Fairwell Hajj of The Prophet (PBUH). They entered with their heads shaved just as 48:27 stated.

Each of these prophecies indicates an understanding of the Qur'an. For example, Surah al-Rum was the basis of discussing the Qur'an being the word of God. A further question arises as to what kind of relationship the Romans and Muslims had. In history the relationship between the Romans and the Muslims had its ups and downs; for instance, the Battle of Mu'ta was a battle between the Muslims and the Romans. In the past The Prophet (PBUH), when he sent an ambassador to the Romans, the Romans would treat the ambassador well. However when he sent al-Harith ibn Umair, the Romans decided to execute al-Harith. This led to the battle of Mu'ta. The Muslim army was led by the Prophet's son Zaid, Ja'far ibn Abu Talib and Abdullah ibn Ruwaha. Ja'far ibn Abu Talib and Abdullah ibn Rawaha looked at Zaid and said that this is the day that they would achieve martyrdom in the way of Islam, even with the smaller mass we hold to the Romans. In this battle Ja'far lost both his arms and that is why he was given the title "Ja'far al-Tayyar," or Ja'far, the One Who Flies in Heaven. He is buried in Jordan where Muslims visit his mausoleum and remember his sacrifice for the Religion of Allah. His martyrdom bears resemblance to Abu Fathlel Abbas' martyrdom, of which Imam Ja'far al-Sadiq (AS) states, "Verily Abbas has a status in the presence of Allah that all the martyrs will envy on the Day of Judgement for he is like Ja'far ibn Abu Talib. Allah will replace his hands with wings."

Here the Romans defeated the Muslims, so The Prophet (PBUH) led an army towards the Battle of Tabuk whilst leaving Ali ibn Abu Talib in Medina. When they reached Tabuk they thought that the Romans were arrogant, having just achieved victory. However, the Romans didn't believe they had won the last battle and didn't even end up coming to Tabuk. The Prophet (PBUH) stayed in Tabuk for a short period whilst managing to bring some to the path of Islam and returned to Medina.

A further relationship with the Romans involves Imam al-Baqir (as Imam al-Baqir (AS) initiated Islamic coins). Prior to this, currency was taken care of by the Romans who were responsible for coins, while the Egyptians were responsible for paper. Roman coins would clearly state, "the Father, the Son and the Holy Spirit." The Egyptians, likewise, adopted the statement, "the Father, the Son and the Holy Spirit" on their paper. Abdel Malik ibn Marwan, the caliph at the time, questioned the Egyptians on this. The Egyptians believed that the Romans were in charge of the coins, thus they had to so that they would not lose the coins. Abdel Malik was in a predicament, and it was suggested to him to ask the son of Ali ibn Abu Talib, Imam Baqir (AS). The Imam therefore told Abdel Malik to start his own currency, with one side of the coin stating, "I swear that there is no God but Allah" and the other side saying, "I swear that Muhammad is the Messenger of God." The fifth Imam also told Abdel Malik to clearly state the year and place of when and where the coin was made. This meant that the Muslims were now able to create their own currency without using the Romans. In 1988 there was an exhibition in the British Museum on the history of coins. One display was of a coin which had the comment, "The first Islamic coin developed in the time of Abdel Malik ibn Marwan by Muhammad, son of Ali."

In addition, a significant aspect of the relationship between the Romans and Muslims is displayed by our twelfth Imam, whose ethnic origin is half Roman. Imam Mahdi's mother Nargis was a Roman princess. So when we read Surah al-Rum we are honouring Nargis, the mother of the Imam of Our Time. Beshr al-Ansari, a companion, narrates that Imam al-Hadi once came to him with a red pouch which had 220 gold dinars. Imam al-Hadi (AS) had instructed him to go to Baghdad where the Furat (Euphrates River) cuts in Baghdad and to observe a ship that will bring a mass of slave girls who were going to be sold. Imam goes on to tell him that one of the slave girls will be wearing a hijab, and whenever someone attempts to remove her hijab she won't allow this. Everyone there offered to buy her. When one offered 300 dinars, Nargis replied saying that even if he was to have all the clothing of King Sulayman she will not accept. Beshr al-Ansari narrates that this occurred in an accurate manner similar to Imam Hadi's account, and that he went in at this point with a letter to give her which was written in the Roman language. Imam also told Beshr that the man selling her will be Umar ibn Yazid and that he should approach him with 220 gold dinars. As soon as Nargis took the letter she embraced it, and Beshr said to her, "How can you kiss a letter when you do not know where it is from?" "Nobody knows the Family of Muhammad and their position, but let me tell you my story," she replied.

"My name is Malika, the daughter of Joshua, my father is the Caesar of Rome and I am from the descendents of the disciple, Simon of Jesus. At the age of 13 my father wanted me to marry my cousin. Whenever the guests came for the ceremony, the palace would tremble. This happened numerous times even with other suitors. One night I saw the Holy Prophet Muhammad (PBUH) in my dream with the Imams of Ahlulbayt as well as Prophet Jesus and Simon. The Holy Prophet asked for my hand; Simon looked at Jesus and accepted, identifying it as an honour. I knew this dream was a reality, however, I didn't see Imam al-Askari (AS). After 14 nights, I saw the lady of light, Fatima al-Zahra (AS), with Maryam al-Sideeqa, and Maryam was saying it was her honour, whilst Lady Fatima responded that Imam al-Askari (AS) would visit after Nargis becomes a member of our religion. I woke up immediately doing the Shahada, and after this I saw Imam al-Askari (AS) every night in my dream. My health deteriorated, and my father was torturing Muslims. He wanted to provide me with any care I requested but I requested that these Muslims be freed, to which he obliged. My health normalised, and in my dream Imam al-Askari made me aware of the war that would take place with the Romans to which I should escape, end up in a ship, be sold at the Furat and meet Beshr al-Ansari with the Roman-written letter." At this moment Beshr curiously asked, "Then how are you conversing in Arabic now?" "My father provided us with tutors of every language, as if Allah (SWT) has destined that I should learn this language of the Qur'an," Nargis stated. Truly she sets an essential example for us today, as all sayyeds do not have to marry a sayyeda in Islam.

In conclusion, I would like to reiterate that Rome has a central role in our religion – for instance with the mother of the Imam of our Time. We pray that Imam's reappearance may be hastened by Allah subhana wa ta'ala and that he may bring justice and dignity to the Muslims.

Lecture 25

Is the Qur'an the Word of God?: Scientific Principles I

In the first part of the analysis of whether or not the Qur'an is the word of God, predictions and prophecies were highlighted in that the prophet comes forward with events prior to their occurrence. A second angle into the analysis focuses on science in the Qur'an, defying the viewpoint that religion and science are incompatible. There are some who also hold an opinion that science and religion are independent of each other. This belief may have stemmed from characters that have not grown up in religious atmospheres. The Qur'an, however, agrees upon a sort of dialogue between scientists and religion. A religion cannot claim to be a religion of God unless it is willing to test different hypotheses in order for the religion to be able to understand the secrets of the heavens and the earth. Albert Einstein, the great physicist, has stated, "Religion without science is lame and science without religion is blind." This therefore means that science needs a conscience, which religion provides. Otherwise scientists could just blow up the planet with an atomic bomb and not regret it at all, i.e., the lack of a conscience.

The Qur'an is regarded by some as only a historical account which provides a set of historical parables. On the contrary, the Qur'an is in no way simply a historical book; the Qur'an is a holistic way of life, and it provides the human being with an understanding of the worlds of ethics, jurisprudence and science. All of these are intertwined within the Holy Qur'an. Whilst part of the Western world was in the Dark Ages, Islam was prospering. Scientific movements were flourishing in areas of the world such as Cairo, Kufa and Andalusia (Spain). Unfortunately, Western syllabuses that take into account the period of the Dark Ages, Islam however flourished and said this was the period of enlightenment. In later periods Western characters came about such as Galileo, Newton and Faraday. Islam, prior to these scientists, flourished scientifically, with the basis of its flourishing being the Qur'an and the Imams. There is a whole PhD discussing Imam al-Sadiq (AS) and his works at the University of Strasbourg in France and how many scientists learned from him. This PhD is entitled, "Ja'far ibn Muhammad, the Great Muslim Scientist and Philosopher." Crystallisation, evaporation, distillation, Pythagorean theory and the theory of the balance of nature were some of the studies carried out by Jabir Hayan and other students of Imam al-Sadiq (AS). For instance, these students discussed the significance of the element calcium before anyone else did.

The religion of Islam came about to convey the Qur'an with scientific discussions one thousand years prior to any one else discovering them, i.e., one thousand years after the revelation of the Qur'an all humans would be grateful for its scientific verses. Chapter 22 of the Holy Qur'an (The Pilgrimage), verse 73, says, "*O mankind, a parable has been set forth for you so listen and ponder carefully, that those whom you call on (the idols) beside GOD can never create a fly, even if they banded together to do so. Furthermore, if the fly steals anything from them, they cannot recover it; weak is the pursuer and the pursued.*" The Arabs, at the time of the revelation of this verse, did not appreciate the scientific miracle of the Qur'an whereas 1400 years later this verse is relative to us as it is telling us that if anyone was to question the Qur'an being the word of God then we can respond with this holy verse.

Why does Allah (SWT) use examples in the Qur'an and what is the aim of the examples? What is so miraculous about the fly in this example? Why does Allah (SWT) mention the fly to the Arabs in particular? What is the famous narrative about the fly which was discussed after The Prophet (PBUH) had died and is related to the event of Karbala? At the start of this verse it says that "a parable or an example was set forth to you so listen and ponder carefully." The Qur'an repeatedly mentions the words "parable" or "example" to explain a concept in a simplified manner. Examples are always illustrated by teachers of mathematics or even in presentations by speakers; they are used to facilitate the comprehension of a particular analogy that is being put forward. For instance, "example" is mentioned in Chapter 62 (Surah al-Jumaa), verse 5: "An example is with those who were entrusted with the Torah, but who subsequently failed, is as the example of a donkey who carries huge burdens of books. How bad are the people who deny the Ayat of Allah? And Allah guides not the people who are disbelievers." This verse was revealed about the children of Israel who carried the Torah on their backs without fulfilling its obligations so that their likeness or example is of the donkey that carries luggage. Allah (SWT) used an example to allow clear understanding of the analogy.

In regards to the importance of the Holy Book, Imam al-Sadiq (AS) has narrated, "An orphan is not one without a mother or father, an orphan is one without any literature." This signifies the importance of the knowledge in our books such as the Qur'an, Nahj al-Balagha, Saheefa Sajjadiya and so on. Another example where Allah (SWT) uses the word "example" is in Chapter 66 (al-Tahreem), verse 11: "God sets forth an example for those who believe — the wife of Pharaoh who said: My Lord, build for me with Thee a house in heaven, and save me from the Pharaoh and his doings, and save me from an unjust people." This was sent to let people know how sometimes if the husband is not religious, an excuse is always made to explain why you are not religious. Thus the Qur'an revealed the verse using Aasiyah wife of Pharaoh as an example. Aasiyah died on the religion of Allah and had a husband who was in no way religious. Therefore, this was another example the Qur'an that the used to explain a concept.

Imam Ali (AS), on the way back from the Battle of Siffeen, tells his son Imam Hassan (AS), "O my son, the heart of a youth is like a cultivated piece of land – whatever you throw on it, it accepts. Therefore I tried to mould your heart before it hardened in order that you were able to learn from my examples and place them in your life." Imam Ali (AS) here knew that the best relationship between a father and child is when the father uses his examples as a sign of wisdom. If a father just tells his child to not do something as it is haram – there will be no conclusion. However, if the father provides his child with an example of his own experience by using a concept then the child will understand and implement it more.

22:73 uses the fly as an example as the Arabs in particular hated flies. They held a belief that the fly was the worst of animals as it was weak, in contrast to the lion which is fearless. Also, the Arabs used to give the idols saffron as food, and flies used to always come and take the saffron which angered the Arabs. To which the Qur'an replied, "If the fly steals anything from them, they cannot recover it; weak is the pursuer and the pursued." This meant that the flies that the Arabs hated would be the cause of the fall of the idols that they worshipped. A fly is used by Allah (SWT) to humiliate the human being in order to remind us of our status. As the poetry by Abu 'Ala al-Ma'arri states, "Men think that they reach power and achieve happiness through power, but a lion ends its life eating from faeces while a fly ends its life eating from honey."

A further account in history about the lowly fly involves al-Mansoor al-Dawaneeqi sitting with the sixth Imam, Ja'far al-Sadiq (AS). Al-Mansoor was sitting with pride when a fly kept bothering him until he was prompted to ask the Imam, "Why did your Lord create the fly?" The Imam replied, "So that they humiliate the oppressors." A Fatimid caliph in Egypt used to be humiliated by the fly as well. Once at a celebration this caliph demanded that a poet recite some of his work. The poet was known as Ibn Hani al-Andalusi, and was one of the greatest poets in the Western world at the time. His poem flattered the caliph with such words as, "You are the one, the Qahaar that angels bow down to." These words affected the caliph's ego, and at the very same minute a fly approached the caliph. When the caliph attempted to catch the fly he fell off his throne. This was as though Allah (SWT) wanted to remind him that there is only One Qahaar who the angels bow down to and that is the All-Knowing Allah (SWT).

Verse 22:73 is revealed not only to say that flies humiliate idols, but even human beings such as caliphs can be humiliated by a fly. An anecdote is given by a scholar in Qum that when he was ready go for his summer leave his teacher requested that he stay behind as it could be the most important summer of his life. During the summer, the teacher gave lessons to him on the study of akhlaaq whilst allowing him to return to his hometown for only one week. The same night of his return back home, the people of his hometown knocked on his door asking questions such as, "How does human faeces taste?" The scholar was surprised at this question, and by the time the last person had come, he still replied, "At first it tastes sour, then sweet, then bitter." "Mawlana, how do you know this?," the person asked, astonished. So the scholar answered, "I look at the flies that approach faeces, who circulate at first, then go straight inside, then at the end the fly disappears." The scholar then noticed that he was calmer than he thought he would be as his teacher had taught him akhlaaq which allowed him to respond to the question by recalling the behaviour of flies.

In the second part of verse 22:73, Allah revealed, *"...if the fly steals anything from them, they cannot recover it."* This is a scientific miracle. Biology and veterinary studies prove that if a fly eats something it consists of enzymes that allow it to consume the food outside its body. These enzymes break food down outside the body before consuming it inside their bodies. This was to highlight that if a fly was to steal anything from the idols, the Qur'an asked the idol worshippers if their idols were able to create a fly. The Qur'an then says that if the idols cannot do this, then let them catch what the fly has stolen from them. On the other hand it is impossible for anyone to take a fly's food as they break down their food externally via substances which they possess, and the fly also has absorbers within its throat that allow its food to go straight inside the body after breakdown. Thus this verse, when it let the Arabs know that their idols could not catch the flies' stolen food, did not know that it had a scientific explanation. On the contrary, the Qur'an provided a scientific discovery which people began to comprehend only a thousand years later after Islam. This verse also imbues a sense of humiliation to human beings themselves, for if a human ever raises their ego they can just recite this verse to remind themselves of their status.

A further scientific influence of the fly involves Abu Hurayrah who in Sahih Bukhari narrates, "When a fly falls into tea, take it out and dip it in again because one wing is a bacteria and the other wing is the antidote." This hadith has also been at the centre of a recent aim to disprove Abu Hurayrah's hadith by a pharmaceutical company in Germany. The investigators bought a fly, and analysed the wings in their biological breeding farms. They found that one wing is truly a bacteria and the other was an antidote. Since then the biological breeders have used the latter wing as an antibiotic in order to help the human immune system in diseases such as AIDS. They have formulated this antibiotic as a tablet which sells at 5000 dollars today. Therefore, there is a probability that Abu Hurayrah may be right. In summary, the 22:73 verse was proving that the Qur'an was the word of God by providing mankind with a scientific discovery a thousand years before the Western world discovered it.

The Ahlulbayt (SA) narrated a number of hadith on the "thubaab," or the fly. One of these narrations takes place when the Prophet (PBUH) gave a wasiya, or recommendation, to Abu Dharr al-Ghafari. "The believer looks at [his] sin like a boulder which has fallen on him whereas an unbeliever looks at [his] sin like a fly on their nose." This means that a believer feels the weight of the world on their shoulders when committing a sin, like in the station of nafs al-lawaama, the station of a soul that feels self-guilt. An unbeliever feels like the sin is a fly on their nose, like humans who, when a fly comes close, simply brush it off. This allows the human being to reach the station of nafs al-amaara, meaning committing sin is a norm. If your soul allows you to commit a sin, know that you are slowly going upon the path of an unbeliever. A second hadith in Sahih Bukhari is narrated by Abdullah ibn Umar ibn Khattab where someone from Iraq had come to him and asked, "O Abdullah, are we allowed to kill a fly?" "It is interesting that the people of Iraq are wondering about the permissibility of killing a fly when they killed the grandson of the Prophet (PBUH)," he replied.

It is surprising for Abdullah ibn Umar to say this since he did not stand alongside Imam Hussein (AS). He stayed in his home rather than aiding the Imam in Karbala. However this stayed with him and he regretted it later on. Abdullah thus in his response wanted to let the people know how they were worried about a small fly but they did not worry about killing the grandson of the Prophet. Umar ibn Saad himself used to be afraid of stepping on flies, so he used to wear slippers that contained spikes at the heel, yet he still allowed his horsemen to trample on the body of our beloved Imam Hussein (AS). Abdullah ibn Umar was able to still help Mokhtar al-Thaqafi as he was his in-law, so when Mokhtar was in prison he promised he would avenge the killing of Imam Hussein when he would flee. When Mokhtar caught ten of the soldiers in Umar ibn Saad's army, he had asked them what crime they committed in Karbala. They replied that they were the horsemen that were sent by Umar ibn Saad to trample on the bodies, including our Imam's body.

Lecture 26

Is the Qur'an the Word of God?: Scientific Principles II

In the first part of the analysis, the fly was looked at in order to stress the scientific principles in the Qur'an. The Qur'an also gives examples with the spider, and thereafter is followed by the mosquito. The verse which this analysis will look upon now is the verse discussing the position of the mosquito (in Chapter 2, verse 26). This verse states, "Indeed, Allah is not timid to present an example – that of a female mosquito or what is smaller than it. And those who have believed know that it is the truth from their Lord. But as for those who disbelieve, they say, 'What did Allah intend by this as an example?' He misleads many thereby and guides many thereby. And He misleads not except the defiantly disobedient." In particular Allah (SWT) focuses on the female mosquito here, rather than discussing the male mosquito. The question then arises, why is Allah (SWT) always so concerned about discussing small insects and animals?

Allah (SWT) always gives parables about mosquitoes so that He can allow us to reflect, and secondly to show humility – the latter because human beings tend to feel that that which they are physically greater than they deserve to be arrogant towards. Likewise human beings portray this arrogance towards other creations of Allah (SWT). Some places in the world do not take care about animals or even plants. When Allah (SWT) discussed the fly, then spiders, then the mosquito…He wanted to foster the attribute of respect in human beings, for the more you respect His creation, the more you will respect the Creator. The means with which to best respect God is by showing respect to what God has created. The Western world displays a greater humility than the Eastern world, as they respect animals, and the animals that are pets in the Western world are usually in neglect in the Eastern world.

The Qur'an usually states that the servants of Allah (SWT) walk and talk on earth in a humble state. The servants of Allah (SWT) speak and listen with humility. Humbleness is one of the greatest traits for a human to have. If one studies the greats in history one finds that they were only successful due to their humility. Prophet Jesus (AS) was once seated with his disciples and began to wash their feet. One of the disciples said, astonished, "O Prophet of God, what are you doing?" Prophet Jesus replied with the beautiful line – "Plants grow on soft land, not on mountainous terrain." This response by Jesus means that plants are only able to grow somewhere where it is soft and not hard. Likewise if you want to invite someone to your religion, they will only come towards the religion if you are soft-hearted with them.

When Bilal al-Habashi had come to recite the athaan (call of prayer) for Prophet Muhammad (PBUH), people would come to Bilal and say, "O Bilal, you have surely achieved the highest position as the mu'ethin of the Prophet (PBUH)." Bilal replied, "Yesterday I was an Abyssinian slave and nothing more. Whatever positions you want to put me in, I remain the same person as I was. One day I was a slave and now I am the slave of Allah (SWT)." Thus, when God mentions insects in the Qur'an, it is a reminder for human beings to be aware of arrogance and to remain humble on earth because something as small as an insect can have a devastating effect on your life.

Chapter 2, verse 26, is another verse that sets forth an example using an insect. It presents the importance of the female mosquito, which can be used to prove the Qur'an are the true words of Allah (SWT). Why is it that in Islam we stress God before scientific principles? Why did Allah say He "is not timid to present an example – even that of a mosquito?" Were there people making fun of the Qur'an? Why did the Qur'an mention the female mosquito and what is so special about its creation? Were there any other female animals Allah mentions in the Qur'an which were scientific miracles as well? How does Amir al-Mu'mineen talk about the mosquito in Nahj al-Balagha? What powerful message does he give us about the mosquito which many people do not understand until today? Why do the Ahlulbayt (AS) mention the wings of the mosquito when talking about the tragedy of Karbala?

Regarding the first aspect, people always ask Muslims why they mention God in any scientific discussion as the principle of God is a delusion. Modern day atheists such as Dawkins, Hitchens, Harris and Dennett differ from past atheists such as Hume in that modern day arguments are less academic and more spiteful. Modern day attacks against religion target sexual abuse and wars, however these arguments are pointless and can even be used against them. Atheists tend to question Muslims on God in the equation of science; they say that the big bang is what initiated the world and not God. In metaphysics, however, for the universe to exist it has to have a beginning and everything that has a beginning has to have a cause. If one constantly goes back in an infinite regression towards the first cause, however much you go back, this will result in infinity to some and in Allah (SWT) for Muslims. Even if the initiation involved a chemical reaction, what was the cause of this reaction? As Muslims, we believe that firstly the argument always goes back to the universe and this universe, to exist, must have a cause. There must be a necessary existence as our existence is only a possibility, so Allah is necessary as the first cause.

We also take account of Allah (SWT) in our discussion of science with issues such as animals. In Islam, when one observes an animal, the reasoning of its creation must be analyzed. For instance, how can these animals all accidentally come to life? Likewise, a watch consists of many delicate intricacies within it, if one was to say that flying objects came together onto a hand to form a watch, this would sound ridiculous. The watch requires a designer who puts its intricacies in place. Further than that, when Muslims consider God in science, they take any scientific issue or any animal and consistently contemplate upon a creation greater than it by using their imagination. Using your imagination, you reach a conclusion that the greatest of them all will result in God. Thus Islam uses a philosophical outlook to show that God acts as a barometer in scientific issues. Even transcendental theories say that logic, ethics and science all need a barometer. For example, God devises ethics for us, otherwise, if we didn't use the ethics of God, everyone would come up with their own ethics. Some atheists say that they don't need to believe in God in order to be good. Good, in their opinion, would be giving to the poor. But someone else's opinion could be that charity is not good, so what is the measure of what's good and not good for us? Some atheists reply that society lets us know what is good, but anyone can change society's ethics over time. Thus humans need God as a barometer in ethics. Likewise with science. A science without God can end up destroying humanity. Some atheists have brought destruction in society when they ironically claim that religion brings destruction.

But if Muslims believe that science is inclusive of God, then do they consider evolution? There are two types of evolution, one which believes in complete change from one species to another and one where there's an evolution of an animal that adapts to its environment and possible mutations which make it bigger or smaller. The macro-evolution of one species changing to another is not agreed upon in Islam, but a micro-evolution of small changes in a species due to its environment is accepted. Therefore, God is the centre of scientific discussion in Islamic thought, yet Muslims encourage scientific discoveries too. Chapter 2, verse 26, says, "Indeed, Allah is not timid to present an example – that of a female mosquito." One may ask how Allah (SWT) could be shy towards anything. At the time of the revelation which mentions the fly verse, Jews in the Arab world mocked the verse as well as the verses of the spider. Allah (SWT) responded to these people, as they were arrogant towards His words, and revealed that He would mention another insect, a mosquito.

Mosquitoes have been researched widely in science. Ronald Ross received a Nobel Prize in 1902 for the discovery of the malaria virus. Malaria affects everyone no matter how healthy or wealthy one is. Allah (SWT) specifically mentions the female mosquito which ingests the blood of the human and can be deadly. The male mosquito is insignificant as it lives on floral nectar. The female mosquito carries this deadly act out by first sniffing the area. If it likes the smell, it will continue – otherwise, if it didn't, it will turn away. The area that the mosquito usually attacks is a thin layer of skin which has a lot of blood. After sniffing, the female mosquito places an anaesthetic on the area and then bites into the layer with its upper mandible and lower mandible. These mandibles are the insect's needle-like mouth, which can cut like a knife. This was the same creation that Allah (SWT) discussed in relation to non-believers who mocked the Holy Qur'an. The female mosquito can in fact destroy the human being, and any other creation, due to its great potency. The mosquito cannot only cause malaria, but it can also cause yellow fever, which is another fatal disease.

The female mosquito, moreover, flaps its wings 500 times per second whereas flies flap their wings three miles per hour, and display one hundred eyes, but only sense humans through heat. Allah (SWT) is saying that this mosquito that the disbelievers are mocking is created in the most intricate way, and He is not embarrassed to mention the female mosquito. This female mosquito is so potent that human beings were not able to discover this until a thousand years later after the revelation of the Qur'an. The biology of the mosquito is so extensive in its other systems, such as the respiratory and reproductive, that if one were to study all of its physiology, one would conclude that Allah (SWT) created it in the utmost delicate way. Nevertheless there are ignorant people who believe that this creation was an "accident."

Some people attack religion as a whole when they dislike an act that they believe religious people participate in. George Bernard Shaw, the playwright and co-founder of the London School of Economics, once said, "Islam is the best religion with the worst followers." Sometimes the followers are not true followers who hold the banner of Islam, instead they hold extreme views of terrorism – but the religion itself has firm principles. Allah (SWT) provides a "sign" for mankind – that this Holy Qur'an reinforces the creation of the female mosquito in this way. Furthermore, Allah (SWT) speaks of other female animals in His Book. The feminine role is purposely studied by Allah to allow a justification of what only the female can uniquely do. For instance, He mentions the verse about the "female bee," as only the female can collect the honey from the hives of the trees and mountains. Another example is when Prophet Solomon speaks to the "female ant" who dominates the ant colonies. Allah (SWT) says that the "female ant" spoke to Prophet Solomon. Only a thousand years later were humans able to determine that the female is the head of the colonies as a whole. Allah (SWT) thus is reminding humans of the power of His Holy Book by mentioning the female. Every angle the Qur'an has taken includes a scientific step which the Lord of the creation knows better than the creations know themselves. If there are still aspects of the world that humans have not yet understood, this does not suggest that our Lord is incorrect; it means our minds have still not advanced above certain limitations. The human intellect only uses a maximum of ten percent of the brain, thus Allah reminds us to remain patient until one day reaching the sciences of the heavens and earth.

Additionally, Imam Ali (AS) has two sermons in Nahj al-Balagha which are in relation to the mosquito. In one he beautifully states, "If all the animals on earth and all the birds and the beasts and the stable cattle and the pastured ones and all the origins of the species and the dull and the sagacious minds got together to create a mosquito, they would not be able to find the way into its being nor how to create it. They leave disappointed and sad whilst reaching a stage where they know they are so weak that they can't even destroy it." The Commander of the Faithful also states wisely in Sermon 42, "How wretched is the son of man; his death is hidden from him, his ailments are concealed from him, yet a mosquito bite pains him. His sweat gives off a bad smell, his choking eventually causes his death and his actions are preserved." Imam here is noting that mankind should remain humble and remain in thankfulness towards their Lord.

Mankind is so insignificant he does not know when and where he will die. No matter how much he has built in this life he will reach death one day. Yazid ibn Mu'awiyah believed he was absolutely powerful after killing our third Imam, massacring Medina and throwing burning catapults at the Ka'aba. Not surprisingly, Yazid's death was so shameful that he was killed whilst hunting alone, yet he always believed he was invincible against death. The Imam then goes on to say that our "ailments are concealed as some people suffer from conditions they were not anticipating," such as Abdel Malik ibn Marwan. He did not know that he had had a condition whereby if he drank water, it would kill him. This was something he did not anticipate, and it caused him great frustration. Humans also carry a body odour, and the human is humiliated when they sweat.

"His choking will cause his death" – an example of someone who died like this was an Umayyad caliph named Sulayman ibn Abdel Malik who was sitting at home with his wife Hababa, a slave girl. He had refused to lead Salatul-Jum'uah due to his arrogance. He always thought his life was unshaken, however Hababa died whilst choking on a pomegranate when seated besides him. Imam says, "A mosquito bite pains you." One mosquito can pain you and can cause a human being to reflect that he should always be thankful and in prostration say, "Ya Allah, you are the Most High and all praises be to you."

So when the disbelievers, including the Jews, mocked Prophet Muhammad (PBUH) and the words of the Qur'an, Allah replied proudly about the female mosquito in verse 2:26. The Ahlulbayt (AS) have mentioned the mosquito on many occasions as the Arabs reflected on how the mosquitoes were part of their lives. Some hadiths relate the tragedy of Karbala to the wing of a mosquito. In one hadith from Imam al-Baqir (AS), he narrates, "He who remembers us, and in whose presence we are remembered, and in those who shed a tear the size of the wing of a mosquito, Allah (SWT) will promise this person a house in Paradise and the barrier between Paradise and Hell will be the tear of that person." This tear for the grandson of the Prophet will allow a person to reach heaven. It must be noted that the interpretation of this hadith means that a believer must not forget all his other duties in Islam such as the Furoo' al-Deen of prayer, fast, hajj, etc.

The great scholar Allama al-Hilli used to ponder over a similar hadith of Imam al-Baqir (AS) which says, "A tear for Imam Hussein the size of the wing of a mosquito will cure a sin the size of an ocean." Allama al-Hilli used to equally wonder about the days where he used to visit Masjid al-Sahla in Kufa, the centre of the government of our Imam. It is prophesized that our Imam will reappear on a Tuesday. Al-Hilli decided to go for forty Tuesdays and thought to himself that if he would see the Imam he would enquire about the hadith on "the tear the size of a mosquito wing." On the fortieth Tuesday al-Hilli reached Masjid al-Sahla and saw a man who questioned where he was heading. Al-Hilli replied that he needed answers from someone he was looking for, but this man insisted on attempting to answer them, whatever the questions may be. So al-Hilli explained how it was difficult to understand the hadith which says that crying tears the size of a mosquito wing for Imam Hussein cures a sin the size of an ocean. The man looked at al-Hilli and replied, "There was a king of the children of Israel who went out with them to war. He lost his soldiers and was stuck in a forest. Then he found one small house in this forest. He knocked on the door and explained his situation, to which a reply came from a woman saying she lived there with her son and one animal. The king let her know he will give them everything they desire when he would later reach his kingdom. That family sacrificed their only animal for the king, and when he later reached his kingdom, he had forgotten to reward them. So the son of that lady went to the king's palace and reminded him of their aid towards him. The king turned to his two advisers and asked what he should do; one said land and the other said give treasure. To this the king suggested the advisors had been unjust as that mother and son gave him everything they had, so he said, 'Everything

I own should be given to them.'" The man then looked at al-Hilli, referring to him by his name, and said that if a normal king can be so just towards that one animal sacrifice, then how just will the king of kings Allah (SWT) be towards the man who sacrificed everything he had on the tenth of Muharram. In return Allah (SWT), without a doubt, will give everything to our Imam by removing the sins of those who repent and cry for his sacrifice. Lastly, this man told al-Hilli to tell his Shi'a that I will be there for them if they visit Masjid al-Sahla for forty Tuesdays. Al-Hilli was weeping whilst the man spoke, and when he looked up, the man had disappeared.

Lecture 27

Is the Qur'an the Word of God?: Historical Accuracy

The first way to prove that the Qur'an is the word of God is through predictions and prophecies. The second is via its scientific principles, and the third aspect is through historical truthfulness. If someone was to present to you a particular narrative or historical account, you would expect it to come with facts and figures to highlight its valid significance. The stories also must be filtered from contradictions so that one may render it accurately so that it is truly the word of God. To reach historical accuracy, one uses different methods, e.g., through archaeologists, or through historical coins or even papyrus or manuscripts. Likewise, hieroglyphics can also be used to test history; some say it was a dead language by the time of the Prophet Muhammad (PBUH). This would suggest that when the Prophet tells a story which was once known through hieroglyphics that it would add reliability to this story. Historical tools can be crafted to be used in order to investigate the people of 'Aad, who lived in the city of Iram full of tall buildings, or those of Thamud living in mountainous areas, or Pharaoh's kingdom. These historical accounts, and many more in the Qur'an, are numerous, however, how does one test their truthfulness? One must not just use the Qur'an but research other sources as well that are valid to people as a whole.

When the Prophet Muhammad (PBUH) came forward with the Qur'an, the people queried him on the nations that had come previously in order to test the accuracies of the Book. For instance, they questioned the Holy Prophet on "Thul Qurnain," or the Companions of the Cave. Those who had tested the Prophet on historical accounts were not necessarily religious as some of them believed in Greek philosophers such as Ptolemy or Pliny. Additionally, some people also question if the Prophet did not merely reproduce the Bible's historical narratives. In response, the argument for the Qur'an being the word of God can be seen through an analysis of narratives and comparisons of it with other Books of God.

There are several historical examples in the Qur'an that this analysis will be focusing on. The first is verse 50 in Chapter 12 which say, "So the king said, 'Bring him to me.'" This verse is in Surah Yusuf, which is named by Allah (SWT) as the "best of stories." It is known as the best of stories as everyone can relate to the story and be taught a lesson. If someone is young, then they can relate to Yusuf when he was young and handsome, like if someone is envious of you as Yusuf's brothers were to him. If someone is of an older age, they can also relate to it. For example, in being accused of an attack you did not commit. Further examples from Yusuf's story include forgiveness. The verse above, in particular, is an example of proving historical accuracy in the Qur'an.

When Yusuf goes into prison because of the accusation of Zulaykha, he meets two prisoners who are accused of plotting to kill the king. Prophet Yusuf (AS) informs them not to worry and will guide them towards Allah (SWT). They describe their dreams and ask if their dreams can be interpreted. One dreams of a bird eating on top of his head and the second dreams of serving the king with drinks. The Prophet replies by saying, "I will interpret your dreams, however let me first tell you about Allah (SWT)." The Prophet knew that they did not believe in God and the one who had birds eating from his head would end up being crucified. So Yusuf wanted to bring them towards Allah (SWT) before the Day of Judgement. Yusuf then explains the dreams. The latter who will serve drinks to the king, Yusuf requests that he remembers him when he leaves the prison. Years passed by and this prisoner did not remember him after he had left their cell until one day the king himself sees a dream. The king's dream involved seven skinny cows eating seven fat cows and he saw a seven year of harvest and famine. The servant recalled Yusuf's dream interpretation and here Yusuf interpreted the dream and was appointed as minister with the condition that the accusation of Zulaykha be removed. Here verse 50 was revealed, "So the king said, 'Bring him to me.'" This in itself displayed a historical accuracy in that the Qur'an did not say, "Pharaoh said, 'Bring him to me.'" It stated, "The king said, 'Bring him to me.'" On the contrary, the Bible said, "Pharaoh said, 'Bring Joseph to me,'" even though there were no Pharaohs in the time of Prophet Yusuf (AS).

In the Qur'an, when the word "Pharaoh" is used, it is usually with Prophet Musa (AS). "Pharaoh said to Moses, 'Come to my palace.'" But with Prophet Yusuf, the Qur'an wanted us to distinguish the era and the titles which were held in order to prove its historical accuracy. Moreover, the first Pharaoh was Amenhotep VI who was in leadership two hundred years after the era of Prophet Yusuf. Before this they used to be called Hyksos, these were kings of Egypt...and pharaohs come much later. Thus the Qur'an showed its dominant historical accuracy above other books which claim to be the word of God.

A second historical accuracy in the Qur'an is on Haman, Qarun and Pharaoh (Fir'awn). Haman is mentioned six times in the Qur'an and he was the henchman of Pharaoh. Prophet Moses' Lord kept helping him, and so Pharaoh decided to build a spiral staircase so that he would meet this Lord. Pharaoh asked Haman to build this staircase for him, but people died whilst building this staircase because in those days they didn't have the protective gear of today. When the staircase reached Pharaoh's satisfactory height, he decided to use a bow and arrow to shoot above. He hit a bird and blood dripped down. In his utmost ignorance, he believed that this blood was from the Prophet's Lord. This mentioning of Pharaoh in the Qur'an is with Haman, however in the Bible there is no mention of Haman. The only mention they have of Haman is in the final parts of the Old Testament, where they state that a man named Haman, who had lived 1100 years after Moses, used to torture the children of Israel. For centuries, the Qur'an was attacked for talking about Haman in Moses' era. Until in 1799 the Rosetta stone was discovered which allowed the determination of Egyptian hieroglyphs. This was due to the fact that the Rosetta Stone consisted of ancient hieroglyphs, the middle portion being demotic, and the lowest script translated in Greek, thus it could be de-coded. After decoding this, they found that Pharaoh was a man of oppression and beside him was a man by the name of Haman. Therefore again the Qur'an has shown another historical accuracy above what is in the Bible.

A third analogy involves the people of Thamud. They are mentioned by some of the great Greek historians before Prophet Muhammad (PBUH). When Prophet Muhammad (PBUH) had come, many people were unsure as to who the people of Thamud were, but in the Qur'an AllahT(SWT) does not just call them Thamud but names them "the people of the Stoneland." A whole chapter in the Qur'an was revealed with the title of "al-Hijr," or "the Stoneland," in Surah 15. When Allah (SWT) talks about al-Hijr, he says Thamud were the people, and al-Hijr was the city. Here Allah wanted to give us a historical fact. Allah said, when we told these people of the violent storms that will come on them they started to carve out houses from the stones. Many historians wondered to whom this was directed to until they found the Rum Valley. Petra in Jordan was what the Prophet Muhammad (PBUH) was referring to in His Book. They came to this conclusion that, as the Rum Valley had the carvings of stone in the mountains, and they had recognised that this was what the Prophet was referring to. Prophet Muhammad (PBUH) didn't just say Thamud straightaway. He said, "The people of the Stoneland," as he wanted to highlight that they will be carving out these monuments.

A fourth historical accuracy involves the people of 'Aad. The belief was that these people were seized and destroyed so you cannot find this city as it is lost. However, in 1990 an article was reproduced with the title, "Lost Arabian City: Found." Nicholas Clapp, an archaeologist, had the works of a man named Thomas who had studied the area, and had studied the city which was originally near the area of "Happy Yemen," or Arabia Felix. Thomas went to study this area and Nicholas Crapp took over this study in the Huntington Library in California, whilst utilising the technology of NASA. Nicholas set out to search this lost city which the Qur'an refers to as 'Iram. For example, in Chapter 89, verses 6 and 7, it says, "Have you not considered how your Lord dealt with 'Aad, with Iram who had lofty pillars?"

These verses allow us to note that the people of 'Aad lived in Iram which had tall buildings. Clapp had studied this and found that there was a city which was lost but could now be found in the area of Yemen; whoever had lived there was wealthy – as were the people of 'Aad. Clapp first traced the footsteps which related to the same period as those of 'Aad. He then went to Huntington Library to get the Greek drawings of that area. The Greek drawings showed that there were inhabitants living there, and lastly Clapp asked NASA to zoom into this and revise any pillars coming out. NASA discovered there were people living there and surrounding them were tall buildings. Clapp concluded that this was proof it was the city of Iram which was once destroyed and was known for its tall buildings. Many people didn't believe there was a true city of Iram, but Allah (SWT) wanted to show the reliability of the book, and 1400 years after the Qur'an was revealed the lost city was found.

A further historical accuracy regarding the people of Saba' can be analysed. When Prophet Solomon (AS) saw the hoopoe bird and asked where he had been, the hoopoe responded by saying that it had been somewhere where it was in awe of a kingdom as magnificent as Solomon's. The bird then explained to him that there was a kingdom with a queen named Balqis, the Queen of Sheba. Surah 34, which is called Saba', is related to this city. The people of Saba' did not believe in Allah as they worshipped the sun. Solomon received gifts from Balqis so that she could bribe him; however, Solomon sent her a letter inviting her towards the submission to One God. Balqis' advisors told her they have an army ready to destroy Solomon. Saba' was one of the four great civilisations of southern Arabia, and their motto was "reconstruction and dedication." The people of Saba' people were also wealthy, as the city had a dam which was a place of irrigation, as stated in Chapter 34, verses 15-17: "For the people of Saba', there was a sign in their homeland. Two gardens on the right and on the left, and they were able to irrigate as they had a good land."

Archaeologists studied the dam, and found this dam had a width of sixty metres, and its length was 620 metres. Irrigation in the dam was carried out; the southern side had 5400 metres, and the northern had 4300 metres (See above verse re: "right and left side"). The remains of this dam are still available today. Instead of thanking Allah (SWT) for this blessing, the people of Saba' became more arrogant until a major flood came which destroyed the dam and their cultivation, which the Qur'an has called "Sayl al-Arimi." When archaeologists visited the area, they found it was exactly as how the Qur'an had described it in Surah al-Saba'. No other book described the area of Saba', with its dam of two gardens on the left and right used for irrigation, and the "Sayl al-Arimi" flood, like the Qur'an.

Further than this, a recent papyrus has been found which refers to Moses as a magician when he was amongst the magicians; the Qur'an is the only book which says the people of Moses call on him as a magician. Chapter 43, verse 49, says, "O Magician, make a covenant with your Lord and surely then we will be rightly-guided." No other book says the people of Pharaoh identify Moses as the "Magician." They say he was in a war with magicians, but after this, they do not call him a "magician." The papyrus that has been found says, "The people of Egypt will eventually call Moses by the title of Magician."

Thus, with all of these historical accuracies, it can be easily concluded that the Qur'an is in no way a copy of the Bible as the Qur'an consists of dominant accuracies. Even if the prophets mentioned in the Qur'an have the same names as the prophets in the Bible, the Qur'an is still paramount above the Bible as there are differences in the stories. Lut in the Bible is a wise man who sleeps with his two daughters, whereas Lut in the Qur'an is a Prophet who doesn't come near his daughters in such a manner. If the Qur'an copied the Bible then it would have the same story about Lut. In addition, the Bible states that Noah was a drunkard in the vineyards, however, in the Qur'an, Noah is a prophet and all prophets in Islam are infallible from sin as they are the guides for mankind. Furthermore, Dawood, or David, commits adultery in the Bible, but the Qur'an does not have this account. Some misconceptions arise about Prophet Dawood, but the truth is that Dawood married a widow so to remove the custom of not marrying a widow. In response to those that say Prophet Muhammad (PBUH) himself wrote the Qur'an, the Prophet was not taught in any educational institution. Allah (SWT) purposely did this so that, if anyone was to accuse the Prophet and the revelation of being false, they would have no reason to as the Prophet had not ever picked up a pen with his right hand.

Lecture 28

Dhikr: The Importance of Remembering God

"This is the Book about which there is no doubt, a guidance for those conscious of Allah."

Chapter 2, verse 2, concerns the topic of dhikr, which in Arabic means remembrance. Remembrance of Allah (SWT) is regarded as one of the highest spiritual acts within Islam as well as all the Abrahamic faiths. The religion of Islam seeks to cover two aspects – the physical and the spiritual – in recognising that the human is made up of both body and soul. Religion provides a program in which you can strengthen or purify your body and soul. Arguably one of the most important acts which strengthens you is dhikr. Dhikr can be manifested in a number of different ways. As an example, if you were to go to a Sufi congregation, their form of dhikr is to stand in a circle and chant the names or attributes of God. Another form in which dhikr is manifested is through du'a, or supplication, as God mentions this in the Qur'an, in 2:186, "And when My servants ask you, [O Muhammad], concerning Me – Indeed I am near. I respond to the invocation of the supplicant when he calls upon Me. So let them respond to Me [by obedience] and believe in Me that they may be [rightly] guided." Another form of dhikr is prayer, or prayer. As the Qur'an says, "Indeed, I am Allah. There is no deity except Me, so worship Me and establish prayer for My remembrance."

Also what we call the dhikr of "tasbeeh" is the same in Christianity with the rosary beads. Many nuns and other Christians use rosary beads to remember Allah (SWT), marking the fact that Mary, mother of Jesus, would remember God with a rosary bead in her hand. Likewise Fatima al-Zahra (AS), due to the hardships in her work at home, asked her father if she could have someone to help her, which led the Prophet to give her the "tasbeeh of Fatima." This was a form of dhikr – thirty-four times "Allahu Akbar," thirty-three times "Alhamdulillah" and thirty-three times "Subhanallah." Our sixth Imam has a narration that says, "As soon as you finish prayer, immediately go into my grandmother Fatima's tasbeeh and you will be protected from the flames of Hell." Therefore you find that tasbeeh is a form of dhikr.

There is a narration that states that one day the companions came to The Prophet (PBUH) and said, "Oh Prophet of God, the rich Muslims can free slaves, give charity and go to hajj. We are the poor Muslims. What can we do?" The Prophet (PBUH) replied, "I'll give you something better than this. Whomever recites Allahu Akbar one hundred times it is as if he has freed a hundred slaves. If you recite Alhamdullilah a hundred times it is as if he's given a hundred horses with charity on them to the poor. If you recite Subhanallah a hundred times it's as if you have sent people to hajj. But whoever says La Ilaha Ila Allah will be the best of people on the Day of Judgement."

Therefore you found The Prophet (PBUH) sought to build this religion which has a spiritual essence, and the main act which brings you spirituality is dhikr. The examination of the root of dhikr will be upon the following: what is the importance of the presence of the heart when you make dhikr? Does God need our remembrance? What is the best act of remembrance which we have neglected? What does Allah (SWT) mean when He says in 2:152, "So remember Me; I will remember you?" In which positions in life does Allah relate this verse to? What's the origin of Du'a Jawshan al-Kabeer? Why was it given to our Prophet? How is it a form of memory?

The first topic that arises is the importance of the heart in an act of dhikr. Some believe that dhikr is just a set of oscillating tongue movements, however it is much more than this. Our sixth Imam says, "The heart is the Qiblah of the tongue." Imam al-Sadiq means here that what you say should be directed by your heart. In Islam dhikr is not complete if the heart is not involved. For example, on the night of Laylat al-Qadr, the recitation of "Astaghfurallahi wa atubu ilayh" and "Astaghfurallahi rabbi wa atubu ilayh" are carried out. The former istighfar is said seventy times, which accounts for seventy sins one has made. It translates as "Forgive me, Allah, and now I am returning to you." Thus a thought like this should come in the person's heart towards a sin they have committed and then they should ask for repentance. "Returning to you" means that you have committed yourself to a change to come back towards Allah and you will not return to sin again. The latter istighfar, translates as "Ya Allah, forgive and nourish me while I return to you."

The true believer is one whose heart trembles in the memory of Allah (SWT). Surah 8 of the Qur'an is titled, "al-Anfal," which means "the Spoils of War." It was revealed in relation to the events that took place after the Battle of Badr. Different groups of the companions thought that the spoils of war should go to them. Verse 8:1 was revealed, which says, "They ask you, [O Muhammad], about the bounties [of war]. Say, 'The [decision concerning] bounties is for Allah and the Messenger.' So fear Allah and amend that which is between you, and obey Allah and His Messenger, if you should be believers." This meant that the spoils of war should go to the Prophet and Allah. When the companions heard the remembrance of Allah, their hearts trembled. Surah 8:2 says, "The believers are only those who, when Allah is mentioned, their hearts become fearful, and when His verses are recited to them, it increases them in faith; and upon their Lord they rely." The believers are those whose hearts tremble, and at the same time are calm when they remember Allah, "With the remembrance of Allah, your heart becomes certain."

Also, in the night of Qadr, when you are saying, "Allahumma al'an qatalat Amir al-Mu'mineen," this does not mean you are cursing the killers of Imam Ali. This means you are asking for the removal of mercy upon the killers of the Imam, which must be said whilst pondering upon the words. Furthermore, when we send la'na, or the removal of Allah's Mercy, upon someone we have to ensure that we are not like those who may have the Mercy of Allah removed from them, for example, if we sin against our family, or if our desires have overtaken us. Therefore, when it comes to remembrance, your heart must reflect on what you are saying, otherwise the dhikr is incomplete.

The second topic concerns God and if He needs our remembrance.

The answer is that Allah (SWT) does not need us to remember Him, rather we are the ones who benefit from dhikr because we are a sculpture that needs perfection, and we reach perfection by remembering Allah. There are three areas in the life of the human being which require the remembrance of Allah. The first area is when God breathed his spirit into you when you were just clay, and this gave you a conscience. This conscience can go either way in your life – nafs al-lawaama is the alive conscience, or nafs al-amaara the dead conscience, or nafs al-mutma'ina which is a certain conscience. This conscience develops in the remembrance of Allah (SWT). The second area is when Allah created you with a "fitra," which means the primordial nature that searches for perfection. It is innate in every human to yearn for perfection; this "fitra" is only matured through remembrance, or dhikr, of Allah. The more you remember Allah, the more perfect your fitra is. The third area is of the most utmost importantance, which is the ability to become lower than an animal or higher than an angel. Some humans act like animals as they do not consider what Allah has given them. The human has imagination, anger and desires which are three potent traits, which when set loose, can destroy a community, whilst feeling guiltless in doing so. Samara ibn Jundub' was one of the governors of Mu'awiyah ibn Sufyan. One day two people were brought to him – one was a supporter of Samara while the other was Samara's enemy. Samara was asked which one he would kill and he said, "Both, as for my supporter I will kill him so he reaches Paradise quicker, and my enemy will go to Hellfire quicker." The human being can reach so low that they show no remorse in killing people. This human being requires dhikr. Remembrance of Allah means they gain accountability for their acts on the Day of Judgement. When it comes to the best act in remembering Allah (SWT), it itself is mentioned as a way of remembrance in the Qur'an. There are many titles of the Qur'an, and one is "al Dhikr" or "the Reminder." This is seen in Surah 15:6, which says, "And they say, 'O you upon whom the message has been sent down, indeed you are mad."

Al Dhikr means that Allah wanted us to remember Him through His Holy Book by storing it in our hard drive. When the Holy Book is put on our head on the Night of Qadr, it is a way of showing our respect to the Qur'an due to its being our guidance. Allah termed the Qur'an "the Reminder" so that the more verses we memorise and understand, the more we remember Allah in every area and action of our life. For example, when the Danish newspaper released offensive cartoons of our Prophet, and then you have a person who hasn't memorised the Qur'an just burning their books to retaliate in kind. Whereas someone who has memorised and understood the Qur'an would remember Surah 6, verse 108, which says, "And do not insult those who invoke other than Allah lest they insult Allah in enmity without knowledge. Thus We have made pleasing to every community their deeds. Then to their Lord is their return, and He will inform them about what they used to do." This verse states that if we were to abuse their leaders, they would turn around and abuse Allah. Thus this ayah gives us the notion to not retaliate. This is an example of how the Qur'an can serve as a reminder to the believer.

A second example of remembering the Qur'an is when your mother calls you and asks for a favour. If the Qur'an is not stored as a reminder in your hard drive, then the person may become frustrated with their mother. On the other hand, if the Qur'an acts as a reminder, then it will be remembered that Allah has said, "And We have enjoined upon man good treatment to his parents. His mother carried him with hardship and gave birth to him with hardship, and his gestation and weaning [period] is thirty months. [He grows] until, when he reaches maturity and reaches [the age of] forty years, he says, 'My Lord, enable me to be grateful for Your favor which You have bestowed upon me and upon my parents and to work the righteousness of which You will approve and make righteous for me my offspring. Indeed, I have repented to You, and indeed, I am of the Muslims.'" This will allow the latter person to do what his mother asks and develop in life.

A third example of the Qur'an serving as dhikr is when someone comes to propose to your daughter from a different community. If the Qur'an acts as a reminder, then Surah 49, verse 13, would remind the person to not hesitate in giving his daughter, "O mankind! Indeed We have created you from male and female and made you peoples and tribes that you may know one another. Indeed, the most noble of you in the sight of Allah is the most righteous of you. Indeed, Allah is Knowing and Acquainted." Allah wanted us to get together if we are of different tribes, cultures and classes.

A fourth example of dhikr using the Qur'an is if you have a cousin who hates you, then there happens to be a fight between the two of you. If the cousin strikes you, and you cannot be reminded by the Qur'an of how you should behave, then you would strike him back. However, if you always have the Qur'an stored in your hard drive, then you would not retaliate and remember the story of Habeel and Qabeel in 5:28, "If you should raise your hand against me to kill me, I shall not raise my hand against you to kill you. Indeed, I fear Allah, Lord of the worlds." Thus, in this example, remembering the Qur'an would make you realise that just like Habeel feared Allah, you should fear Allah and not hit him back.

A fifth example of the Qur'an serving as dhikr is when someone asks a person to be forgiven. If the person does not have the Qur'an as a way of life, they will not forgive them. However, if a person is constantly reminding themselves of the Qur'an, then they would forgive as per 3:159: "So by mercy from Allah, [O Muhammad], you were lenient with them. And if you had been rude [in speech] and harsh in heart, they would have disbanded from about you. So pardon them and ask forgiveness for them and consult them in the matter. And when you have decided, then rely upon Allah. Indeed, Allah loves those who rely [upon Him]." This verse is Allah emphasising to the Prophet of his soft-heartedness and how this brought people to the religion, whilst also forgiving them. Therefore, the best way of dhikr is remembering the Qur'an in order to determine your way of life.

Subsequently, in verse 2:152, the line "So remember Me. I will remember you" contains three beautiful interpretations. The first interpretation is that Allah wants us to remember Him in ease so that He may remember us in times of hardship. Unfortunately most people only remember Allah when they require benefits, but do not remember Allah in order to thank Him for their blessings. There is a narration that three people set out on a journey; there was a major sandstorm so they had to find shelter, and so they sat down in a cave. A rock had fallen which blocked the cave opening. The three looked at each other and one of them said, "Allah says to remember Him in times of ease so that He remembers us in hardship. So let us remember and be thankful for all those times we had blessings so that Allah will remove this hardship." Another of the men said, "Ya Allah, I remembered you in the time of ease. Remember me in this time of hardship. When I was near my beautiful cousin and I saw her in front of me, I was going to come and touch her until she told me to fear Allah. As soon as she said this I thought of how arrogant I was to commit a sin while Allah is watching me. Ya Allah, I was in a time of ease and I could have taken it further but I remembered you. Ya Allah, remember me in this time of hardship."

When the man had said this, part of the rock moved to the side. Then the second man spoke, "Ya Allah, I am a person who you know very well looks after my parents and is an only child. My parents are very old. One day I went to take their food when they had both slept, but I knew had I gone up I would wake them. So I decided to stay in the same place so they wouldn't wake up the whole night. Ya Allah, I remembered you in a time of ease because You said whoever looks after their parents, You will look after them on the Day of Judgement. Ya Allah, remember me in this time of hardship." Again the rock went to the side to reveal more of the outside. The final man then spoke, "Ya Allah, I used to own a farm. I had a worker who worked for me. This worker was good. When I came to give him his wages, he said that he wanted more and he left. Ya Allah, from those wages I went to buy more animals for my farm. One day I saw this person and I told him that all the animals and produce that I have made from his wages will go to him now. Ya Allah, I remembered you in a time of ease. Ya Allah, remember me in a time of hardship." The whole of the rock moved to the side and revealed the outside fully, so they were all able to leave. Therefore the first interpretation of verse 2:152 was that if you remember Allah in ease, Allah will remember you in hardship.

The second beautiful interpretation of verse 2:152 is "Remember Me above the ground, I will remember you below the ground." Every step made on earth is watched by a Lord who is a witness to your actions. Every relationship you build is watched. We all want Allah to remember us below the ground because everyone will be asked about their sins. Surely there will be a time when we will be below the ground, which is narrow and dark, while we will be questioned. The fourth Imam did not forget Allah (SWT) throughout his life; the earth was honoured to have Imam Zain al-Abideen (AS). Whenever Imam would leave his house, the governor of Medina Hisham ibn Isma'il would nudge and push him or even make others throw things at him. Never once did the Imam respond to them.

When Umar ibn Abdelaziz became governor of Medina, he caught Hisham and said, "If there is anyone who has been oppressed by Hisham, let them come and take their vengeance on him." The companions of the Imam would remind him of the past, but still the Imam would not go, rather he replied, "If Hisham is hungry, tell him I'll feed him. If he is thirsty, tell him I'll quench his thirst. If he has an outstanding loan, I'll pay the loan for him." Hisham ibn Isma'il was chained after this, and he saw the Imam walking towards him. Hisham said terrified, "Ali ibn Hussein, do to me what you like." Yet the Imam whispered, "If you are hungry, I will bring you food everyday. If you are thirsty, I'll quench your thirst, and if you are in need of a loan, I can pay you." The humility of the Imam was so great that it reached this level. This type of humility should be manifested in all of us because Allah wanted us to be humble while we walk on this earth. Now Jannat al-Baqee' is full of the fourth Imam's followers who surround his grave everyday, even when there are those who do not allow visitations.

The third interpretation of the verse is that Allah (SWT) says, "Remember Me in obedience, I will remember you in Mercy." This refers to our prayer and our worshipping acts which show our obedience to Allah. Any human being who remembers Allah (SWT) with obedience, Allah will remember him forever with Mercy. Looking at our second Imam, who signed the treaty with Mu'awiyah, and which must have been difficult... However, the Imam did so out of obedience to Allah. Imam Hassan knew that if there was fighting that this would have been the end of the Ahlulbayt and the religion of Allah. He imitated The Prophet (PBUH) with the Sulh al-Hudaybiya. So Allah in turn remembers the Imam with His Mercy, thus al-Baqee' is honoured by the presence of the Imam's grave, and in Egypt the great granddaughter of the Imam, Nafisah, is visited by many followers too.

Imam Hassan's son Zaid had a son named Hassan, and Hassan's daughter was Nafisah. She was married to Ishaq, the son of our sixth Imam. Nafisah would fast in the day and pray at night. When people asked her why she would worship so much, she would reply, "To prepare for the grave." Nafisah left Medina to go Palestine in order to visit the grave of Prophet Ibrahim, and then settled in Egypt. The people of Egypt would always say that they were reminded of Imam Hassan when they would see her akhlaaq and obedience to Allah.

When Imam remembered Allah, Allah remembered him when he gave him Nafisah. A Jewish man has narrated that he was living in Egypt when his daughter became blind. He didn't believe in Islam but had asked about the most religious person they had. The people would reply Nafisah, the great granddaughter of Hassan. The narration states that this Jewish man asked if he could take the water that fell from Nafisah's wudhu'. When they gave it to him, he asked God, "O God, if this Nafisah is the daughter of Hassan, the grandson of Imam Hassan, then I ask you to cure my daughter from her blindness." When the man placed the water on his daughter's face, the daughter was able to see again. Nafisah was a source of baaraka to the people of Egypt. When she died, her husband wished to take her to Medina yet he saw a dream of the Prophet coming to him. The Prophet asked him to leave Nafisah in Egypt for she will be a source of Ahlulbayt in Egypt. Until today, followers of the Ahlulbayt still go there.

In conclusion, no one remembered Allah like the Holy Prophet (PBUH) and His Holy Progeny. The School of Ahlulbayt is proudly the School of Supplication. Today in the world people are becoming Sufis or Kabbalists or Buddhists. This type of conversion is because they want to be spiritual, but the origin of spirituality stems from Muhammad (PBUH) and His Family. Through their supplications we know how to remember Allah and when to remember Allah. An example of this is the beautiful Du'a Jawshan al-Kabir. This du'a is recited on the Night of Qadr. The origin of this du'a is from when The Prophet (PBUH) was fighting in a battle, and the armour he was wearing was so heavy that it was uncomfortable for him. Jibra'il came to The Prophet (PBUH) and said, "Oh Prophet (PBUH), we can see your discomfort and the "jawshan" that is hurting you, so we will give you a du'a that will bring success to you and your Ummah. Whoever recites this du'a in the holy month of Ramadan we will protect them from the fire of Hell." The du'a sent down was "Du'a Jawshan al-Kabir." Imam Hussein (AS) has a hadith that states, "My father Ali ibn Abu Talib says that when a person dies they should have "Du'a Jawshan al-Kabir" on their kafan because that du'a is a protection for the body after the person has passed away. Then my father said to me, 'O my son Hussein, recite Du'a Jawshan al-Kabir because within it is Allah's Greatest Name and through that your supplication will be answered. O my son Hussein, when a person recites this du'a and performs the dhikr of Allah's Greatest Names, Allah will send seventy thousand angels to perform istighfar for that person for every action performed.'"

Lecture 29

Examining Prophet Dawood's Judgement

The story of the legal judgements of Prophet Dawood (AS) is amongst one of the most magnificent stories in the Qur'an. When examining the stories of the Prophets in the Qur'an, the aim is to dissect history whilst analysing its contemporary significance. All of the Prophets have many different areas in their life histories which can be applied in our own lives. There are those who complain that history is highlighted more, however the stories of the Qur'an allow for both aspects to be looked at. Prophet Dawood has many parts of his biography which can be used in our lives today. For example, he used to recite the Zabur, or Psalms, with a melodious voice. In the same way the Prophet recited the Zabur with a melodious voice, the Holy Qur'an must also be read with a voice of passion and zeal. Another example of his life is when he was a valiant warrior against the army of Goliath, which can be taken by youth today as the ability to sacrifice at a young age. These aspects of Prophet Dawood's life thus can be made contemporary.

Likewise, the aspects of Dawood's legal judgements can be studied in order to provide them with contemporary significance. Prophet Dawood is revered in all the Abrahamic faiths of Judaism, Christianity and Islam. Through these he is given a number of titles; he is seen as a Prophet of God, a king and a judge. This examination will focus on his title of judge, and how Allah (SWT) developed his expertise at being a judge in the community. The judge occupies a prominent position in society; there isn't a legal system in the world that can continue without a judge at the helm of the system. The judge has a role in ensuring that the constitution is one which is stable, and that equity and justice is available within society. The judge has to ensure that our property, life, religion, honour and intellect is protected. Therefore the judge is pivotal in society; in Surah 38 of the Qur'an Allah discusses the development of Prophet Dawood as a judge.

The story of Prophet Dawood is very similar to the issues in society today. His story will be examined with the following questions – why does God choose his Khalifa on earth? Why do the people not choose the Khalifa? What was the situation when Prophet Dawood (AS) had to give a judgement? Is it true that Prophet Dawood married ninety-nine wives and decided to commit adultery with the one hundredth? The importance of looking at two sides of an argument in any community case. The power of reconciliation when you hear both sides of an argument. The verse in question is Surah 38, verse 26, "O Dawood! We did indeed make thee a caliph on earth so judge thou between men in truth (and justice). Nor follow thou the lusts (of thy heart), for they will mislead thee from the Path of Allah. For those who wander astray from the Path of Allah is a Penalty Grievous for they forget the Day of Account." This verse says that the caliph is established by Allah (SWT). This means that the community does not decide who the Khalifa is as one School in Islam believes. This School believes that after the Prophet passed away, the community leaders had to come together to elect a successor. This School in Islam believe this because of Surah 42, verse 38, which says, "And those who have responded to their Lord and established prayer and whose affair is [determined by] consultation among themselves, and they spend from what We have provided them."

This verse states that their "affair is determined through consulting among themselves." However, this verse was not revealed about leadership, rather it was revealed about the Ansar of Medina. When they faced difficulties in the early age of Islam, they consulted each other in order to decide which steps to take. Surah 3, verse 159, is also suggested to be about leadership by other Schools in Islam, "So by mercy from Allah, [O Muhammad], you were lenient with them. And if you had been rude [in speech] and harsh in heart, they would have disbanded from about you. So pardon them and ask forgiveness for them and consult them in the matter. And when you have decided, then rely upon Allah. Indeed, Allah loves those who rely [upon Him]." On the contrary, this verse has nothing to do with leadership and Khalafa, rather it concerns the Prophet who talks to the Muslims and consults them in order to hear their opinions and need, yet the ultimate decision is always Allah's. As the Qur'an says, "He [Muhammad] does not speak of his own will, he speaks of revelations sent from Allah."

Within the School of Ahlulbayt leadership and Khalafa is believed to be a decision made solely by Allah; just like everything else, the Prophet says the decision comes from Allah. The School of Ahlulbayt do not believe that the community decides who the caliph is because the community will not choose the best person; in some cases in Islamic history the community chose inappropriate caliphs who were not religious. Moreover, some of the community may not even attend the election; this reason, as well as others, supports the idea that only God can choose leadership. Almighty Allah knows His creation better than the creations know themselves. If the creation chooses the caliph, they will not choose the best, but rather they will choose the caliph that is most similar to themselves and their sentiments. The reason why they were unlikely to choose Imam Ali (AS) after the Prophet is because Imam killed their fathers at Badr, Uhud or Khandaq. Whereas in the Qur'an, Allah (SWT) clarifies that He is the one who appoints His leaders on earth. Surah 28, verse 68, says, "And your Lord creates what He wills and chooses; not for them was the choice. Exalted is Allah and high above what they associate with Him."

This verse states that the choice is with Allah. When Allah appointed Adam as caliph, Allah did not ask Habeel and Qabeel to consult among themselves. Likewise, when Allah made Prophet Ibrahim an Imam, this was his decision. Surah 2:124 says, "And remember that Abraham was tried by his Lord with certain commands which he fulfilled. He said: 'I will make thee an Imam to the Nations.' He pleaded, 'And also (Imams) from my offspring!' He answered, 'But My Promise is not within the reach of evil-doers.'" When Allah (SWT) chose Prophet Dawood (AS), Allah says in 38:26, "[We said], 'O David, indeed We have made you a successor upon the earth, so judge between the people in truth and do not follow [your own] desire, as it will lead you astray from the way of Allah.' Indeed, those who go astray from the way of Allah will have a severe punishment for having forgotten the Day of Account."

Allah chose Dawood as Khalifa on earth, emphasising that only Allah is able to do so. This is because Allah sends the legislation, and thus knows who will protect it. Every single Prophet of God announced his successor before he passed away because it is Allah's appointment and not man's. Prophets of God are not legislators. They are those who announce the legislation, while Allah is the legislator. It is only logical to say that Prophet Muhammad (PBUH) also announced his successor before he passed away; it is unlikely that the final Prophet, with the most important Message, would leave the matter of his succession to the Ummah. The appointment of Prophet Dawood includes two hadith, one of which we reject and the other we accept. Both relate to the Qur'anic verse 38:22-23, which says, "And has the news of the litigants reached you? When they climbed over the wall into (his) mihrab (a praying place or a private room). When they entered in upon David, he was terrified of them. They said, 'Fear not! Indeed this, my brother, has ninety-nine ewes, and I have one ewe'; so he said, 'Entrust her to me,' and he overpowered me in speech."

This verse is about how two angels visited Dawood. One said to him that he has one sheep whereas his brother has ninety-nine and he wants to take his one sheep. They asked the Prophet if this would be accepted. The question arises as to why these angels came to ask Dawood about their situation. One narration believes that the angels were teaching Dawood a lesson because he had married ninety-nine women and he had wanted another woman who was the wife of his general, Uraya. This narration believes that this woman had come out only dressed in a robe, so the Prophet sent Uraya to war ensuring he was at the frontline so that he could have his wife. So when the angels came to ask him, this made the Prophet realise he was wrong to go for the hundredth woman. However, this is a ridiculous narration, and it from the "Israelite traditions." These traditions came to us from people who converted from Judaism and Christianity to Islam. The Israelite traditions included Biblical traditions; the story of Dawood sending Uraya to war because he liked his wife is a story from the Bible. Ka'ab al-Ahrar, Tamim al-Dari and Wahab ibn al-Munabah came forward with these narrations from the Biblical books. Even if these narrations are in Arab traditions, they should not be taken to be true because the only book which is Sahih is the Qur'an. Thus, Israelite traditions must be rejected as they do not reflect what is in the Qur'an.

Once, Imam Ali al-Ridha (AS) was in the courtroom of the Abbasid caliph al-Ma'moon. This caliph had a court poet named Ali ibn Jaham. Al-Ma'moon told Ali ibn Jaham to question the eighth Imam on anything he desired. He tried to question the Imam, and after a few questions he gave up. So the Imam asked him a question. "What do you say about Prophet Dawood and the angels that came to visit him? One of them said he had one sheep while the other had ninety-nine and wanted to take his one sheep, so the first angel asked if this would be fair. What do you say about that incident?" Ali ibn Jaham said, "It's clear that Prophet Dawood had ninety-nine wives, and he wanted another one by oppressing the general." The Imam replied, "Inna lillahi wa inna ilayhi raji'oon. Uraya was the general of Dawood, and he died in battle. His wife became a widow. In that culture a widow was not allowed to marry. Allah ordered Prophet Dawood to break that tradition so that society could be raised with equality."

Only a hundred years after The Prophet (PBUH) had passed away, people narrated stories about the Prophets of God. There are even false traditions about The Prophet (PBUH) himself that are unbelievable. So the Imam explained to them how Prophet Dawood was ordered to marry Uraya's wife. Similarly, Prophet Muhammad (PBUH) married widows such as Um Salama. The angels asking the question about the hundredth sheep being taken relates to an incident when two brothers came to Prophet Dawood. There is a difference of interpretation in this area. One of the narrations states that one brother came to Dawood saying, "I have one sheep; my brother has ninety-nine. Now my brother has guests round his house and he wants to take my one sheep. Is this fair?" Prophet Dawood immediately answered, "This is not fair. This is oppression."

When Allah sent the same story to Dawood with angels, this was so that he would be reminded to not just hear the side of one angel, but to also hear the side of the latter angel. Hearing the side of one person is not sinning but the Prophet's greatness as a caliph on earth must be appointed with the knowledge of hearing both sides of the story. It is impossible to judge without hearing both sides and hence Allah (SWT) sent those angels to Dawood's mihrab to make this clear to Dawood. In our communities many judgements are based on one side of a story. As an example, two partners in a business or a marriage break up. One of the partners is your best friend who comes to describe the whole story to you; from this you negatively judge the other side. However this is not enough, the other side of the story must be heard too. A person who is Islamic will remind you to go and hear the opposite side of the story.

Thus here Allah (SWT) wanted Dawood, as a caliph, to remember his responsibility to listen to both sides of a story. Consequently, Prophet

Sulayman (AS) took this trait from his father Dawood. One day a case was brought to them. Someone had come to them who was complaining that his field was always being destroyed by another man's sheep. When Sulayman asked the other side of the case, he admitted that his sheep go into his field to graze on the grass. Dawood heard the story and said that in his opinion the sheep should be given to the person with the field. Sulayman said that in his opinion (21:78) he should let the sheep be in his field until the amount of produce that he has lost is gained; when he has gained everything back, then let him return the sheep again. This incident is beautiful for the fact that two Prophets of God have both given solutions in different ways. This relates to how today two different scholars may provide solutions in legislations. Thus, if we apply this to scholars today, we must not question the different judgements they hold, and their judgements generally must be accepted. Moreover, Dawood and Sulayman, in both providing solutions without dispute allows for an aspect of open-mindedness in Islam.

One day Prophet Sulayman was approached by two women who each said the same baby belonged to them. Sulayman heard both sides before he reached a conclusion and said, "Fine. If the baby belongs to both of you, then let us cut the baby in half." One of the women immediately stood up and rejected this idea by admitting, "No, do not do it. This baby does not belong to me. Take the baby." Sulayman discovered that this was the real mother so he awarded her with the baby because a real mother would rather sacrifice her baby than allow him to be hurt. There is a famous poet that says Amir al-Mu'mineen was the same as this woman with the Khalafa. He wanted to protect it so much that he would rather give it away then allow for its destruction. Therefore, in Islam it is important to look at both sides of the story in order to reach a conclusion.

The caliphs in the religion of Islam were advised to look at both sides of the story. Umar ibn Khattab narrates on one occasion that Ali ibn Abu Talib helped him in a situation which allowed him to understand the concept of listening to both sides of an argument. "When I was told about five people who had committed adultery in the Islamic state, I decided that they all should be executed," Umar said. Imam Ali (AS) then reminded him that he should hear their side and that it was possible that not all of them had committed the act. The first person said he was a Christian living in the Muslim state. The second said that he was Muslim and married. The third admitted he was a Muslim who was single. The fourth said that he was a slave and the last said that he was a bit insane. Ali ibn Abu Talib declared then that they each have a different judgement. "The Christian living in the Muslim state must be beheaded. We give the greatest rights to non-Muslims in a Muslim state, but if they contravene their rights, they face punishment. The second is Muslim and married, so he has to be stoned to death. The single Muslim must be given one hundred lashes. The slave must be given fifty of the lashes. The law does not apply to the last one as he is insane." When Umar ibn Khattab heard this, he said, "If it was not for Ali then Umar would have perished." Umar had heard one side, yet recognised later that it was vital that we hear from both sides.

Amir al-Mu'mineen allowed fair judgement when it came to a Christian man who took the Imam to court when the Imam had been caliph. Qadhi Shurayh was the judge at the time; Ali ibn Abu Talib explained to him how this coat of mail belonged to him. The Christian then said it belonged to him and then the judge asked if they had witnesses. Ali ibn Abu Talib's sons were not deemed to be appropriate witnesses by the judge so the judge awarded the case to the Christian. When the Christian left the courtroom, he looked at Imam and said, "Today I have seen God's justice on earth. I am a Christian living in an Islamic state who took the caliph to court and the decision went against him." In this situation, Imam Ali (AS) highlighted the fact that that, although he was caliph, he has his side while the Christian has his side too. In Islamic law, and in any community case, whenever you hear a story both sides must be taken on board. If only one side is taken, you can damage someone's life.

If one hears both sides of the story, their role is to be able to reconcile the two sides of the case. Imam Ali (AS), in his wasiya, or final will, says, "I advise you to be conscious of Allah and steadfast in your religion. Do not yearn for this world nor should you be seduced by it. Do not resent anything that you have missed in it. Proclaim the truth and work for the next world. Oppose the oppressors and support the oppressed. I advise you, my family and my relatives, to be conscious of Allah, to remove your differences and strengthen your ties for your reconciliation of differences is greater than fasting and prayer."

Here Imam Ali (AS) is saying that reconciliation is greater than recommended (mustahab) fasting and prayer. It is mandatory on someone, once they have heard both sides, to aim to reconcile them. However, there are certain differences that are irreconcilable. Imam al-Baqir (AS) had a problem with his cousins who were the grandsons of Imam Hassan (AS). Imam Hassan's grandsons opposed the fifth Imam. Abdel Malik narrates that he went to the fifth Imam and attempted to reconcile them. However the fifth Imam told him, "It cannot be resolved. It is like the children of Israel...when a man had two daughters, they were both married to men who did not get along. One of the daughters asked her dad to pray for rain as her husband was a farmer. The second daughter asked her father to pray for no rain because her husband would make pottery. So the father couldn't resolve this. In the same way the father couldn't reconcile them, you cannot reconcile me and my cousins."

On the other hand, reconciling two brothers of the same faith is the greatest act in the religion. Abu Hanifah contributed to Islam with a school of fiqh that 31% of the Muslim world adheres to. He was the master of fiqh for the people of Kufa. He produced graduates such as Muhammad ibn Hassan Shaybani and Abu Yusuf. Even though he made a major contribution to the religion, he could not get along with his son-in-law. Abu Hanifah's original name was Nu'man ibn Thabet, but Hanifah was his daughter's name. One day Hanifah advised her father why Allah allows a man to marry four wives and why women cannot marry four, so he named himself after his daughter. It was difficult for Abu Hanifah to get along with his son-in-law, no one tried to reconcile them. The companion of our sixth Imam, Mufadhel ibn Umar al-Kufi, narrates how he was walking once when he saw Abu Hanifah and his son-in-law quarrelling. He asked them why they were quarrelling and discovered it was about 800 dirhams, so Mufadhel gave 400 dirhams each to both of them which made them come together. They said to Mufadhel, "God bless you Mufadhel for performing such an act." Mufadhel answered, "Do not bless me. Bless Ja'far ibn Sadiq for he said to me, 'Whenever you see any of our followers quarrelling, ensure you work your hardest to bring them back together.' No one has endeavoured to reconcile you, so it was my responsibility to try and bring you together."

Imam al-Sadiq in another hadith says to his students, "There was once the poorest man in the city; he had nothing left to feed his family, so he sold some rope he had at home. The man was able to sell the rope for two dinar. He was on his way to buy some bread but then he saw two Muslims fighting each other. When he asked them why they were arguing, it turned out that one of them owed the other one dinar. The man gave them each one dinar. When he went home, he told his wife what he had done, and she replied, "Jazak Allah kheir," and gave him her dress to sell. When he had left, no one would buy the dress except the man selling fish who made a deal with him that he would give him some of the fish for the dress. At home, when the wife was cutting the fish, a ring fell out of it. When they took this ring to the market, they found the ring was a treasure so the man was able to sell it. On his way back, he saw a man poor man who was pleading with him due to his hunger so the man sympathised with him and gave him all the money he had just received for the ring. When the man was going into his house, he saw the same beggar who told him, "I am an angel sent by God to tell you that when you reconciled the two [Muslims] you carried out the best act." When you are in a community that is riddled with broken relationships then that community is not far from breaking completely. But reconciling is performing the best of acts, because the Qur'an says in 49:10, "The Believers are but a single Brotherhood: So make peace and reconciliation between your two (contending) brothers; fear Allah, that ye may receive Mercy."

The very principles of The Prophet (PBUH) and his Holy Progeny were the principles of reconciliation throughout their lives. When they faced an enemy they tried to perform a Sulh, like Sulh al-Hudaybiya by the Prophet (PBUH) who was questioned about this by his own companions. But as soon as he had done this Allah sent the revelation of "the Opening." Amir al-Mu'mineen, before the battle of Jamal, tried to reconcile with the opposition, with Talha and Zubayr. Only twenty-five years after the Prophet had passed away, everyone wanted to fight the Imam. Imam Hassan (AS) also tried to reconcile with Mu'awiyah with a treaty similar to that of his grandfather, yet they did not stand by the agreements, such as the cursing of Ali. On the tenth of Muharram, Imam Hussein (AS) tried to reconcile the differences in the Ummah. The Imam reminded the opposition who his grandfather was. He reminded them that The Prophet (PBUH) had said, "Hussein is from me and I am from Hussein. God loves whoever loves Hussein." But they did not want to reconcile with any of the Ahlulbayt. They left Imam Hussein in the land of Karbala. As the famous poet says: "Silk sits on the throne of Damascus, Whilst knowledge lies on the ground of Karbala."

Lecture 30

The Islamic Philosophy and Definition of Eid

The discussion concerning the festival of Eid is a fascinating discussion in Islamic thought. It requires a thorough discussion as it provides both a historical and contemporary significance. Millions around the world celebrate Eid and exchange greetings in a time where families meet up – as well as friends. The community is united, and you find it to be one of the most beautiful periods in the Islamic calendar, highlighting to us the importance of festivals in religious thought. Virtually every religion has festivals which are on days that people acknowledge the guidance they have received within that religion.

The essence of these festivals is a spiritual message. For example, in Christianity, Christmas is the birth of the Messiah, which has a spiritual essence. The birth of the Messiah will provide justice, honour, and prosperity, thus the spiritual concept of Jesus being born again in your life is also felt. Hanukkah in Judaism is about celebrating the Maccabees, who resisted the temptation to worship more than one God as the Greeks were doing at the time, and thus also providing a spiritual message. Divali in Hinduism concerns the new lease of life, hence the lights on the candles which are paraded around their community. Nirvana in Buddhism is spiritually commemorated by recognising the purification of the soul which Buddha achieved at the age of eighty.

Each of these festivals are spiritual, yet unfortunately today the spiritual essence is seen to be wavering and instead has become more of a material concept. For example, Christmas was originally a spiritual festival but over the years people began looking forward to Christmas sales. The churches may be empty whilst people may be going to shop. There is no problem with buying things for your family but the festival itself has a spiritual concept. Divali may also be just used to excessively party instead of focusing on its spiritual message. This materialism has also affected Eid in Islam, whereby Eid originally had a spiritual message, yet now it's become about excessive spending. Some may also party so as to release the frustration of thirty days of fasting. Some schools in Islam believe in the authenticity of Sahih Muslim's narration about the incident of how the Prophet was celebrating Eid. Muslim narrated that the first caliph walked into The Prophet (PBUH)'s house to see two dancers performing and singing the same song that the Ansar sang in the Battle of Bu'ath. The first caliph asked, "Oh Prophet (PBUH), how could the instrument of Satan be played in your house?" The Prophet (PBUH) replied, "O Abu Bakr, for everyone there is a festival. For us, Eid is the festival. So we are allowed this on the day of Eid."

However, this narration is not taken on board by the School of Ahlulbayt. It is impossible that the Prophet (PBUH) would make an exception to the whole of his moral principles on the day of Eid. The theory that music is prohibited every other day except Eid is an ignorant concept. Some Middle Eastern countries even drink alcohol on the day of Eid because they believe the Prophet allowed it as a day of exception. On the contrary, the day of Eid had a particular spiritual reverence. Like every religious festival, Eid has a definition which requires an examination, and that will be accomplished by posing the following questions: Who was the first Prophet to discuss the word Eid? Why did he discuss it with his disciples? Why does the School of Ahlulbayt have a number of Eids? What is the philosophy of each one of these? What is the meaning of the word Eid? Why was it used? How does it affect our lives? What is the beautiful hadith of Amir al-Mu'mineen when it comes to making every day in your life Eid?

The first and only Prophet in the Qur'an to ever use the word Eid was Prophet Jesus (AS). Prophet Jesus used "Eid" in relation to a discussion which he had with his disciples. Narrations show that Prophet Moses (AS) and Jesus (AS) both had twelve disciples; likewise Prophet Muhammad

(PBUH) had twelve disciples. Jesus' disciples included John, Simon and Jonah; Jesus would send them to different districts so that they could spread the message of God. Surah Yaseen, verse 14, says, "When We sent to them two but they denied them, so We strengthened them with a third, and they said, 'Indeed, we are messengers to you.'" This verse was revealed about the disciples of Prophet Jesus (AS). Half of Surah Yaseen is about the disciples, and how he sent two of them which the people denied, and so he sent a third disciple.

Whenever Prophet Jesus would leave a congregation, five thousand people would follow him. This five thousand would be divided into groups. One group were his disciples, a second would be those afflicted with diseases (e.g., the lepers), the third would be the general followers and the fourth group would mock his claim of being the King of the Children of Israel. One day those who would mock him came to the disciples and asked them if they truly believed that Jesus was the Prophet of God. The disciples replied that they believed in him without a shadow of a doubt. So the fourth group asked that, if he was what he claimed to be, then let him send down food from the heavens. Some of these disciples came to Prophet Jesus and they asked him if he could request that his Lord send food down from the heavens. Surah 5, verse 112 onwards recounts this dialogue. "[And remember] when the disciples said, 'O Jesus, son of Mary, can your Lord send down to us a table [spread with food] from the heaven?' [Jesus] said, 'Fear Allah , if you should be believers.' They said, 'We wish to eat from it and let our hearts be reassured and know that you have been truthful to us and be among its witnesses.'" The disciples wanted food from heaven to be sent not because they did not believe but so they would feel reassured. The moment they said this to Jesus, he recited this du'a, "Said Jesus, the son of Mary, 'O Allah, our Lord, send down to us a table [spread with food] from the heaven to be for us a festival (Eid) for the first of us and the last of us and a sign from You. And provide for us, and You are the best of providers.'"

The Qur'an states that Jesus asked God to send down food from heaven so that it may be an "Eid" for them. Jesus wanted this day of celebration to be not just for them but for every generation, "for the first of us and the last of us." Thus he wanted it to return every year and to be a "sign" from God. Hence, any day which is a guidance for the Islamic society should be called an "Eid" for the people. Our Holy Prophet (PBUH) narrates an incident whereby his daughter Fatima recognised Jesus' du'a for food in a difficult situation. One day Fatima al-Zahra (AS) was asked by Amir al-Mu'mineen (AS) why she and the children's face were pale. She said that the past couple of days there had been hardly any food and she had not told him because she thought it would trouble him.

When Imam left to buy some food with the one dinar he had borrowed, he met Miqdad who was in a distressed mood. The Imam asked why Miqdad was down; Miqdad replied that his children and wife had nothing to eat. Imam immediately took out the one dinar and gave it to him. Imam then went to pray Salat al-Maghrib. After the prayer, The Prophet (PBUH) asked Imam if he could come over to their house, and the Imam accepted. When Imam entered the house and told her, Fatima remembered the prayer Jesus made which asked for food to be sent from heaven so that it may be Eid. The narration by The Prophet (PBUH) states that Fatima went into the kitchen and prayed, "Ya Allah, when Jesus, son of Mary, asked that if you send food from heaven, it will be a day of Eid, and you met his request by sending down food from heaven. Ya Allah, I am the daughter of your Prophet. I am asking when your Prophet has come and I have nothing to give him. I ask you with the same du'a of Jesus." The narration states that Jibra'il descended and brought food towards her. Therefore, you find that the first Prophet who mentioned Eid in the Qur'an was Prophet Jesus.

If food sent down from heaven is considered to be Eid, then a Prophet of God leaving guidance for the Ummah should be a day of Eid as well. In the School of Ahlulabyt, there are a number of Eids on the basis that any day where The Prophet (PBUH) left guidance for his nation should be acknowledged. The first day of Eid in the School of Ahlulabyt is Eid al-Mubahila, when The Prophet (PBUH) taught us about inter-faith guidance, and he wished this day to be a Eid for the recognition of Islam's open-mindedness. In Eid al-Mubahila, the Christians of Najran visited the Holy Prophet, and as they lived in the Islamic state, they had to pay the "jizya." In fiqh if you are a non-Muslim, you pay a tax of "jizya" which allows you to worship according to your own religion. When they visited the Prophet, they asked him what his opinion was of Jesus. The Prophet replied that he was a Prophet of God. They said that they believed Jesus was the Son of God because he didn't have a father. The Qur'an replied that Jesus was like Adam so he is not the Son of God (3:59), "Indeed, the example of Jesus to Allah is like that of Adam. He created Him from dust; then He said to him, 'Be,' and he was."

The Christians did not agree, so they came to a Mubahila with the Prophet. Mubahila is when great leaders from both sides come and are willing to sacrifice their souls for the future of their religion. The Christians brought all their priests and dignitaries. The Prophet (PBUH) brought Amir al-Mu'mineen, his daughter Fatima, and his grandsons with him. His holy family represented the religion for him. The Qur'an says in 3:61, "Then whoever argues with you about it after [this] knowledge has come to you, say, 'Come, let us call our sons and your sons, our women and your women, ourselves and yourselves, then supplicate earnestly [together] and invoke the curse of Allah upon the liars [among us].'"

The Holy Prophet had brought Imam Hassan and Hussein as his "sons," Fatima as his "women" and Imam Ali as his "self." The idea here was that the Christians wanted to engage in a Mubahila. When they looked at the five of them – The Prophet (PBUH) and his daughter's family – they were astonished. One of the Christian Fathers said, "By God, I am seeing such faces that if they were to pray to God to move the mountain, God Almighty would do that for them. Oh you people of Najran, if you wish to contest with Muhammad in this prayer of invoking curses upon the liars, then I warn you that you may be destroyed. It would be better that you surrender to them and obey them." This day is seen as a day of Eid because it was a day of guidance that came to mankind from the Lord of the Heavens to the people of the earth.

The second Eid in the School of Ahlulbayt is Eid al-Ghadeer. Our sixth Imam says, "There is no event as great as the Eid of Ghadeer." This day provided guidance from Allah to the people. Prophethood was coming to an end, but the protection of Prophethood was going to commence. For twenty-three years, The Prophet (PBUH) taught the message of the Qur'an and now he would leave the Ummah with the interpretation of the Qur'an. The Prophet (PBUH) did not want to leave them in a precarious situation where the interpretation of the Qur'an would be difficult. On the Day of Ghadeer, The Prophet (PBUH) declared that, in the same way that they had accepted his authority, that they must equally accept the leadership of his son-in-law, Ali ibn Abu Talib.

The Prophet (PBUH) stated on Ghadeer Khum after his farewell pilgrimage, "O my people! Allah is my Mawla and I am the mawla of the faithful, and I have a superior right and control over their lives. And this Ali is the mawla of all those of whom I am mawla. O Allah! Love him who loves him and hate him who hates him. O my people! I will precede you, and you shall also arrive at the pool of Kawther, the pool wider than the distance between Basra and San'a', and there are on the pool as many goblets of silver as stars. When you shall reach me, I shall interrogate you about your behaviour towards the two invaluable assets after my death. The major asset is the Book of Allah, the Mighty and Glorious, one end of which is in the hand of Allah, the Exalted, and the other end which is in your hands. Grasp it tightly and do not go astray and do not change or amend it. The other asset is my Progeny, who are my Ahl al-Bayt. Allah the Gracious and Omniscient has informed me that the two will not part from each other before they reach me at the pool." Every year we commemorate this. If it were not for the announcement of Imam Ali (AS) as the successor to Prophet Muhammad (PBUH), Muslims would be in a precarious situation in their knowledge about the origin of Islam and the interpretation of the Qur'an. Allah (SWT) told the Holy Prophet that Ali was his successor, which became an Eid for the "first and last of us" as Prophet Jesus stated.

The third Eid within the School of Ahlulbayt is Eid al-Adha. This day of Eid is in honour of the sacrifices that Prophet Ibrahim (AS) made with his son Isma'il (AS) and reminds us if to see if we have sacrificed for Allah (SWT) as well. Have we defeated Satan in the same way Ibrahim did? When Muslims go on the hajj pilgrimage to throw seven stones at Jamarat, they are throwing away seven bad deeds. Eid al-Adha was an Eid that taught us that this religion was built on an aspect of sacrifice.

The fourth Eid in the School of Ahlulbayt is Eid al-Fitr. This Eid reminds us of the purification of our souls that we should have reached at the end of Ramadan. In Salat al-Eid, the chapters which are recommended to be read are Surah al-Shams and Surah al-A'ala because both of them consist of verses which relate to how Eid is celebrated as our souls have been purified through the month of Ramadan. In Surah al-Shams, the relevant verses are, "By the Soul, and the proportion and order given to it, and its enlightenment as to its wrong and its right. Truly he succeeds that purifies it. And he fails that corrupts it!" Surah al-A'ala has a similar verse which states, "But those will prosper who purify themselves." These verses are read in the Prayer of Eid so that you acknowledge that it is a day of celebration because thirty days of fasting have been carried out, thus disciplining the soul.

There are four reasons as to why he word "Eid" is used for the Islamic festival. The first comes from the idea that the word "eid" comes from the Arabic word "ya'ood," meaning "that which returns." Thus eid is that which returns every year. For some of us, this annual Eid is simply culture, but for those who understand the spiritual essence…they set a new year's resolution or set a target to accomplish. The second opinion in reference to the word "eid" is that it means God's Mercy returns to you every year. Mercy can be seen on the Night of Qadr when Allah opens the door of blessings for us, but we do not know which day it really is so we carry out the deeds over the course of a few days. Allah also says to protect the middle prayer, however, we are not certain which of the five this is, and so we pray and protect them all. Likewise, Eid was made a day of celebration whereby Allah has promised His Mercy to be sent down to us.

The third opinion is that the Muslims return Mercy to each other. The community will be united when they tell each other, "May Allah accept all your deeds" and "May Allah make your days the best of days." When zakat is paid at the end of the month, Mercy is shown between you and the needy of the community. So Eid is a Mercy where one human returns it to another human. Our fourth Imam, on the night of Eid, would sit all his slaves down and ask them if he had ever hurt them. "Never," they would say to him, and then he would ask if his akhlaaq had ever hurt them. Still they would say, "Never." After these questions, Imam would ask them to pray to Allah for him so that He would show Mercy to Imam on the Day of Judgement. Lastly, he would ask them to be free and leave the house, but the slaves would refuse to leave as their freedom was in the house of Zain al-Abideen. On Eid it is not just recommended to gather in prayer but also to walk barefooted to the prayer. Thus, the Muslim should show equal humiliation to everyone else on Eid. It is also recommended to have the Eid prayer in an open space so that Mercy is exchanged between everyone. The fourth reason Eid was named this way is because it refers to a type of horse in Arabia known as "khayl al-eidiya." This horse was seen as a horse of honour and principle, and thus they concluded that the festival day is a day of honour so they named it "Eid."

The main point with the word eid is that the Muslims recognise the signs of Allah and thank Allah for what He has given them. Amir al-Mu'mineen has the following beautiful hadith, "Every day is a day of Eid when you do not disobey Allah (SWT)." Hence, one should not just look forward to the Eids in the Islamic calendar; one can instead look forward to everyday when one has not disobeyed Allah. The fourth Imam, in Du'a Tawba, (Repentance) says, "O Allah, this is the position of the one whose sins alternate between his hands, who Satan has gained mastery over. He has fallen short of what you have commanded through neglect, or he has committed that of which you have commanded him not to do out of delusion."

When we commit sins everyday, we either commit them out of neglect, or out of delusion. Out of neglect is when you ask Allah to forgive you when you have committed a sin out of negligence. Out of delusion is when you believe you can get away with sin everyday as if no one is watching you. Once a man came to Imam Hussein (AS) and said that he could not stop sinning. The Imam replied, "If your self takes you to sin, keep sinning. But remember five factors when you are about to sin. Sin only in that place where Allah cannot see you. The second factor is to not sin on this land as this is Allah's land. The third factor is to not enjoy the food that Allah provides for you. The fourth is when the angels of death come to take you, ensure that you walk with them. The fifth is that, when the Book of Deeds is given to you on the Day of Judgement, you cannot deny any of it."

There is no place where Allah cannot see us. When we carry out extra acts in front of our managers at work, it is because we know that they are watching, but Allah (SWT) is watching us all the time. Should we show Him our sins? If Allah has created this world for us, then we cannot go against Him on the land which He owns. Also, if Allah has given us the blessings of food, we cannot sin against Him because that would be exploiting His bounty. If you have not committed any sins, then you would be confident to walk with the angels of death. When the man had heard all of this, he admitted that he had been delusional. The Lord saw Him wherever he went, and gave him the earth to walk on, and to enjoy the bounties therein, and these should not be gone against in arrogance.

Made in the USA
Las Vegas, NV
26 August 2022